A Suffrage Reader

A Suffrage Reader

Charting directions in British suffrage history

Edited by
CLAIRE EUSTANCE, JOAN RYAN
and LAURA UGOLINI

Leicester University Press
London and New York

Leicester University Press
A Cassell imprint
Wellington House, 125 Strand, London, WC2R 0BB
370 Lexington Avenue, New York, NY 10017-6550

First published 2000
© The editors and contributors 2000
Chapter 5 is reprinted by permission of Duke University Press.

Apart from any fair dealing for the purposes of research or private study or criticism or review, as permitted under the Copyright, Designs and Patents Act 1988, this publication may not be reproduced, stored or transmitted, in any form or by any means or process, without the prior permission in writing of the copyright holders or their agents. Except for reproduction in accordance with the terms of licences issued by the Copyright Licensing Agency, photocopying of whole or part of this publication without prior written permission of the copyright holders or their agents in single or multiple copies whether for gain or not is illegal and expressly forbidden. Please direct all enquiries concerning copyright to the publishers.

British Library Cataloguing-in-Publication Data
A catalogue record for this book is available from the British Library.

ISBN 0-7185-0177-2 (hardback)
    0-7185-0178-0 (paperback)

Library of Congress Cataloging-in-Publication Data

A suffrage reader : charting directions in British suffrage history /
  edited by Claire Eustance, Joan Ryan and Laura Ugolini.
    p. cm.
  Includes bibliographical references.
  ISBN 0-7185-0177-2 (hardcover). — ISBN 0-7185-0178-0 (paperback)
  1. Women—Suffrage—Great Britain—History. 2. Suffragists—Great Britain—History. I. Eustance, Claire. II. Ryan, Joan.
III. Ugolini, Laura.
JN979.S87 1999
324.6′23′0941—dc21   99-13307
                                                                                         CIP

Typeset by BookEns Ltd, Royston, Herts.
Printed and bound in Great Britain by Biddles Ltd, Guildford and King's Lynn

Contents

Acknowledgements	vi
Notes on Editors and Contributors	vii
Abbreviations	x
Introduction: Writing Suffrage Histories – the 'British' Experience *Claire Eustance, Laura Ugolini and Joan Ryan*	1
1. Reflecting on Suffrage History *Sandra Stanley Holton*	20
2. 'Crossing the Great Divide': Inter-organizational Suffrage Relationships on Merseyside, 1895–1914 *Krista Cowman*	37
3. 'Suffragettes Are Splendid for Any Work': The Blathwayt Diaries as a Source for Suffrage History *June Hannam*	53
4. Teetotal Feminists: Temperance Leadership and the Campaign for Women's Suffrage *Margaret Barrow*	69
5. 'Doing Justice to the Real Girl': The Women Writers' Suffrage League *Sowon S. Park*	90
6. Suffragette Experience Through the Filter of Fascism *Julie Gottlieb*	105
7. 'It Is Only Justice to Grant Women's Suffrage': Independent Labour Party Men and Women's Suffrage, 1893–1905 *Laura Ugolini*	126
8. Between the Cause and the Courts: The Curious Case of Cecil Chapman *Angela V. John*	145
9. Journeying Through Suffrage: The Politics of Dora Montefiore *Karen Hunt*	162
10. Suffrage Autobiography: A Study of Mary Richardson – Suffragette, Socialist and Fascist *Hilda Kean*	177
11. 'What a Lot There Is Still to Do': Stella Browne (1880–1955) – Carrying the Struggle Ever Onward *Lesley A. Hall*	190
Index	206

Acknowledgements

The editors would like to thank all the contributors to the 'Seeing Through Suffrage' conference for their enthusiasm and encouragement. We also thank Janet Joyce and Sandra Margolies at Cassell for their help and support. Special thanks should go to June Balshaw, Philip de Jersey, Mick Ryan and Eleanor Hardy.

We are grateful to the following for assistance or permission to use material: the Bodleian Library, Oxford (H.W. Nevinson papers); the Hon. Simon Howard of Castle Howard (Castle Howard Archives); The National Trust (Blathwayt Diaries at Dyrham Park); the Fawcett Library and, particularly, David Doughan, for sharing his ideas; and the Museum of London.

Claire Eustance's original ideas for a conference became a reality through the inspiration, support and hard work of other members of the University of Greenwich's Male Support for Women's Suffrage research project: June Balshaw, Angela John, Sean Mortimer, Laura Ugolini, Carolyn Spring and Paul Stigant. Thanks must also go to David Sneath, Alan Bull, Kath Sinnott, Edith Stollery, Mary Worley, Jenny Bache, Anne Stonebank, Anneyce Knight and Maria Francis. Financial grants by the British Academy (Humanities Research Board), the Lipman-Miliband Trust and the Royal Historical Society (Research Support Committee) helped enormously in covering the cost of inviting keynote speakers to the conference.

Notes on Editors and Contributors

Margaret Barrow is Subject Specialist and User Education Librarian at the University of Manchester Institute of Science and Technology. She has a long-standing interest in the role of women in society, and recently received her PhD for a thesis on the women's temperance movement in England. Her publications include *Women 1870–1928: A Guide to Printed and Archival Sources in the United Kingdom* (London, Mansell, 1981).

Krista Cowman teaches in the School of Cultural Studies at Leeds Metropolitan University. She is currently completing a book on women's political activity on Merseyside c. 1890–1920. Her publications include a chapter in Mary Joannou and June Purvis (eds), *The Women's Suffrage Movement: New Feminist Perspectives* (Manchester, Manchester University Press, 1998).

Claire Eustance was an organizer of the Seeing Through Suffrage Conference. She is a British co-editor of the journal *Gender & History*. She wrote a chapter for and edited with Angela V. John, *The Men's Share? Masculinities, Male Support and Women's Suffrage, 1890–1920* (London, Routledge, 1997). Her other publications on suffrage and gender history include a chapter on the Women's Freedom League in the collection edited by Mary Joannou and June Purvis, *The Women's Suffrage Movement: New Feminist Perspectives* (Manchester, Manchester University Press, 1998).

Julie Gottlieb was awarded a PhD for her thesis 'Women and fascism in inter-war Britain' by the University of Cambridge in the spring of 1998. She has published reviews in the *Times Literary Supplement* and contributed biographical entries for the forthcoming *Cambridge Guide to Women's Writing in English*, edited by Lorna Sage. Her article 'Women and fascism in the East End' will be published in a forthcoming issue of *Jewish Culture and History*. She is currently an SSHRC Post-doctoral Fellow in the Department of History, University of Toronto. Her book *Feminine Fascism: Women in Britain's Fascist Movement, 1923–45* will be published by I.B. Tauris in 2000.

Lesley A. Hall is Senior Assistant Archivist in the Contemporary Medical Archives Centre at the Wellcome Institute for the History of Medicine, London. She is an Honorary Lecturer in the History of Medicine at University College London. She holds both a professional Diploma of Archive Administration and a University of London PhD in the history of medicine. Her publications include *Hidden Anxieties: Male Sexuality 1900-1950* (Oxford, Polity Press, 1991) and (with Roy Porter) *The Facts of Life: The Creation of Sexual Knowledge in Britain 1650-1950* (New Haven, Yale University Press, 1991) as well as numerous articles and reviews. She is currently working on a biography of Stella Browne and an edited volume of her scattered writings.

June Hannam is Principal Lecturer in History at the University of the West of England. She is joint reviews editor for *Women's History Review* and Chair of the South West Women's History Network. Her publications include *Isabella Ford, 1855-1924* (Oxford, Blackwell, 1989) and, with Ann Hughes and Pauline Stafford, *British Women's History: A Biographical Guide* (Manchester, Manchester University Press, 1989). She has published widely on women and the Independent Labour Party and on feminist politics in the nineteenth century. She is currently collaborating with Karen Hunt on a book on women and British socialism (1880-1930).

Sandra Stanley Holton is a Senior Australian Research Council Fellow in the History Department at the University of Adelaide. Her publications include *Feminism and Democracy: Women's Suffrage and Reform Politics in Britain, 1900-1918* (Cambridge, Cambridge University Press, 1986) and a series of articles in *Australian Historical Studies*, *Women's History Review*, *American Historical Review* and *Victorian Studies*. Her most recent book is *Suffrage Days: Stories from the Women's Suffrage Movement* (London, Routledge, 1996). She is currently working on a life of Alice Clark, industrialist, suffragist and pioneering historian of women's work.

Karen Hunt is a Senior Lecturer at Manchester Metropolitan University and teaches women's history, social history and women's studies. Her *Equivocal Feminists: The Social Democratic Federation and the Woman Question, 1884-1911* was published in 1996 by Cambridge University Press and she is collaborating with June Hannam on a book on women and British socialism (1880-1930). Her next project is a biography of Dora Montefiore.

Angela V. John is Professor of History at the University of Greenwich. She is a founder member of the editorial collective of the journal *Gender & History*. Her publications include *By the Sweat of Their Brow: Women Workers at Victorian Coal Mines* (London, Croom Helm, 1980; Routledge,

1984); *Elizabeth Robins: Staging a Life* (London, Routledge, 1995) and, co-edited with Claire Eustance, *The Men's Share? Masculinities, Male Support and Women's Suffrage, 1890-1920* (London, Routledge, 1997). She edited *Unequal Opportunities: Women's Employment in England 1800-1918* (Oxford, Blackwell, 1986) and *Our Mothers' Land: Chapters in Welsh Women's History, 1830-1930* (Cardiff, University of Wales Press, 1991). She is currently working on a biographical study of Henry Nevinson, Margaret Wynne Nevinson and Evelyn Sharp.

Hilda Kean is a tutor in History and course director of the MA in Popular Memory and Public History at Ruskin College, Oxford. She has researched and published widely on the suffrage movement, auto/biography and representation. She has written *Challenging the State? The Socialist and Feminist Educational Experience* (London, Falmer, 1990); *Deeds Not Words: The Lives of Suffragette Teachers* (London, Pluto 1990); *Animal Rights: Political and Social Change in Britain since 1800* (London, Reaktion, 1998). She is co-editing with Geoff Andrews and Jane Thompson *Ruskin College: A Century of Contesting Knowledge and Dissenting Politics* (London, Lawrence and Wishart, 1999). She is currently researching a family and local history of East London.

Sowon S. Park is a research fellow at Queen Elizabeth House, University of Oxford. She has written a DPhil thesis on suffrage fiction and her works on the topic are 'Suffrage fiction: a political discourse in the marketplace' in *English Literature in Transition*, and 'The first professional: the Women Writers' Suffrage League' in *Modern Language Quarterly*, March 1997.

Joan Ryan is a Principal Lecturer in History at the University of Greenwich. Her research has mainly concentrated on the industrial employment of women, particularly in the interwar years. She has also published on the early women police and contributed to an Italian collection on nineteenth-century suffrage issues.

Laura Ugolini completed her PhD on Independent Labour Party men and women's suffrage, 1893-1914, in 1997. She has contributed a chapter to *The Men's Share?*, edited by Angela V. John and Claire Eustance. She is currently a Research Fellow in the School of Humanities and Social Sciences at the University of Wolverhampton.

Abbreviations

AFL	Actresses' Franchise League
ALRA	Abortion Law Reform Association
ASS	Adult Suffrage Society
BCL	British Commonwealth League
BDWSU	British Dominions Women's Suffrage Union
BUF	British Union of Fascists
BWTA	British Women's Temperance Association
CLWS	Church League for Women's Suffrage
CUWFA	Conservative and Unionist Women's Franchise Association
CWSS	Catholic Women's Suffrage Society
ELFS	East London Federation of Suffragettes
FCSU	Forward Cymric Suffrage Union
ICW	International Council of Women
ILP	Independent Labour Party
IOGT	Independent Order of Good Templars
IWSA	International Woman Suffrage Alliance
LRC	Labour Representation Committee
LWSS	Liverpool Women's Suffrage Society
MLWS	Men's League for Women's Suffrage
MPU	Men's Political Union for Women's Enfranchisement
NAC	National Administrative Council (of the Independent Labour Party)
NSWS	National Society for Women's Suffrage
NUSEC	National Union of Societies for Equal Citizenship
NUWSS	National Union of Women's Suffrage Societies
RSPCA	Royal Society for the Prevention of Cruelty to Animals
SDF	Social Democratic Federation
SPG	Six Point Group
UKA	United Kingdom Alliance
US	United Suffragists
VFWF	Votes for Women Fellowship
WBCG	Workers' Birth Control Group
WCG	Women's Co-operative Guild
WCTA	Women's Christian Temperance Association
WCTU	Women's Christian Temperance Union
WEA	Workers' Educational Association
WFL	Women's Freedom League
WILPF	Women's International League for Peace and Freedom
WLA	Women's Liberal Association
WLF	Women's Liberal Federation
WNLA	Women's National Liberal Association
WSPU	Women's Social and Political Union
WSS	Women's Suffrage Society
WTAU	Women's Total Abstinence Union
WWSL	Women Writers' Suffrage League

Introduction: Writing Suffrage Histories – the 'British' Experience

Claire Eustance, Laura Ugolini and Joan Ryan

I

Suffrage history is enjoying a renaissance in Britain.[1] Over two decades of broadening perceptions and definitions coupled with the unique appeal of 'women's suffrage' mean that connected dialogue is now possible on subjects as seemingly diverse as the reforming agendas of 'radical unitarians' in 1830s and 1840s Britain and the aims of supporters of the British Union of Fascists a century later. For a number of scholars, women's suffrage now forms a backdrop for exploring how the creative media of literature, drama and visual arts were used by and for women. Thanks to years of dedicated research it is possible to draw parallels between the ideas and actions of suffrage activists as well known as Sylvia Pankhurst, as infamous as Mary 'Slasher' Richardson, as far travelled as Dora Montefiore and as settled as Emily Blathwayt. Suffrage history has also become a means of exploring broader conceptual themes: for example, transformations in gender relations, or the development and deployment of concepts of nationalism, morality, professionalism and individualism.

The work of Kjell Östberg and Irma Sulkunen provides fascinating insights into the suffrage campaigns in Sweden and Finland respectively. Their work, together with the international collection *Suffrage and Beyond*, edited by Caroline Daley and Melanie Nolan, has served as a timely reminder that the campaigns in Britain did not take place in a vacuum. Such work has sealed the lid on outdated assumptions which have tended to represent the British campaign as a yardstick against which the suffrage campaigns in all other countries or regions must be measured. On the contrary, it is important to acknowledge how the state of women's citizenship in other countries influenced the British experience. From as early as the 1850s British women were learning from and co-operating with suffrage activists and women's rights campaigners based in France, the United States, New Zealand and Australia.[2]

The collection of essays which make up this *Suffrage Reader* provide fresh insights into the British experience of women's suffrage free from the ideological baggage which had placed Britain at the centre of global events. All chapters take as their starting-point campaigns for women's suffrage in Britain and stretch across a period of more than seventy years, demonstrating just how fluid definitions of 'suffrage history' have become. Where once British suffrage historiography concentrated primarily on the decade or so before the First World War, this collection begins in the 1880s and goes beyond the landmark date of 1918 to explore the continuing significance of suffrage for individuals and organizations, in some cases up to the 1950s. Even so, these dates should not be taken as indicative of any attempt to place proscriptive boundaries on suffrage history. On the contrary, recent research has demonstrated how a great deal can be added to understandings of histories of women's suffrage and to concepts of citizenship and rights in Britain by exploring the motivating forces and the ideas articulated by women and men active much earlier in the nineteenth century.[3]

Any account or reappraisal of suffrage history in Britain has always had to contend with a number of uncomfortable but enduring historical 'truths'. Put simply, women's suffrage histories have been marginalized in conventional political narratives and subjected to frequent challenges regarding their legitimacy. This is evident through omissions, occasional token references and even blatant attacks on some of the more (in)famous activists. Dating from the first moves by suffrage activists to record their experiences, to the work of feminist historians in the 1970s and beyond, more enlightened accounts have been produced to counter the misrepresentations.[4] And yet, in spite of all the evidence to the contrary, some detractors have continued to question the significance of women's demands for enfranchisement, in terms of both their scale and their impact. This complicated legacy has ensured a distinctive niche for suffrage history within the broader project of women's/feminist history. However, this has not been without its difficulties; an occasional tendency to manipulate - even glorify - the suffrage movement in order to promote some notional sense of feminist history, while ignoring conflicts and inequalities in its history, resulted over the years in a certain amount of ambivalence towards the subject among subsequent generations of feminist and gender historians.

The perspectives on British women's suffrage developed in this book are important contributions to the ongoing process of acknowledging difference, diversity, disillusionment and conflict among women and men, as well as alliances and shared goals and ideas. More generally, the book delineates the integration of the ideas and experiences of suffrage into a more inclusive history of women's and men's political, cultural, sexual and socio-economic lives. In the first chapter of this collection Sandra Holton, a renowned suffrage historian, gives her own interpretation of the developments in British suffrage history since the 1970s. The themes she maps out, which balance integration and separateness, establish important foundations which chapters in this collection build upon. As Holton indicates, studies of women's suffrage are on the verge of significant transformations as long-neglected questions of national identity, nationalism and imperialism are addressed. With many of the older, often unspoken, assumptions underpinning histories of the British women's suffrage campaign now being challenged, a reassessment of the ways the campaign developed a distinctive national identity is imperative. The remainder of this introduction is framed accordingly.

II

David Doughan, Reference Librarian of the world-renowned suffrage resource the Fawcett Library, posed an important question when he asked why demands for women's suffrage became *the* issue that dominated feminist activity in Britain and North America in the early years of the twentieth century. He pointed out that while suffrage was an issue in other countries, particularly across Europe, it did not overwhelm other demands and campaigns undertaken by and for women to the degree witnessed in Britain.[5] In seeking possible answers, David Doughan has distinguished between the political traditions of these countries and the political system that existed in Britain. Other contributors to such debate have demonstrated in different ways how the style of government in Britain and related perceptions of democracy and citizenship influenced British women's suffrage campaigns. In her work on the 1830s, Kathryn Gleadle has demonstrated how demands and campaigns for women's suffrage were intricately bound up in the broader changes in Britain's political landscape and its political culture. Both women and men were involved in the enthusiastic campaigns that eventually resulted in the 1832 Reform Act. Demonstrations of their disappointment and critique of the outcome of 1832, through Chartist politics and protests in the 1830s and 1840s, and later through writing and domestic politics, meant that women's voices became much more identifiable and distinct in the 1850s and 1860s.[6] While a growing separateness in women's protests was becoming discernible, nevertheless women's demands and campaigns, including those for the vote, remained firmly located within the changing landscape of British politics. Jane Rendall has identified the 1867 Reform Act as a defining moment for the British suffrage movement, while showing that it also marked the 'shifting boundaries of national and racial identities, and changing perceptions of the role of the British state'.[7]

By the mid-Victorian period, suffragists were sharing with a wider liberal culture ethnocentric notions of progress and 'civilization'.[8] It followed quite naturally that because of the significance and importance placed in Britain on democracy and representation by progressive opinion, it was this that activists focused on as a means to effect change. Consequently the vote became the rallying point for diverse groups of British women and men seeking reform on many different, and often conflicting, fronts. Some conceived of the vote in terms of extending political rights to women, or at least to certain groups of women. Some demanded full adult suffrage. For others the vote was a means by which to re-negotiate sexual rights or, as in the case of Stella Browne (see Chapter 11), a way to challenge the very meanings conventionally attached to the nature of womanhood. Other advocates of women's suffrage prioritized the economic reorganization of society, and activism through the labour movement. All of these positions were influenced by and negotiated through a variety of factors, including class location, age and generation.[9]

It may seem ironic, given their formal exclusion from Parliamentary decision-making, that the vast majority of organized women campaigners in Britain from the 1830s onwards revered and respected the principles and traditions of the British political system. Such behaviour becomes more understandable if one considers the ways in which by the end of the nineteenth century some women were being incorporated into the body politic, for example through participation in local government or party politics (albeit to a limited extent and in ways dictated by an elite group of men). Further light is shed by looking at the process through which suffrage activists became politicized. Many middle-class activists such as Dora Montefiore, the subject of Karen Hunt's chapter, had been tutored in liberal ideals of progress and peaceful change from an early age by family members. Even when the political stance and class origin of the women demanding the vote diversified, and women like Stella Browne turned to socialism, the vision of full citizenship rights for women remained grounded in ideals of reform rather than revolution. It was only after enfranchisement that severe disillusionment led a few former suffrage activists to question the basic foundations and justice of the British democratic tradition. Julie Gottlieb's discussion of three former suffrage activists in Chapter 6 provides a fascinating insight into the conditions and experiences that led some women to fascism. At the other end of the political spectrum, well-known suffrage activists Sylvia Pankhurst and Charlotte Despard chose to embrace communism and Irish republican politics respectively.

For Victorian and Edwardian British women of all classes, gaining the parliamentary vote carried with it additional significance born out of the age. Voting rights represented full and proper status as members of the British nation. Politicized in an age imbued with imperial notions of British might and supremacy, many suffrage activists wanted British women to have a full share of this legacy and to bring their feminine qualities and knowledge to bear upon a national and imperial stage. At the same time, it is in this context, as Barbara Caine points out, that the class assumptions of the emerging feminist movement in Britain are thrown into sharp relief. Working-class activists were often deprived of real power in many suffrage organizations by the exclusionary practices of middle-class women, many of whom assumed that it was women of their class who constituted 'true' British womanhood.[10] And yet in every general pattern there is an exception: in Chapter 3 June Hannam offers an alternative to the conventional image of working-class suffrage activist Annie Kenney as Christabel Pankhurst's passive tool. Hannam also suggests that the friendship and co-operation between Kenney, the ex-factory worker, and the genteel Blathwayt family in some ways actually reverses conventional relations of power and authority between classes. To view the question at another level, divisions between British suffrage activists should not be over-stressed. Equally striking was the unifying factor between British suffrage activists – female and male, working-class and middle-class – namely a shared sense of belonging to a common British experience; a national and ethnic self-awareness against which gender and class politics were fought out. Eighteenth-century 'patriotic' discourses, used to oppose the 'corruption' of Walpole's government or the 'tyranny' of George III, have parallels among nineteenth- and twentieth-century suffrage activists. Although it has been argued that by the last quarter of the nineteenth century the language of 'patriotism' had been appropriated and incorporated within a conservative discourse, the effectiveness with which 'radical' causes such as women's suffrage laid claim to such a language should not be underestimated.[11] Anti-suffragists could characterize women's enfranchisement as a 'national danger' and emphasize women's supposed inability to deal with international and imperial matters.[12] However, suffragists also showed themselves to be adept at turning the language of nationhood and of Empire to their advantage, even though their success often remained at a moral rather than at a practical level. They could, for example, justify their claim to the vote in terms of a special British tradition, with Britain as the birthplace of parliamentary democracy and of representative institutions. It was not unusual for activists, both male and female, to conjure images of the ancient rights of English subjects, something practised by the Women's Freedom League in the early twentieth century when its members attempted to petition Edward VII.[13] For some male suffrage supporters, as Angela John points out in Chapter 8, women's suffrage represented the completion of a British democratic process begun many years before with Magna Carta. Similarly, in her work on the Women's Tax Resistance League Hilary Frances has observed that tax resisters saw themselves as belonging to a long and specifically English and Scottish tradition of opposition to unjust and tyrannical government. They claimed their antecedents with the signing of Magna Carta, the Reformation, the Dissenters and the Covenanters of England and Scotland.[14] In this collection, Laura Ugolini shows that by the beginning of the twentieth century, despite their explicit rejection of the liberal-radical emphasis on political reforms, the male socialists of the Independent Labour Party were also appealing to this British tradition of 'radical' protest to justify women's claim to the vote. The use of such slogans as 'taxation without representation is tyranny' was not uncommon.

Of course, patriotic discourses were rarely deployed unproblematically. One infamous example is the small section of the militant movement, given voice by Christabel Pankhurst, who launched a series of deeply jingoistic attacks on Britain's opponents during the First World War. Her speech on 'international militancy' made in New York in 1915, with its attack on the Kaiser and Germany and its defence of Herbert Asquith's government, reflected the extent of her about-turn on the urgency of suffrage. Despite the venom of Pankhurst's speech, her faith in the 'worthy' British Constitution (if not in the Liberal government) was made in the same mould as that of many suffrage activists of her age.[15] When a suffrage measure was finally passed by the House of Lords in early 1918, Millicent Garrett Fawcett, by then one of the longest-serving suffrage veterans, demonstrated by her choice of words a more downbeat but no less sincere investment in the integrity of British democracy. She remarked that 'it was a continually and deeply felt reproach that this country, the Mother of Parliaments, hung back from the application of the principle of free representative institutions to her daughters'.[16]

Of course, among those who could be said to constitute the British suffrage movement in its broadest sense there was great variation in what it meant to be part of the British nation. National identities are as much cultural constructs as gender and class identities. Equally, 'Britishness' is not a simple or immutable category, but rather must be understood as a sense of belonging to a continuously renegotiated 'imagined' political community.[17] And it is clear, from the important work that has been produced on the suffrage campaigns in Wales, Scotland and in regions of England, that any notion of 'British' suffrage history must operate on a number of shifting but interconnected levels. Suffrage activists' identification with an explicitly 'British' political constituency in the nineteenth and twentieth centuries was superimposed over and coexisted with older national identities relating to being 'English', 'Scottish' or 'Welsh'. Because of the longevity and intensity of the campaigns to free Ireland from English-centred government, the overlaying of different national identities across the British Isles did not exist among Irish women's suffragists to the same degree. The distinctiveness of the Irish campaign was perceptible through the existence of a separate mass membership society in Ireland, unlike in England, Scotland and Wales, which shared major societies. There were various degrees of co-operation between Irish and English suffrage activists, particularly in the early twentieth century;

however, any encroachment or attempt to incorporate Ireland into the campaign on the British mainland was very often met with indifference and occasionally with indignation.[18]

Varying degrees of identification with long-standing national identities may have been a defining feature of the British suffrage movement, but this does not seem to have hindered the development of constructive relationships and friendships between Scottish, Welsh or English women's suffrage activists. Ignorance and insensitivity on the part of London-based leaders and activists were just as likely to be criticized by activists in non-metropolitan regions of England as by Scottish and Welsh suffrage activists. Furthermore, while England may have been identified as the centre of government and influence over the British Empire, there is no evidence that English influence was either successfully imposed or accepted by members of the women's suffrage movement in Scotland or Wales.[19] On the contrary, Leah Leneman has pointed out that Scottish suffrage activists were prominent and influential at a national level over the long history of the campaign for women's suffrage in Britain.[20] Moreover, Scottish and Welsh activists were particularly creative and imaginative in their use of images, symbols and rhetoric, often drawn from history and folklore, that would have been easily associated in the public's mind with Scottish and Welsh national characteristics. It was not uncommon for Scottish suffragists, whatever their organizational loyalties, to make use of traditional symbols of tartan, heather, thistle, of songs, or of appeals to a distinctive Hibernian history. During Winston Churchill's by-election campaign in Dundee in 1908, the Scot Mary Phillips, a Women's Social and Political Union (WSPU) activist, noted how she had reminded the electors of the 'traditions of Scotland, of the fights for freedom in which our forefathers led, and in which our foremothers were never far behind the men of England in striking a blow for justice for women!'[21] Welsh suffragists also placed great importance on their roots; members of the London-based Cymric Suffrage Union deliberately forged an identity for themselves as *Welsh* suffrage activists, in opposition to their representation by Welsh Liberals as 'outsiders'.[22]

Krista Cowman's and June Hannam's chapters in this volume offer convincing evidence of how misleading it is to represent a nation-wide/national movement solely and simply through the dictates and policies and practices of the 'centre'. To do so not only neglects the richness and diversity inherent in suffrage history, but also overlooks a defining feature of the character of the British suffrage movement. Even before the movement became a 'national' one, the impetus for suffrage activities from the 1860s did not come from a 'centre', but rather from a number of connected organizations in cities as diverse as Manchester, London, Bristol and Edinburgh. As the British movement became an increasingly nationwide one towards the end of the nineteenth and into the twentieth century, it continued to maintain shape and meaning through the activities of different local groups and branches in the different regions. If anything, regional allegiance caused more problems for the national societies than the more historic tensions that occasionally surfaced between, say, England and Wales. Rather than displaying unswerving loyalty to any one organization and its principles, it was not unusual for grass-roots activists in different localities and regions to co-operate and make alliances with other suffrage societies or political groupings in their area. In Chapter 2, Krista Cowman illustrates how some instance of co-operation could even overcome huge religious distinctions such as those in Liverpool, where bonds developed between women from both sides of the Catholic–Protestant divide.

Equally, in many areas across Britain it is not possible to understand the suffrage campaign without reference to local government politics, patterns of employment, culture and the presence and activities of other organizations. Still significant is the pioneering work of Jill Liddington and Jill Norris, who established how in Lancashire the suffrage campaign was connected with local labour and liberal politics, to patterns of employment in textile factories and to pre-existing forms of female organization, including trade unions and the Women's Co-operative Guild.[23] Local labour politics clearly influenced the actions of the Women's Freedom League branch in Middlesbrough, which in 1908 tried to subvert the organization's rules on an all-female membership by letting sympathetic Independent Labour Party (ILP) men take an active part in branch meetings and activities.[24]

For many suffrage activists, male and female, the first site of loyalty and identification was with their locality. As June Hannam demonstrates in Chapter 3, the Blathwayts' sense of permanence in their West Country home, despite the years spent by the family in imperial service, was symbolized by the planting of the 'suffragette arboretum'. There were of course notable exceptions; Dora Montefiore's story, which is discussed by Karen Hunt in Chapter 9, is distinctly cosmopolitan, as is evident from Montefiore's ability to stride not only through different suffrage organizations and different political groups, but also through countries and even continents.

Other activists identified with specific organizations that they felt best reflected their interests and concerns. The Women Writers' Suffrage League (WWSL), discussed by Sowon Park in Chapter 5, was established in 1908 to represent professional writers and welcomed all women who had sold at least one text. Park demonstrates convincingly how the WWSL's influence and impact, particularly in terms of professionalizing British women's writing, was greatly disproportionate to its size and lifespan. Other interest-based organizations active in the suffrage campaign could have much less strictly defined parameters, including those appealing to different religious affiliations. The

Church Leagues in particular witnessed a rapid expansion in membership during their lifespan in the early twentieth century and are one group of many to be more or less ignored in older narratives of British suffrage history. In this collection Krista Cowman has begun to redress this oversight. Margaret Barrow's study of the leadership and membership of the British Women's Temperance Association (see Chapter 4) adds another dimension to the spectrum of organizations and societies connected with the suffrage campaign in Britain. And, of course, suffrage activists were often members of more than one society or were members of many simultaneously, and Karen Hunt's and June Hannam's chapters are particularly illustrative of how loyalties and identifications, particularly with suffrage militancy, could shift and change over time.

In addition to offering support for women's suffrage via their political parties, or mixed organizations like the People's Suffrage Federation or the Church Leagues, men could join specific men-only organizations like the Men's League for Women's Suffrage, the more militant Men's Political Union or the Northern Men's Federation for Women's Suffrage. The extent to which men were an integral part of Britain's women's suffrage campaign has recently been the subject of an edited collection of essays.[25] Still somewhat marginalized within narratives of suffrage history, this subject is addressed in this collection by Angela John and Laura Ugolini. Their chapters demonstrate how male supporters drew on experiences or motives distinct from those that inspired women. These could include a commitment to notions of 'manliness' or 'gentlemanliness' – or actions based on their status as fully voting citizens. Angela John's chapter on Cecil Chapman (Chapter 8) shows how his suffragism was based on his position above local, particular or sectional interests. The authorities may have perceived his role as an impartial dispenser of justice to be inconsistent with his suffrage activities, and yet to Chapman the two were clearly compatible.

Whatever the complexities of individual motivations, suffrage activists' sense of national identity could provide a dynamic and multilayered sense of belonging to a greater whole. Edwardian suffragists in particular were accomplished in adapting this multiplicity into strategies that could reaffirm the strength and legitimacy of the demands for female enfranchisement. It was no coincidence that as suffrage societies grew more diverse and disparate in the twentieth century, strategies emerged which encouraged participants to see themselves as members of a powerful and influential national movement. This became even more important when contact between distant branches was weakened by press silence, or when sections of the movement were alienated by the actions of others, as increasingly became the case between activists at opposite ends of the constitutional–militant spectrum. One way of mitigating such divisions was to appeal to a sense of shared national gender identity and a shared history. For example, in 1910 suffrage activist Louisa Thompson conjured up a particular image of a homogeneous British womanhood, located firmly within a tradition of British radicalism, stating to *Vote* readers, 'The revolt of British women against political tyranny ... is as tremendous in its meanings as was the revolt of the Chartists, and as far-reaching in its nature.'[26] Similar strategies worked for members of the remote Shetland branch of the National Union of Women's Suffrage Societies (NUWSS), who gained inspiration by the feeling that they were part of a movement 'that linked women the length and breadth of the land'.[27]

During the Edwardian phase of the suffrage campaign in Britain, a sense of national cohesion was also given form and substance via a series of mass participation events. The spectacle of the Women's Coronation Procession of June 1911 included members from at least 28 suffrage organizations, who united in advance of what was considered by many to be impending victory. This spectacle was perhaps the most successful in blending the local, regional, national and imperial elements of the British nation. Local societies carried banners commemorating local events or personalities; activists from Wales who wore traditional dress embodied easily recognizable national identities. In addition to all these diverse images the Historical Pageant and the Pageant of Empire demonstrated to onlookers and participants alike suffragists' claims to be part of both a proud British political tradition and a wider imperial one.[28]

National identity backed up by cultural signifiers or by notions of imperialism gave the activists in Britain a means to identify themselves as a community and also to distinguish themselves from other nations. This could be used to strengthen arguments in favour of women's suffrage. In 1910 Margaret Heppler, a member of the NUWSS executive, lamented that while women in Australia and New Zealand, 'our compatriots in ampler Britains beyond seas', had the vote, British women were told that their enfranchisement would 'bring our country to ruin'. Heppler emphasized the similarities between the lives of British and Antipodean (though excluding Aboriginal) women in order to condemn the former's votelessness.[29]

Responses of feminists and suffragists to imperial issues were not always as simple or universal as the celebratory nature of events such as the 'Pageant of Empire' of 1911 would suggest.[30] Nevertheless, the vast majority of British suffrage activists seem to have come to terms with the reality of empire. Empire served not only as a potential field of action for the energies and distinctive qualities of enfranchised women, but also as the 'other' against which suffrage campaigners could compare and define themselves. In her ground-breaking work Antoinette Burton has shown how British feminists claimed a special understanding of and empathy with Indian women because of their common femaleness, while at the same time adopting 'Orientalist' assumptions about Indian culture and customs. According to Burton, British women's claims to speak on behalf of Indian women served both to ratify public spaces as imperial and as a means of justifying British women's right to participate in these spaces.[31] Indian women became for British feminists 'the symbol of subjection in a decaying civilization'.[32]

The different and interlinked manifestations of national identity – imperial, British, English, Welsh, Scottish, regional, local – were integral to the objectives of suffrage activists across Britain and to the very nature of the movement. However, campaigners did not isolate themselves from contact with activists and organizations in other countries. On the contrary, recent studies have emphasized the pervasiveness and importance of international contacts within the nineteenth- and twentieth-century suffrage campaigns. June Pettitt's research on transnational networks in France, Britain and the United States in the 1850s shows how such contacts were being developed even before there was any semblance of a mass suffrage movement in Britain.[33] Similarly, Sandra Holton has traced a series of transatlantic networks that had important repercussions for the developing campaign in Britain, particularly for militancy. Dating from the second half of the nineteenth century, and over three generations, friendship networks were established between members of the extended Bright family and American suffrage activists, notably Elizabeth Cady Stanton. These networks linked the two sides of the Atlantic with ties based on 'private hospitality together with shared values, memories, experiences, jokes and reading … mutual aid and moral support'.[34]

Ellen DuBois has emphasized the internationalism of organizations committed to women's enfranchisement, such as the Women's Christian Temperance Union (WCTU),[35] although in this collection Margaret Barrow draws attention to fears about an 'Americanization' of the BWTA in the latter decades of the nineteenth century. On many other occasions family and friendship networks based around suffrage activism consistently crossed national boundaries without raising controversy. This is demonstrated in Lesley Hall's reassessment of Stella Browne's attitudes towards and involvement within the suffrage movement. Hall suggests that part of the explanation for Browne's interest in issues of sexuality, marriage and motherhood may be traced to her connections with radical German feminist groups, in particular those centring on Dr Helen Stöcker, in the period prior to the First World War.

The formalization of such links by the establishment of an international alliance of suffrage societies had been advocated as early as 1899, when it became clear that the International Council of Women (ICW), an umbrella organization of heterogeneous women's bodies established in 1888, was divided on the issue. Eventually a permanent organization, the

International Woman Suffrage Alliance (IWSA), was established in 1904 in Berlin, where the third meeting of the ICW was taking place. Six countries that had national suffrage organizations joined, including Britain. Millicent Garrett Fawcett, the president of the NUWSS, was elected vice-president with the German Anita Augsburg.[36] British members of the alliance saw the organization as enabling suffrage activists to meet across national boundaries, united by their common femaleness and experience of oppression. Mary Sheepshanks, a Newnham graduate, vice-principal of Morley College, NUWSS activist and since 1913 editor of *Jus Suffragii*, the organ of the alliance, put the matter forcefully: 'In all countries women are faced with similar problems, industrial, social, ethical, political, and in nearly all they are ... helots, whose services are required, whose property is taxed, who are amenable to all laws, but who must be dumb and helpless in their country's government.'[37] Commenting on the Women's Peace Conference at The Hague in 1915 (which many IWSA members attended), Emmeline Pethick-Lawrence noted the similar dresses and personalities of the delegates: 'There was nothing in general appearance to distinguish one nationality from another.'[38] The reason for this may lie in the fact that, at least in the pre-war period, delegates at international conferences came from remarkably similar backgrounds. They were in the main wealthy, older Christian women. In some ways this description fits Dora Montefiore, the subject of Karen Hunt's chapter. The ease with which she undertook her physical, as well as political, 'journey' from Australia to Europe, a 'journey' that involved also participation in IWSA affairs, was that of a well-to-do, middle-class woman in her forties.

Yet, as Leila Rupp has shown, despite the feeling that women from different parts of the world were not 'strangers' to each other, since they had 'a common aim and a common suffering',[39] there remained within the Alliance boundaries and exclusions. In spite of an increase in the number of affiliated societies to 51 by 1929, including organizations from India, China and Japan, the IWSA remained dominated by Europe and the United States. Nor did the internationalist agenda of the IWSA necessarily entail the abandonment of notions of nationhood. National sentiment could be reinforced most dramatically by visual means, and through spectacle: the use at congresses of flags, national anthems, or 'traditional' songs and dances in national dress.[40] Individuals could be active in this organization without relinquishing their sense of a separate national identity. Millicent Garrett Fawcett, for example, also held deeply patriotic and imperialist beliefs, and was described by a contemporary as a 'worshipper at the inner shrine, the holy of holies, all that England stands for to her children, and to the world'.[41]

For suffrage activists based in Britain, the beliefs of leaders like Fawcett influenced a trend which saw increasing interest in women's lives and experiences in other countries. Suffrage newspapers published articles that took as their subject women from other countries: women in China appeared to be a particularly popular subject for members of the militant suffrage society, the Women's Freedom League (WFL). In 1913 it was announced that the WFL newspaper, *The Vote*, was in 'personal communication with nearly forty international friends who represent about thirty countries', many of whom had promised articles concerning women's work in various countries.[42] Much of the ethnocentric assumptions underlying the thinking of British suffragists can also be found in an international context, alongside more complex views. According to Rupp, particular ideas about the nature of 'progress, civilisation and the emancipation of women' posited European women, or women of European descent, as providing help and support to their more oppressed sisters. 'In this way, white women both shouldered a burden and placed themselves in charge.'[43] This greater involvement in international networks and coverage of women's lives in other countries served to reflect back a particular image of the British movement. Many activists liked what they saw and shared a desire to make a British women's movement, in whatever form, as strong and powerful as possible.

In 1914 the international stage was transformed for British suffrage activists from a setting of consensus and co-operation to one of conflict, as the European powers entered a state of war. In Britain, all activists would have felt the call of wartime patriotism – whether they rejected or embraced it – and as the magnitude of the conflict became clear, the First World War proved to be both a watershed and a testing ground for the British suffrage campaign. Suffrage activists' responses to the conflict were influenced by long-standing loyalties, some developed through the suffrage campaign and others of longer duration. Although leaders of the WSPU found no difficulty in switching their primary loyalty away from suffrage towards an intensely patriotic war effort, members of the rank and file did not follow blindly. Millicent Fawcett directed the NUWSS away from suffrage into a considered patriotic policy summed up in the union's 1915 annual report. The report stated that the Union's work 'includes little direct suffrage propaganda', although also claiming to 'have done work of first-rate importance to the interests of women and to the furtherance of the cause of their [women's] enfranchisement'.[44] Prominent NUWSS members Helena Swanwick and Mary Sheepshanks rejected what they saw as the fostering of 'national pride at the expense of humanity'[45] and found new purpose in the Women's International League for Peace and Freedom (WILPF), an organization which campaigned for a negotiated end to hostilities. Other suffrage activists expressed their support for the war, but did so in different ways. The writers Cicely Hamilton and May Sinclair, for example, embraced the fighting and violence as a 'mystical cleansing' which left little space for either feminism or suffragism.[46] A wide range of opinion existed among members of the

WFL, with Charlotte Despard, the much-revered president, eventually pursuing a strong pacifist line, while two other influential members, Nina Boyle and Eunice Murray, declared themselves to be 'patriotic women ... intensely concerned in the victory of our national arms'.[47] At one of the first celebrations to mark women's partial enfranchisement, held in Croydon in April 1918 and attended by suffrage activists who had continued to organize throughout the war, it was reported that all those present sang patriotic songs including one called 'God Save Our Splendid Men'. The presence of war was inescapable.[48]

The variety of responses of British suffrage activists to the First World War was mirrored in other ways, and it became increasingly difficult to maintain consensus in the face of a mounting plethora of priorities and concerns. Some concerns, like the rights of women industrial workers, reflected long-established patterns, influenced by gendered and class-based perceptions of politics and also by local and political allegiances. In the context of total war the fragile gender and class alliances which had served to create both the perception and the reality of a mass national women's movement fractured.

Such profound changes in the organization and focus of the British movement, in addition to the partial victory of the 1918 Representation of the People Act, at one stage marked the culmination of histories of suffrage in Britain. Coming at a time considered to be one of the crucial 'cut-off' points between different historical periods, this narrow interpretation of British suffrage history has proved remarkably difficult to shake off. Only in the past decade have the many suffrage and feminist organizations which continued, or were formed, after 1918 begun to receive the attention they deserve.[49] The edited collection by Harold Smith on twentieth-century British *feminism* is indicative of an important cross-over point between suffrage and feminism which is often thought to exist at the '1918' juncture.[50] In this collection, Lesley Hall's study of the life and ideas of Stella Browne, particularly after 1918, provides a valuable study of the overlap and interconnectedness of the two ideologies. Like Hall's, the contributions in this collection from Hilda Kean and Julie Gottlieb emphasize that the field of suffrage history should not stop at 1918, nor yet in 1928 when full equal adult suffrage was finally introduced in Britain. Kean's study of suffrage autobiography traces how, long after women's suffrage had been achieved, the ex-WSPU militant Mary Richardson recounted and retold her suffrage activism to give unity and a sense of cohesion to her life. Gottlieb's chapter offers a different perspective on Richardson and, more broadly, on the authoritarian sections of the militant suffrage movement, by exploring the involvement of three ex-suffragettes in British fascism. Both chapters offer new ways of thinking about the relationship between the suffrage movement, political activity and nationalism.

Following legislation in 1918, and again in 1928, women's suffrage activists, or feminists as many then described themselves, could claim a legitimate interest – as citizens – in the business both of the British Empire and of the international community which came into being after the formation of the League of Nations in January 1920. Women lost no opportunity in establishing new societies through which to exercise their new 'power'. One such organization, the Council for the Representation of Women in the League of Nations, campaigned for female representation at the Assembly and also, with limited success, lobbied the League of Nations on issues deemed of relevance to women world-wide. As in the pre-war suffrage movement in Britain, judgements about women's interests in 'other' countries were based on the perceived need to guide their 'less developed' sisters.[51] A telling indication of how feminists active in the increasingly middle-class women's movement in Britain in the 1920s continued to identify their reforming role with their position within the empire came with the formation of the British Commonwealth League (BCL) in 1925. Formerly the British Overseas Committee of the IWSA, the BCL reaffirmed its pledge to 'work for Political Equality in all parts of the British Empire overseas where women were still without the Vote ... To do our full suffrage work internationally, we must be a suffrage Empire.'[52]

Gendered, racial and class-based constructions of national identity which shaped the fortunes, ideology and actions of generations of British suffrage activists in the period up to 1914 appeared to be remarkably resilient among some sections of the post-war feminist movement in Britain. Where once the promise of citizenship and of a sense of belonging to a 'British nation' was for many suffrage activists a source of strength, by the 1920s circumstances had altered. The realities of British citizenship saw many suffragists and feminists using notions of imperial responsibility not as a strength, but as a means to achieve some recognition and influence in a political environment that continued to be dominated and directed by men.

III

The following chapters serve an important purpose in demonstrating the diversity, fluidity and richness of suffrage history and the historiography of suffrage in Britain over the period from the 1880s to the 1950s. On a broad level they contribute to an understanding of how concepts of citizenship and democracy were underpinned by the interplay of gender, class and race. Equally, the essays which make up this collection provide new ways of mapping the development of feminist ideas and feminist coalitions in the later nineteenth and early twentieth centuries. Following on from Sandra Holton's personal overview of the developments in suffrage history, the second chapter uses a study of suffrage organizations on Merseyside to plot how the mass suffrage movement developed outwards from different regions of Britain, rather than being directed down from a 'centre'. The third chapter, which looks at one family's involvement in the Edwardian suffrage campaign, provides a different regional focus. It also provides an example of how suffrage could subvert traditional class relationships. The next four chapters look respectively at the temperance movement, women writers, women who joined the fascist movement and ILP men. These chapters provide fascinating and unexpected insights into the impact women's suffrage had on the shifting and developing ideological and reforming agendas of these very different groups. The final four chapters contribute separate studies of individuals whose whole lives were coloured by their involvement in the women's suffrage campaign. These chapters explore the experiences and influences that contributed to development of and shifts in each individual's rationale for demanding political change.

This volume offers new ways of understanding the complexities of British suffrage history; it provides a means of beginning to unravel the inconsistencies and prejudice as well as to challenge the powerful alliances which underpin gender relations. By doing so it aims to give new impetus and meaning to the critical feminist edge of suffrage history.

Notes

1. For the purposes of this book, the term 'suffrage history' is used loosely to describe histories of the campaigns specifically for *women's* suffrage in Britain. Its use in this context does not preclude the inclusion in this field of present and future work exploring men's attitudes towards their own enfranchisement, or lack of it.

2. K. Östberg, 'After suffrage: male strategies towards women in politics in Sweden, 1919-1939', and I. Sulkunen, 'Finland – a pioneering country in women's voting rights', papers given at 'Seeing Through Suffrage, New Studies on Gender and Women's Suffrage. An International Conference', April 1996 (hereafter STS, April 1996); C. Daley and M. Nolan (eds), *Suffrage and Beyond: International Feminist Perspectives*, New York, New York University Press, 1994.

3. Specifically, the papers presented at the STS conference by Jane Rendall, Kathryn Gleadle, June Pettitt and Matthew Cragoe. See K. Gleadle, *The Early Feminists: Radical Unitarians and the Emergence of the Women's Rights Movement, 1831-51*, London, Macmillan, 1995; P. Levine, *Victorian Feminism, 1850-1900*, London, Hutchinson, 1987. Research is ongoing; for example, June Pettitt has identified some interesting transnational links between feminists based in the United States, France and England in her work on the Sheffield Women's Rights Association in the 1850s. J. Pettitt, 'Feminism and transnationalism: a case

study of the Sheffield Women's Rights Association, 1851-2', unpublished paper, 1997.

4. For an extremely readable and emphatic rejection of some of the more extreme misrepresentations of the British women's suffrage campaign, see D. Spender, 'Militant and maligned', in *Women of Ideas and What Men Have Done to Them*, London, Pandora, 1982, pp. 546-603. See also the introduction to J. Marcus, *Suffrage and the Pankhursts*, London, Routledge and Kegan Paul, 1987, pp. 1-17.

5. D. Doughan, 'Women's suffrage: an Anglo-Saxon obsession?', STS, April 1996.

6. Gleadle, *The Early Feminists*. See also H. Rogers, *Authority and Authorship: Radical Women and Popular Politics in Nineteenth Century England*, forthcoming.

7. J. Rendall, 'Who was Lily Maxwell? defining the British nation, 1867', STS, April 1996. Explorations of the connections between citizenship, race and masculinity are the subject of a forthcoming book by Catherine Hall, Keith McClelland and Jane Rendall.

8. J. Rendall, 'Citizenship, culture and civilization: the language of British suffragists, 1866-1874', in Daley and Nolan (eds), *Suffrage and Beyond*, pp. 127-50. See also Gleadle, *The Early Feminists*, for a discussion of earlier uses of notion of history, progress and civilization.

9. B. Caine, *English Feminism, 1780-1980*, Oxford, Oxford University Press, 1997, p. 132.

10. *Ibid.*, p. 126.

11. L. Colley, *Britons: Forging the Nation, 1707-1837*, London, Pimlico, 1992; H. Cunningham, 'The language of patriotism', in R. Samuel, *Patriotism: The Making and Unmaking of British National Identity*, Vol. 1, *History and Politics*, London, Routledge, 1989, pp. 57-89.

12. H. L. Hart, *Women's Suffrage and National Danger: A Plea for the Ascendancy of Man*, London, Alexander and Shepheard, 1889. See also B. Harrison, *Separate Spheres: The Opposition to Women's Suffrage in Britain*, London, Croom Helm, 1978.

13. C. Eustance, 'Protests from behind the grille: gender and the transformation of Parliament, 1867-1918', *Parliamentary History*, Vol. 16, Part 1, 1997, pp. 107-26, esp. p. 119.

14. H. Frances, 'Pay the piper, call the tune! The Women's Tax Resistance League', in M. Joannou and J. Purvis (eds), *The Women's Suffrage Movement: New Feminist Perspectives*, Manchester, Manchester University Press, 1998, pp. 65-71.

15. C. Pankhurst, 'International militancy', a speech delivered at Carnegie Hall, New York, 13 January 1915, London, WSPU, 1915, p. 3.

16. *Jus Suffragii*, 1 February 1918.

17. B. Anderson, *Imagined Communities: Reflections on the Origin and Spread of Nationalism*, London, Verso, 1991 (first edition 1983), and Colley, *Britons*.

18. For a variety of interpretations of the Irish suffrage campaign and connections with suffrage societies operating on the British mainland, see R. C. Owens, *'Smashing Times': A History of the Irish Women's Suffrage Movement, 1889-1922*, Dublin, Attic Press, 1984, and M. Ward, '"Suffrage first - above all else!" An account of the Irish suffrage movement', *Feminist Review*, No. 10, Spring 1982, pp. 21-32.

19. More research needs to be done into the ways in which suffrage texts and newspapers used the terms 'Englishwoman' and 'British woman'. Commenting more generally on late Victorian and Edwardian culture, Jane Mackay and Pat Thane have suggested that the interchangeability between the two terms may have been due to a complacent sense of Anglo-Saxon superiority, or a desire to quash regional differences, and also to the very flexibility and vagueness of the rhetoric of 'Englishness' in relation to women. See J. Mackay and P. Thane, 'The Englishwoman', in R. Colls and P. Dodd (eds), *Englishness, Politics and Culture, 1880-1920*, London, Croom Helm, 1986, pp. 191-229.

20. L. Leneman, 'A truly national movement: the view from outside London', in Joannou and Purvis (eds), *The Women's Suffrage Movement*, pp. 37-50.

21. L. Leneman, *A Guid Cause: The Women's Suffrage Movement in Scotland*, Edinburgh, Mercat Press, 1991, p. 61.

22. A. V. John, '"Run like blazes": the suffragettes and Welshness', *Llafur*, Vol. 6, No. 3, 1994, pp. 29-43.

23. J. Liddington and J. Norris, *One Hand Tied Behind Us: The Rise of the Women's Suffrage Movement*, London, Virago, 1978.

24. Verbatim minutes of the Third Annual Conference of the WFL, 1 February 1908, p. 15 (Fawcett Library, London).

25. A. V. John and C. Eustance (eds), *The Men's Share? Masculinities, Male Support and Women's Suffrage in Britain, 1890-1920*, London, Routledge, 1997.

26. *The Vote*, 13 August 1910.

27. Leneman, 'A truly national movement', p. 44.

28. L. Tickner, *The Spectacle of Women: Imagery of the Suffrage Campaign, 1907-14*, London, Chatto and Windus, 1987, pp. 123-31.

29. *Jus Suffragii*, 15 May 1910.

30. See, for example, the work by Jill Liddington and Anne Wiltsher on the anti-militaristic and anti-imperialist beliefs and activities of some suffrage activists. J. Liddington, *The Long Road to Greenham: Feminism and Anti-militarism in Britain since 1820*, London, Virago, 1989; A. Wiltsher, *Most Dangerous Women: Feminist Peace Campaigners of the Great War*, London, Pandora Press, 1985.

31. A. Burton, *Burdens of History: British Feminists, Indian Women and Imperial Culture, 1865-1915*, Chapel Hill, University of North Carolina Press, 1994, especially p. 34. See also V. Ware, *Beyond the Pale: White Women, Racism and History*, London, Verso, 1992.

32. A. Burton, 'The white woman's burden: British feminists and the "Indian woman", 1865-1915', in N. Chaudhuri and M. Strobel (eds), *Western Women and Imperial Complicity and Resistance*, Bloomington, Indiana University Press, 1992, p. 150.

33. Pettitt, 'Feminism and transnational links', unpublished paper, 1997.

34. S. S. Holton, 'From anti-slavery to suffrage militancy: the Bright circle, Elizabeth Cady Stanton and the British women's suffrage movement', in Daley and Nolan (eds), *Suffrage and Beyond*, p. 213.

35. E. DuBois, 'Women's suffrage around the world: three phases of suffrage internationalism', in Daley and Nolan (eds), *Suffrage and Beyond*, pp. 252-74.

36. For further information on the IWSA see L. Rupp, *Worlds of Women: The Making of an International Women's Movement*, Princeton, Princeton University Press, 1997, and M. Bosch, with A. Kloosterman, *Politics and Friendship: Letters from the IWSA, 1902-1942*, Columbus, Ohio State University Press, 1990.

37. *Jus Suffragii*, 1 July 1916. See also 1 May 1914.

38. *Jus Suffragii*, 1 June 1915.

39. *Jus Suffragii*, 15 July 1908.

40. Rupp, *Worlds of Women*, pp. 108-11.

41. From letter quoted in R. Strachey, *Millicent Garrett Fawcett*, London, John Murray, 1931, p. 301.

42. Women's Freedom League, Annual Report, 1913, p. 22 (Fawcett Library, London).

43. Rupp, *Worlds of Women*, pp. 52-80.

44. NUWSS, *Annual Report*, 1915, p. 10.

45. *Jus Suffragii*, 1 November 1914.

46. J. Marcus, 'Corpus/corps/corpse: writing the body in/at war', in H. M. Cooper, A. Munich, A. Merrill and S. Squier (eds), *Arms and the Woman: War, Gender and Literary Representation*, Chapel Hill, University of North Carolina Press, 1989, pp. 124-67.

47. See M. Mulvihill, *Charlotte Despard: A Biography*, London, Pandora, 1989, pp. 116-26; *Jus Suffragii*, 1 November 1915.

48. *The Vote*, 5 April 1918.

49. See J. Alberti, *Beyond Suffrage: Feminists in War and Peace, 1914-28*, Basingstoke, Macmillan, 1989; C. Law, *Suffrage and Power: The Women's Movement, 1918-28*, London, Tauris, 1997.

50. H. Smith, *British Feminism in the Twentieth Century*, London, Edward Elgar, 1990.

51. *The Vote*, 13 March 1925, 4 December 1925, 19 November 1926, 18 February 1927, 11 November 1927.

52. *The Vote*, 26 June 1925. In the 1920s, the WFL was affiliated to the Council for the Representation of Women in the League of Nations and British Commonwealth League.

1 Reflecting on Suffrage History

Sandra Stanley Holton

This chapter is based on a paper written for the plenary session that opened the Greenwich conference 'Seeing Through Suffrage', and it was intended to 'set the scene' in terms of an overview of suffrage history up until then. The editors have asked me to recast it so as to chart my own course through this field over the past 25 years or so. I cannot do proper justice in the space available to all the other researchers who have helped or influenced my own work, so I must simply apologize for any omissions and superficialities that may strike the reader in what follows. The field is now so large and various that it is impossible to be comprehensive, but I hope at least to point out some of the landmarks that have helped direct my own work, and to identify some possible signposts for future work.[1]

Encountering suffrage history

It was reading Sylvia Pankhurst's *The Suffragette Movement* alongside George Dangerfield's *The Strange Death of Liberal England* in the early 1970s that first prompted my interest in this field.[2] These were, I was later to realize, perhaps the two most influential studies to be published up until that time, but each told the story of the suffrage movement from a very different perspective. Sylvia Pankhurst's personal memoir gave the sense of an immense social movement that consistently attracted women of serious purpose prepared to undertake heroic acts of self-sacrifice for the cause of women's enfranchisement. Her picture was of a socially diverse movement, sometimes divided within itself, and with links to the labour movement which were continuous, despite the hostilities between the leaderships of the two movements from time to time. Sylvia Pankhurst looked back through the glass of family memory, and her story was told entirely from the 'militant' perspective associated principally with the Women's Social and Political Union (WSPU) and the breakaway militant group with which Sylvia Pankhurst was most identified, the East London Federation of Suffragettes.

George Dangerfield, in contrast, looked only at the campaign that was waged in the years immediately before the First World War. He linked the suffrage movement to the industrial unrest of the 1911-13 period and to Sir Edward Carson's threatened revolt against attempts to introduce home rule for Ireland, in a trinity of revolt against 'liberal England'. Instead of the story of heroism and dedication to social progress recounted by Sylvia Pankhurst, he told a story of the campaigns as the work of irrational, exhibitionist hysterics. Freudian theory was also invoked to suggest a 'lesbian' impulse to the movement, by which he meant not so much a sexual orientation as a revulsion against the society of men, a withdrawal into a closed world of women. Both studies largely ignored the 'constitutionalist' National Union of Women's Suffrage Societies (NUWSS), formed in 1897 out of a federation of some of the earliest suffrage societies from the 1860s. Only the twentieth-century militants were taken to be of any significance. Constitutionalists, I was to find, had last appeared as a significant presence in the history of the women's movement in Ray Strachey's *The Cause* of 1928.[3]

Here was an object lesson in the way values shape the writing of history, and the importance of rhetorical strategies in establishing the power of an interpretation, whether it be Sylvia Pankhurst's passionate engagement or George Dangerfield's sardonic detachment. When I came later to embark on a doctoral thesis, the suffrage movement immediately presented itself as a likely subject. This interest was confirmed when I began my preliminary bibliographic survey, for I soon encountered an alternative socialist-feminist perspective on the suffrage movement in Marion Ramelson's *Petticoat Rebellion* and Sheila Rowbotham's pioneering textbook on women's history, *Hidden from History*.[4] Each in some sense borrowed from the legacy of the militant school of history, but they also provided a more complex assessment of the class divisions and tensions among suffragists, and looked further back into the nineteenth-century origins of the demand for the vote. The publication of *The Hard Way Up*, the autobiography of a working-class, socialist suffragist, Hannah Mitchell, confirmed the importance of socialist circles to early militancy in the North-West and the solidarity that was secured between working-class and middle-class suffragists in this period, as well as indicating some of the tensions that eventually led to a series of militant breakaway groups, beginning with the Women's Freedom League (WFL), formed in 1907.[5]

Another recently published study, Constance Rover's *Women's Suffrage and Party Politics*, was the first exploration for over sixty years to look in any depth at the parliamentary situation that confronted suffrage campaigners, and the complexity of the position of their cause within each of the two main parties; where the leadership was sympathetic, the rank and file were not, or vice versa. Moreover, the policy of the newly emergent Labour Party moved back and forth on the question during the early twentieth-century campaigns. Subsequently David Morgan's *Suffragists and Liberals* was to demonstrate the complexity of the parliamentary situation that confronted the cause of women's suffrage after the landslide election victory of the Liberal Party in 1906.[6]

Finding a thesis topic

Initially I thought I was going to write about Sylvia Pankhurst, and how and why the story of the WSPU, led by her mother, Emmeline, and older sister, Christabel, had served to obscure the organizational and political complexity of the suffrage movement. But I was especially interested in exploring the troubled relationship between the suffrage and the labour and socialist movements, and initial reading in this field quickly shifted my interests towards the constitutional suffragists of the NUWSS. It seemed that this body had proved especially effective in bringing the Labour Party back to support for women's suffrage in the years immediately before the First World War. My central interest remained the relationship between the suffrage and the labour and socialist movements, and I now realized that this topic could not be adequately addressed through a focus on Sylvia Pankhurst.

I also discovered among the treasures of the Fawcett Library some records of the NUWSS, as well as pamphlet literature, and a specialist book collection that confirmed that there had been no monographic study of the constitutionalists. I had my thesis topic. Research in these records, however, soon made me aware of the importance of the extensive network of NUWSS provincial branch societies to its campaigning. Not only did its methods require elaborate local machinery to organize pressure from the constituencies, but a third generation of leaders emerged from some of its major provincial branches during the early twentieth-century campaigns, and were increasingly influential in their support for co-operation with the Labour Party. The NUWSS story could not be told simply from the perspective of London. In a search for branch records I was fortunate enough to find that the Mitchell Library in Glasgow, where I then lived, had a substantial collection of the records of the Glasgow NUWSS branch society. The Manchester Public Library archives also held extensive records of the society in that city – formed in the late 1860s, one of the first suffrage bodies – together with an important body of correspondence relating to the national leadership.

By great good fortune the papers of one of the most influential of those provincial suffragists who were to move into the NUWSS's leadership, Catherine Marshall, were also discovered at this time, and taken in by what has since become the Cumbria Record Office. These were to prove especially valuable in charting the relationship between the constitutionalists and the Labour Party, for Catherine Marshall became parliamentary secretary of the NUWSS in the crucial years from 1912. Earlier she had helped establish a lively local branch in the Lake District, giving more insight into rank and file campaigning. Her papers had been rescued from an old garden shed and at this time were still unlisted, grimy with the dust of decades, bird droppings and the attentions of mice. They were also quite muddled, so that an important policy discussion paper might follow a laundry list. This made for some anxiety that something important might be missed on my always rushed visits from Glasgow to Carlisle. But it also added to the sense of exploring in new territory, and shortly afterwards Jo Vellacott began the task of sorting, dating and ordering the collection, and making it altogether less intimidating to this novice researcher.[7]

So the direction of my research was determined by gaps and anomalies in the existing literature on the suffrage movement. It was equally informed by the socialist–feminist perspective which predominated in the new women's history that first emerged in the late 1960s, and was very powerfully shaped by previously little-used or unknown sources. These sources were 'discovered' by and read through the impetus of new questions, but they also, for me, represented an intervention from the past into the debate around those questions. The preservation of documentary sources, especially in women's history, is almost always a matter of chance, and such remains from the past necessarily interact with the concerns of the present-day researcher. But they also determine the credibility of any historical interpretation.

Suffrage history from the late 1970s to the mid-1980s

The publication of a fresh source, Hannah Mitchell's autobiography, seems to have been especially influential in shaping much of the research that began to appear from the late 1970s. It raised questions about the nature of relations between the suffrage, labour and socialist movements, and between the suffrage leadership and the rank and file. It also suggested the importance of certain regional centres of campaigning, most especially Manchester. Jill Liddington and Jill Norris's study of the Lancashire and Cheshire Textile and Other Workers' Representation Committee (LCTOWRC), *One Hand Tied Behind Us*, took its title from a comment by Hannah Mitchell on the difficulties of political campaigning for working-class women.[8] This study broke new ground, not simply in examining a previously neglected suffrage society, but in its focus on an important locality for the campaigns, and in the way it contextualized the demand by analysing the economic, social and party-political situation of women textile workers. It also offered the first major challenge to existing frameworks which put the national leadership of the WSPU at the centre of suffrage history. It suggested the class tensions and party political divisions that might disturb both the NUWSS and WSPU at a local level. It demonstrated the importance of provincial branch societies in the innovation of new campaigning methods and fresh policy initiatives.

The dominant paradigm had received a fundamental challenge. Indeed, there was little work at all during this period on the militant wing of the movement. What there was came principally from a radical feminist perspective that valued especially the separate intellectual, social and political worlds which women were creating among themselves, often alongside same-sex loving relationships. Elizabeth Sarah challenged a particularly hostile biography of Christabel Pankhurst by insisting on the power of her critique of male–female relations, and the value of separatist strategies. Martha Vicinus, in a chapter in her influential *Independent Women*, explored the symbolic meaning of militancy, most especially in terms of the claims of women to occupy public spaces, and in the spiritual values that might attach to personal suffering.[9]

The challenge to old paradigms was furthered also by research that was undertaken in this period on the NUWSS. Leslie Parker Hume published the first organizational history of that body in 1982.[10] In this same period the organizational range of the twentieth-century suffrage movement also received fuller acknowledgement in Les Garner's *Stepping Stones to Women's Liberty*, which compared the three largest societies, the NUWSS, the WSPU and the WFL. It also looked at the growing discontents within the movement by 1912, most especially in terms of the founding of the journal *The Freewoman*, and provided a revaluation of the impact of the First World War on the granting of the vote. A growing body of literature also appeared in these years on the links between the suffrage movement and the internationalist and peace movements of the First World War, and the complexities of that relationship. Here again, recognition of the role of constitutionalists was part of the story, for example in Jo Vellacott's exploration of the tensions within the NUWSS.[11]

My own work focused much more, as I have explained, on the internal politics of the suffrage movement, its cross-currents and more particularly the conditions that made possible the co-operation between the Labour Party and the NUWSS from 1912. In *Feminism and Democracy* I developed the arguments put forward in my PhD thesis. I looked, first, at the ideas and values expressed by women through the sixty years or so of suffrage campaigning. Unlike in the United States, these questions had as yet received little sustained analysis.[12]

I took my lead from a comment by Helena Swanwick, a leading constitutionalist, who had wished that the term 'feminist' had never been coined. She preferred to think of herself as a 'humanist', seeing men and women united by their common humanity, and the cause of women as the cause of all.[13] I also found helpful current debates between radical and socialist and liberal feminists about the power and danger of any 'essentialist' account of women; that is, one that asserted that women were by their very nature quite different from men.

Finding similar, if altogether less clearly articulated, tensions in suffragist polemic, I suggested that it was possible to distinguish both 'humanist' and 'essentialist' arguments in support of the enfranchisement of women. While the essentialist case became increasingly evident over the course of the suffrage campaigns, it might often be expressed alongside the humanist position in a single suffragist speech or pamphlet. Nor did the humanist perspective ever entirely disappear; it continued to be forcefully stated by influential figures like Helena Swanwick. I also examined the call to sexual solidarity among women of all classes, most notably in arguments that presented women as a 'sex-class': that is, as a social group with distinct interests *vis-à-vis* all men in the existing sexual hierarchy.[14]

Feminism and Democracy also argued that there had been much greater co-operation between militants and constitutionalists, especially at a local level, than could be allowed for in frameworks which presented the two wings as quite distinct, even oppositional.[15] With regard to relations between suffragists, socialists and labour supporters, I argued that the continued property basis of the parliamentary franchise at this time was the source of early discord. One-third of men, almost all working-class, remained unenfranchised, and as the infant Labour Party needed to expand its constituency the demand for a solely manhood suffrage measure, often disguised by the term 'adult suffrage', appealed to many of its supporters.[16]

It was here that *Feminism and Democracy* went beyond my doctoral thesis, by identifying what I termed a 'democratic suffragist' current. This was evident within all sections of the movement, but came to dominate constitutionalist policy-making in the crucial years of 1912–14. Democratic suffragists sought to marry the adult suffrage and women's suffrage demand within support for a universal suffrage: that is, the vote for all adults, male and female. A similar current of opinion informed a realignment within the militant wing of the movement, I argued, most notably in the formation of important but largely neglected breakaways like the East London Federation of Suffragettes and the United Suffragists. I suggested that it was the strategy of merging the women's suffrage demand in one for universal suffrage that ensured the eventual success of the cause in 1918.[17]

Suffrage history from the late 1980s to the late 1990s

By the second half of the 1980s, then, there had been a significant shift in the interpretative frameworks shaping suffrage history in Britain, a shift that had extended our understanding of the range and complexity of the internal politics of the suffrage movement, that challenged any absolute distinction between militants and constitutionalists, and that increasingly recognized the importance of local movements and provincial suffrage societies. The next decade was to see an equally substantial revision to past frameworks in a constantly growing body of new literature. My own work at this time was influenced by these new directions in three respects: first, a reconceptualization of what might constitute women's politics, and a reconsideration of the relation between the formal politics of public life and the informal politics of personal life; second, the expanded time frame in which suffrage history was being considered, beyond the very narrow focus on the first two decades of the twentieth century that characterized most of the work in the previous decade; and third, in the analysis of the gender and cultural politics of the suffrage campaigns, including the formation of the historiography of this question.

Especially evident in this period is a more extensive interest in the nineteenth-century women's movement and its relation to the suffrage demand, for example in Philippa Levine's *Victorian Feminism*. Patricia Hollis reminded suffrage historians that women had begun to vote and to stand for public office from the 1870s through new local government legislation. Many suffragists who, like Lydia Becker, did not live to see the parliamentary vote for women nonetheless enjoyed extensive periods of public office on School Boards and as Poor Law Guardians. Another landmark was the collection edited by Jane Rendall, *Equal or Different*, which also served to point up the breadth of women's political interests in this period, and expanded our understanding of the ideas that informed the early women's movement.[18]

Johanna Alberti's *Beyond Suffrage* followed the careers of fourteen somewhat later suffragists from the First World War into the inter-war period, emphasizing the importance of friendship networks, and of internationalism and pacifism to the political outlook of many. Kathryn Gleadle explored another neglected aspect of the much earlier origins of the women's movement, in the influential group of Unitarian intellectuals and writers of the 1840s who helped shape the contours of the debate on the position of women. Eileen Yeo analysed the ideas of a particularly influential member of this circle, Anna Jameson, and examined the relationship between such circles and the emerging field of social science. A further important cross-fertilization between the originators of the women's movement and another major reform movement was analysed in Clare Midgley's *Women against Slavery*. Barbara Caine, in a collective biography, *Victorian Feminists*, provided an analysis of the very different perspectives on the position of women that might be found among four leading figures in the nineteenth-century women's rights movement: Frances Power Cobbe, Emily Davies, Josephine Butler and Millicent Garrett Fawcett.[19]

In these ways our understanding of the intellectual and social foundations of the women's movement were significantly advanced. There is also evident in all these works a dissatisfaction with the way women's political activity in this period had previously been conceived. Jane Rendall, in her introduction to *Equal or Different*, argued for the value of a broader definition of what might constitute women's politics in the Victorian period, for example religious and philanthropic activity. Similarly, Philippa Levine detected an emergent, distinctively female political culture in this period, a perception that received confirmation in Patricia Hollis's analysis of women's work in local government. A wider recognition of Victorian women's separate worlds of love and friendship was at the heart of much of this reassessment, for example in Jane Rendall's account of the relationship between Barbara Leigh Smith and Bessie Rayner Parkes. Philippa Levine provided an extensive prosopographical study of the social and political circles in which some of the early advocates of women's rights moved, and demonstrated the importance of kinship and friendship networks to its organizational development, and to the values that came to shape it.[20]

Some of my own research traced a friendship and kinship network among the women of the Priestman-Bright circle. Though it had been important to the founding of a number of the first suffrage societies, and to related bodies like the Ladies' National Association for Repeal of the Contagious Diseases Acts, it had effectively been written out of suffrage histories after 1912, and subsequently forgotten. I identified, through tracing this network, a Radical-Liberal current within the suffrage movement that became increasingly at odds with the more moderate among its leadership. This tension helped explain many of the internal conflicts in this period, conflicts which were eventually to split the National Society for Women's Suffrage in 1888. This current also maintained much closer links with the US suffrage movement and provided support for the early efforts of Elizabeth Cady Stanton and Susan B. Anthony to form an international network of suffrage organizations.[21]

A growing concern with the sexual politics of the suffrage demand was also increasingly evident in work published from the late 1980s. Mary Lyndon Shanley's *Feminism, Marriage and the Law* was especially helpful to my own work on the Bright circle in two ways. First, it confirmed the existence and importance of what I termed the Radical current within the early years of the women's movement, including figures like Josephine Butler and Elizabeth Wolstenholme Elmy. Second, it suggested the existence of a relationship between women's campaigns for reforms of the marriage laws and for repeal of the Contagious Diseases Acts, and a Radical conception of the changes needed to secure the full citizenship of women. The right to possess one's own body, whether as wife or as prostitute, was central to this vision of citizenship, so that the end of coverture and equal civil rights before the law became as fundamental, from this viewpoint, as gaining the vote. Recognizing such perspectives among some of the founders of the women's movement also put a somewhat different meaning on free love from the one it holds today, and I explored this question in an account of the marriage of Elizabeth Wolstenholme Elmy.[22]

A concern with the sexual politics of the women's suffrage movement also informed a significant current of contemporary radical feminist history that emerged in this period. Susan Kingsley Kent, in *Sex and Suffrage*, analysed suffragist polemics around questions such as marriage, the Contagious Diseases Acts and venereal disease. Here more continuities between the nineteenth-century founders and the twentieth-century suffragists became apparent, though often such work did not recognize many of the tensions and conflicts among suffragists on such issues. Similarly, Sheila Jeffreys analysed the accounts of women's sexuality provided by some suffragists critical of male sexual norms. Her *The Spinster and Her Enemies* also emphasized the valuing of female celibacy and same-sex loving relationships between women in this period. Sheila Jeffreys contrasted this to the emerging field of sexology that established heterosexual, penetrative sex as the only normal and healthy expression of sexual desire. Here again, however, the widely divergent views among suffragists remained unacknowledged. A different perspective was offered in Lucy Bland's *Banishing the Beast*, which explored the varying discourses that informed these debates in terms of religious, scientific and medical views on the sexuality of women, and which recognized the variety of opinion within the women's movement more fully.[23]

Another clear departure in this period was the growing interest in the cultural work of the bohemian intelligentsia – actors, artists, writers – as contributing to the success of the suffrage campaigns. In the previous decade Julie Holledge and Sybil Oldfield had opened up this field with their studies of women in the theatre and the world of letters who had become suffragists. The relationship between women's artistic lives and their politics was further illuminated in Angela John's study of the WSPU supporter, actress and writer Elizabeth Robins. This interest in the role of the bohemian intelligentsia in the suffrage movement also informed my own study of the nineteenth-century suffragist and former theatrical Jessie Craigen. This suggested the importance of her considerable powers of public speaking in the 1870s and 1880s when this capacity was not commonplace in the movement. Nor was this contribution only a matter of voice training but reflected also Jessie Craigen's skill in rhetoric, her command of language.

Jessie Craigen's presence also demonstrated the importance that leading suffragists like Lydia Becker put on winning working-class support for the cause from the early 1870s. Her career threw further light, too, on the tensions between Radical suffragists and the more moderate among the leadership, especially in terms of any alliance with the Irish home rule movement. It provided a further instance of romantic friendships, in this case between Jessie Craigen and Helen Taylor, in the formation of a female political culture in this period. It traced the difficulties encountered by those who were dependent on others in the movement for their living. And lastly, it suggested how narrow was the line that the early suffragists had to walk between insisting on women's right to occupy public space and maintaining public legitimacy for their cause.[24]

The cultural work of suffragist writers, artists and actors was also brilliantly explored in Lisa Tickner's *The Spectacle of Women*. Their various skills were put to use for the promotion of votes for women to great effect, in the production of pageants, posters, banners, plays and novels that were so notable a part of twentieth-century suffrage campaigning. Not only did such contributions make for effective propaganda for the cause, Lisa Tickner argues, but they played an essential role in helping to promote representations of the 'new' woman and to counter the stereotypes on which the anti-suffragist case rested, and by which it was often presented to the public.[25]

The meaning of militancy has also undergone significant reappraisal in the past decade, most notably in Liz Stanley and Ann Morley's *The Life and Death of Emily Wilding Davison*. This study of the suffragette who died after throwing herself under the king's horse at the 1913 Derby drew attention to the extensive presence of 'freelancers' and irregulars within the WSPU. These women had inaugurated some of the best-known militant tactics: the hunger strike and window-smashing, for example. While most remained loyal to the WSPU leadership even as that organization began to fragment, they also retained their right to independent action. Here again the perspective of present-day radical-feminist historians is evident, most especially in its methodology of tracing the webs of love and friendship among women, and in emphasizing their implications for forms of political action.[26]

In this way it was possible to reveal the values that were shared by Emily Wilding Davison and her group of friends among such militant freelancers: socialism, vegetarianism, animal rights, for example. Such an analysis also served to undermine the official and orthodox accounts of Emily Wilding Davison as an irrational, demented woman, by revealing the moral imperatives that led her to adopt such extreme measures. A very different perspective on militancy was hereby revealed from those centred on the WSPU leadership, though here too, reappraisal is under way, for example in June Purvis's work on the now iconic figure of Christabel Pankhurst.[27]

My own essay on Emmeline Pankhurst was prompted by a similar concern to understand the significance of militancy. I had long been perplexed by the readiness of many suffragists to endure extremes of suffering for this cause, especially when confronting a government that showed itself more than ready to censor, to harry, and to resort to barely disguised torture in the form of forcible feeding. Rebecca West's account, which stresses Emmeline Pankhurst's identification with the French

Revolution, gave some clue. But, paradoxically, it was reading Ann Oakley's acute analysis of the leading constitutionalist Millicent Garrett Fawcett that proved especially helpful, particularly in terms of its account of constitutionalism as a particular view of history and social change.

My discussion of Emmeline Pankhurst became in a sense contrapuntal to Ann Oakley's, and focused on the influence of Thomas Carlyle's history of the French Revolution. Here was an account that celebrated the Terror (the first work in English to do so), and that emphasized the importance of individual revolutionaries in exerting their will to bring about major political and social change through individual acts of heroism. This was the lesson from history that Emmeline Pankhurst sought to follow in her promotion of suffrage militancy, while also, I argued, propounding a distinctively female heroic which eschewed violence against persons. Here, then, was a 'Romantic feminism', most especially in terms of the historical burden it placed upon the individual militant.[28]

All the above influences and concerns were at work when I came to write *Suffrage Days*. I had three aims. First, I wanted to recover some of the stories of suffragists whose contributions had been lost to history, work that I continue presently in my ongoing research on Alice Clark and on her great-aunts, the Priestman sisters. For me, such recovery remains an essential element in the project of women's history. Second, I hoped to construct a narrative that would convey something of the new lines of interpretation that had emerged over the previous decade or so: the importance of the webs of love and friendship on which the movement was built; the existence of a Radical-Liberal current that continually challenged the more moderate leadership from the inception of the campaigns in the late 1860s; the sexual politics of women's suffrage; the relation between this demand and the changing social constructions of gender identities; the previously neglected continuities between the nineteenth- and twentieth-century phases of the campaigns; the fluid boundaries between the militant and constitutionalist wings of the movement; the complex relations between the suffrage and the labour and socialist movements; the importance of the democratic suffragist strategy to the eventual winning of votes for women; the role of suffragists in internationalist, pacifist and humanitarian aid efforts during the First World War. Third, I sought to challenge any presumption that suffrage history had been 'done', that there was little more work needed, and little left to say on the topic.

And happily, the field continues to prompt fresh and exciting work. Extensive interest in analysing the nature of the militancy and the cultural significance of the twentieth-century struggle for votes, for example, continues. Part of this research agenda involves filling in many of the gaps that remain in our knowledge of the militant wing: for example, in exploring its breakaway groups like the WFL, or in undertaking further local studies. But such work continues to go beyond the formal-political, institutional and intellectual-history approaches of earlier years. Issues of gender identities and gender contestation are much more central, for example, to recently completed doctoral theses, like those of Claire Eustance on the WFL and of Krista Cowman on the suffrage movement in Liverpool.[29]

The role of gender identities in the suffrage campaigns is the focus also of the major project recently completed at the University of Greenwich to investigate the role of men within the movement. *The Men's Share?*, edited by Angela John and Claire Eustance, breaks entirely new ground in asking what men's support for women's enfranchisement might reveal about understandings both of masculinity and femininity, and the possible limits to male supporters' conception of the liberation of women. Elsewhere, Claire Eustance has looked at the symbolic significance of the grille behind which women visiting Parliament had to sit until 1917. There she has forcefully argued the need to explore changing social constructions of masculinity in order more fully to understand the relation between women's suffrage and the transformation of Parliament during the period of the suffrage campaigns.[30]

My own interest in such questions was further fostered by the seminar series that was part of the Greenwich project. There I contributed a paper on Laurence Housman that helped me think through some of the themes I was to pursue further in my *Suffrage Days*, most especially in terms of alternative male sexualities and the politics of gender difference. In the essay I contributed to *The Men's Share?*, however, I looked more widely at the nature of the 'suffragette' identity and its implications for male participation in militancy, most especially in terms of the female heroic on which suffrage militancy was based. I looked, too, at how male suffragists sought to uphold old ideals of chivalry, while promoting new ways of thinking about what it was to be manly. I recounted the attempts of the authorities to throw into question the manliness of suffragists like William Ball and Hugh Franklin, who endured lengthy periods of forcible feeding leading in the first case to a temporary loss of sanity and in the second to a period of voluntary exile in France.[31]

It is only to be expected that such sea changes in the concerns of suffrage history should also have brought about a new and expanding interest in suffrage historiography. Not surprisingly, given the importance of Sylvia Pankhurst's historical work, much of this has focused on the construction of a 'militant' perspective on the movement's past.[32] Kathryn Dodd has provided a fascinating analysis of how Sylvia Pankhurst adopted a variety of forms to suit her particular political and literary purposes.[33] June Purvis is approaching suffrage historiography with a somewhat different set of concerns, and has offered a long-overdue reassessment of some of the more hostile historical accounts of the WSPU leadership, and of the social composition of militant prisoners.[34]

Historiographical issues have also been central to some of my own most recent work. In a chapter on the late nineteenth-century Women's Franchise League I followed David Rubinstein in questioning the periodization we had inherited from earlier generations of historians. I argued that the history of the League not only lent support to Rubinstein's argument that the 1890s was not a period of dormancy, but also represented significant continuities between the Radical suffragists of the Victorian period and the militants of the early twentieth century, continuities that Sylvia Pankhurst's work had served to obscure to a significant degree.[35]

It is also the case that alternative perspectives within early suffrage history have largely been ignored, aside from Kathryn Dodd's pioneering analysis of Ray Strachey's *The Cause*. Accordingly, another aspect of my own recent work has focused on what I have termed the 'constitutionalist' school of suffrage history. In a further article I look at the sense of national identity embodied within its historical frameworks.[36] This interest was prompted by Jane Rendall's discussion of the languages of race adopted by the early suffragists, together with Antoinette Burton's and Vron Ware's recent work on the relation between the women's movement and British imperialism.[37] I took as my starting point Charlotte Carmichael Stopes's *British Freewomen*. Here I have found that the new languages of racial difference and imperial destiny were deployed in the constitutionalist case for women's enfranchisement by reference back to the supposed cultural and genetic legacy of the ancient Britons, and to then current ideas about hierarchies of race. Brought together in suffragist polemic, these ideas imbued the female Briton with a particular historical destiny in the vanguard of the advance from 'barbarism' and towards the spread of civilization.[38]

Conclusion

Over the course of the past three decades the new history of the women's suffrage movement has expanded further on the fresh feminist perspectives on intellectual and political history frameworks with which it began. Drawing variously on theories of sexual politics, of gender difference, of representation and of post-colonialism, these new investigations have remapped the field of suffrage history, which has become far more reflexive, and hence more interested in its own history. And the basic work of recovery continues, as it must, directed by the ever-changing intellectual and political concerns of the present day.

Notes

1. A fuller acknowledgment of my debts to other scholars may be found in S. S. Holton, *Suffrage Days: Stories from the Women's Suffrage Movement*, London, Routledge, 1996, especially pp. 279–90.

2. E. S. Pankhurst, *The Suffragette Movement: An Intimate Account of Persons and Ideals*, London, Virago, 1977 (first published 1931); G. Dangerfield, *The Strange Death of Liberal England*, London, Paladin, 1975 (first published 1935).
3. R. Strachey, *The Cause: A Short History of the Women's Movement in Great Britain*, London, Virago, 1978 (first published 1928).
4. M. Ramelson, *Petticoat Rebellion: A Century of Struggle for Women's Rights*, London, Lawrence and Wishart, 1967; S. Rowbotham, *Hidden from History*, London, Pluto Press, 1973.
5. H. Mitchell, *The Hard Way Up: The Autobiography of Hannah Mitchell, Suffragette and Rebel*, London, Virago, 1977 (first published 1968).
6. C. Rover, *Women's Suffrage and Party Politics in Britain, 1866–1914*, London, Routledge and Kegan Paul, 1967; D. Morgan, *Suffragists and Liberals*, Oxford, Blackwell, 1975.
7. My research on local records needed to be condensed in the book that followed, but for a fine study of the Scottish movement see L. Leneman, *A Guid Cause: The Women's Suffrage Movement in Scotland*, Aberdeen, Aberdeen University Press, 1991. On Catherine Marshall, see J. Vellacott, *From Liberal to Labour with Women's Suffrage: The Story of Catherine Marshall*, Montreal, McGill-Queen's University Press, 1993.
8. J. Liddington and J. Norris, *One Hand Tied Behind Us: The Rise of the Women's Suffrage Movement*, London, Virago, 1978.
9. E. Sarah, 'Christabel Pankhurst: reclaiming her power', in D. Spender (ed.), *Feminist Theorists: Three Centuries of Women's Intellectual Traditions*, London, Women's Press, 1983, pp. 256–84; M. Vicinus, *Independent Women: Work and Community for Single Women, 1850–1920*, London, Virago, 1985.
10. L. Parker Hume, *The National Union of Women's Suffrage Societies*, New York, Garland Publishing, 1982.
11. L. Garner, *Stepping Stones to Women's Liberty: Feminist Ideas in the Women's Suffrage Movement, 1900–18*, London, Heinemann Educational Books, 1984; J. V. Newberry, 'Anti-war Suffragists', *History*, Vol. 62, 1977, pp. 411–25.
12. S. S. Holton, *Feminism and Democracy: Women's Suffrage and Reform Politics in Britain, 1900–1918*, Cambridge, Cambridge University Press, 1986. Two comparative-historical accounts were my principal guides at this time: R. Evans, *The Feminists*, London, Croom Helm, 1977; O. Banks, *Faces of Feminism*, Oxford, Martin Robertson, 1979, together with B. Taylor, *Eve and the New Jerusalem: Socialism and Feminism in the Nineteenth Century*, New York, Pantheon, 1983; B. Caine, 'John Stuart Mill and the English women's movement', *Historical Studies*, Vol. 18, 1982, pp. 52–67, and 'Feminism, suffrage and the nineteenth-century women's movement', *Women's Studies International Forum*, Vol. 5, 1982, pp. 537–50. See also D. M. C. Worzala, 'The Langham Place circle: the

beginnings of the organized women's movement in England, 1854-1870', unpublished PhD thesis, University of Wisconsin, 1982, a pioneering study of the ideas of the British movement.

13. H. M. Swanwick, *The Future of the Women's Movement*, London, G. Bell, 1913, p. vii, and *I Have Been Young*, London, Victor Gollancz, 1935, p. 207. The term 'feminist' gained currency in Britain, as in the United States, only from 1910 on. See Holton, *Suffrage Days*, p. 157 and p. 271, endnote 43.

14. Holton, *Feminism and Democracy*, pp. 9-28.

15. *Ibid.*, pp. 29-52.

16. *Ibid.*, pp. 53-75.

17. *Ibid.*, pp. 124-50. Compare with the very different account of the wartime suffrage movement in M. Pugh, 'Politicians and the women's vote, 1914-18', *History*, Vol. 59, 1974, pp. 358-74.

18. P. Levine, *Victorian Feminism 1850-1900*, London, Hutchinson, 1987; P. Hollis, *Ladies Elect: Women in English Local Government 1865-1914*, Oxford, Clarendon Press, 1987; J. Rendall (ed.), *Equal or Different*, Oxford, Basil Blackwell, 1987.

19. J. Alberti, *Beyond Suffrage: Feminists in War and Peace, 1914-29*, London, Macmillan, 1989; K. Gleadle, *The Early Feminists: Radical Unitarians and the Emergence of the Women's Rights Movement, 1831-1851*, London, Routledge, 1995; E. J. Yeo, 'Social motherhood and the sexual communion of labour in British social science, 1859-1950', *Women's History Review*, Vol. 1, 1992, pp. 63-88; C. Midgley, *Women against Slavery: The British Campaigns, 1789-1870*, London, Routledge, 1992; B. Caine, *Victorian Feminists*, Oxford, Oxford University Press, 1992.

20. J. Rendall, 'Friendship and politics: Barbara Leigh Smith Bodichon (1821-91) and Bessie Rayner Parkes (1829-1925)', in J. Rendall and S. Mendus (eds), *Sexuality and Subordination*, London, Routledge, 1989, pp. 136-70; P. Levine, *Feminist Lives in Victorian England*, Oxford, Basil Blackwell, 1988.

21. S. S. Holton, '"To educate women into rebellion": Elizabeth Cady Stanton and the creation of a transatlantic network of Radical suffragists', *American Historical Review*, Vol. 99, 1994, pp. 1113-36, and 'From anti-slavery to suffrage militancy: the Bright circle, Elizabeth Cady Stanton and the British women's movement', in C. Daley and M. Nolan (eds), *Suffrage and Beyond: International Feminist Perspectives*, Auckland, Auckland University Press, 1994, pp. 213-33.

22. M. Lyndon Shanley, *Feminism, Marriage and the Law in Victorian England 1850-1895*, London, I. B. Tauris, 1989, and for a somewhat later period see C. Dyhouse, *Feminism and the Family in England 1880-1939*, Oxford, Basil Blackwell, 1989; S. S. Holton, 'Free love and Victorian feminism: the divers matrimonials of Elizabeth Wolstenholme and Ben Elmy', *Victorian Studies*, Vol. 37, 1994, pp. 199-222, in which my

argument was also very much informed by C. Pateman, *The Sexual Contract*, Stanford, University of California Press, 1988.

23. S. Kingsley Kent, *Sex and Suffrage in Britain, 1860-1914*, Princeton, Princeton University Press, 1987; S. Jeffreys, *The Spinster and Her Enemies*, London, Pandora, 1985; L. Bland, *Banishing the Beast: Sexuality and the Early Feminists*, New York, New York Press, 1995.

24. J. Holledge, *Innocent Flowers: Women in the Edwardian Theatre*, London, Virago, 1981; S. Oldfield, *Spinsters of This Parish: The Life and Times of F. M. Mayor and Mary Sheepshanks*, London, Virago, 1984; A. V. John, *Elizabeth Robins: Staging a Life, 1862-1952*, London, Routledge, 1995; S. S. Holton, 'Silk dresses and lavender kid gloves: the wayward career of Jessie Craigen, working suffragist', *Women's History Review*, Vol. 6, 1996, pp. 125-46.

25. L. Tickner, *The Spectacle of Women: Imagery of the Suffrage Campaign, 1907-1914*, London, Chatto and Windus, 1987. The current interest in representation and the suffrage movement is evident also, for example, in some of the contributions in M. Joannou and J. Purvis (eds), *The Women's Suffrage Movement: New Feminist Perspectives*, Manchester, Manchester University Press, 1998.

26. L. Stanley with A. Morley, *The Life and Death of Emily Wilding Davison*, London, Women's Press, 1988.

27. J. Purvis, 'Christabel Pankhurst and the Women's Social and Political Union', in Joannou and Purvis (eds), *The Women's Suffrage Movement*, pp. 157-72.

28. R. West, 'A reed of steel', in J. Marcus (ed.), *The Young Rebecca*, London, Macmillan, 1992, pp. 243-62; A. Oakley, 'Millicent Fawcett and her 73 reasons', in *Telling the Truth about Jerusalem: A Collection of Essays and Poems*, Oxford, Basil Blackwell, 1986, pp. 18-35; S. S. Holton, '"In sorrowful wrath": suffrage militancy and the romantic feminism of Emmeline Pankhurst', in H. L. Smith (ed.), *British Feminism in the Twentieth Century*, Aldershot, Edward Elgar, 1990, pp. 7-24.

29. C. L. Eustance, '"Daring to be free": the evolution of women's political identities in the Women's Freedom League, 1907-1930', unpublished PhD thesis, University of York, 1993; K. Cowman, 'Engendering citizenship: the political involvement of women on Merseyside 1890-1920', unpublished PhD thesis, University of York, 1995.

30. A. V. John and C. Eustance, 'Shared histories - differing identities: introducing masculinities, male support and women's suffrage', in A. V. John and C. Eustance (eds), *The Men's Share? Masculinities, Male Support and Women's Suffrage in Britain, 1890-1920*, London, Routledge, 1997, pp. 1-37; C. Eustance, 'Protests from behind the grille: gender and the transformation of Parliament, 1867-1918', *Parliamentary History*, Vol. 16, 1997, pp. 106-26.

31. Holton, *Suffrage Days*, and 'Manliness and militancy: the political

protest of male suffragists and the gendering of the "suffragette" identity', in John and Eustance (eds), *The Men's Share?*, pp. 110-34.

32. Notably in J. Marcus, 'Introduction', in her *The Pankhursts and Women's Suffrage*, London, Routledge and Kegan Paul, 1987; L. E. N. Mayhall, 'Creating the "suffragette spirit": British feminism and the historical imagination', *Women's History Review*, Vol. 4, 1995, pp. 319-44; H. Kean, 'Searching for the past in present defeat: the construction of historical and political identity in British feminism in the 1920s and 1930s', *Women's History Review*, Vol. 3, 1994, pp. 57-80.

33. K. Dodd, 'The politics of form in Sylvia Pankhurst's writings', in her *A Sylvia Pankhurst Reader*, Manchester, Manchester University Press, 1993, pp. 1-30, and for further re-evalutions see R. Pankhurst, 'Sylvia Pankhurst in perspective: some comments on Patricia Romero's *E. Sylvia Pankhurst: Portrait of a Rebel*', *Women's Studies International Forum*, Vol. 11, 1988, pp. 245-62; I. Bullock and R. Pankhurst, *Sylvia Pankhurst: From Artist to Anti-fascist*, London, Macmillan, 1994; B. Winslow, *Sylvia Pankhurst: Sexual Politics and Political Activism*, London, UCL Press, 1996.

34. J. Purvis, 'A "pair of infernal queens"? A reassessment of dominant representations of Emmeline and Christabel Pankhurst, first-wave feminists in Edwardian Britain', *Women's History Review*, Vol. 5, 1996, pp. 259-80, and 'The prison experiences of the suffragettes in Edwardian Britain', *Women's History Review*, Vol. 4, 1995, pp. 103-34.

35. D. Rubinstein, *Before the Suffragettes: Women's Emancipation in the 1890s*, Brighton, Harvester Press, 1986; S. S. Holton, 'Now you see it, now you don't: the Women's Franchise League and its place in contending narratives of the women's suffrage movement', in Joannou and Purvis (eds), *The Women's Suffrage Movement*, pp. 15-36.

36. K. Dodd, 'Cultural politics and women's historical writing: the case of Ray Strachey's *The Cause*', *Women's Studies International Forum*, Vol. 13, 1990, pp. 127-37; S. S. Holton, 'The making of suffrage history', in J. Purvis and S. S. Holton, *Votes for Women: New Feminist Essays on Suffrage History*, London, Taylor and Francis, 1999.

37. J. Rendall, 'Citizenship, culture and civilisation: the languages of British suffragists, 1866-1874', in Daley and Nolan (eds), *Suffrage and Beyond*, pp. 127-50; A. Burton, *The Burdens of History: British Feminists, Indian Women and Imperial Culture, 1863-1915*, Chapel Hill, University of North Carolina Press, 1994; V. Ware, *Beyond the Pale: White Women, Racism and History*, London, Verso, 1992.

38. C. Carmichael Stopes, *British Freewomen: Their Historical Privilege*, 4th edition, London, Swan Sonnenschein, 1909; S. S. Holton, '"British freewomen": national identity, constitutionalism and languages of race in early suffragist histories', in E. J. Yeo (ed.), *Radical Femininity: Women's Self-Representation in the Public Sphere*, Manchester, Manchester University Press, 1998, pp. 149-71.

2 'Crossing the Great Divide': Inter-organizational Suffrage Relationships on Merseyside, 1895–1914

Krista Cowman

It is frequently asserted that the history of British women's suffrage is complete.[1] There are two obvious challenges to this assumption. First, advances in the discipline of history alert us to the fact that the last word on any historical topic is almost unreachable. Second, the notion of history implicit in this assertion is a gendered one. One could not, for example, imagine a situation in which the French Revolution or Chartism were said to be 'finished'. The emergence of women's history as some distinct category throws such assumptions into stark relief, because it provides a theoretical framework in which new work on suffrage can progress. There have been many advances in suffrage history over the past two decades, both in the reinterpretation of existing materials and in the discoveries of fresh archival sources.[2] Although these have added much to existing knowledge of the movement, they also remind us how much more still remains to be discovered.

Much of the work undertaken by historians in recent years has focused almost exclusively on the actions and policies of single suffrage organizations. To an extent this has been necessary and desirable. Although there were more than 50 suffrage organizations in Britain at the outbreak of the First World War, as yet the history of only two, the Women's Social and Political Union (WSPU) and the National Union of Women's Suffrage Societies (NUWSS), can be found in monographs.[3] A third large national society, the Women's Freedom League (WFL), which outlived both the WSPU and the NUWSS, and continued into the 1960s, has no published full-length study to date.[4] The histories of smaller and shorter-lived groups such as the United Suffragists, the Liberal Women's Suffrage Union and the Catholic Women's Suffrage Society are found only in article form.[5] The majority of suffrage organizations, including the People's Suffrage Federation, the Votes for Women Fellowship and the Conservative and Unionist Women's Franchise Association, remain almost totally unresearched.

An important parallel development to revisions of suffrage history with a national perspective was begun with the publication of Jill Liddington and Jill Norris's *One Hand Tied Behind Us*.[6] This was largely concerned with replacing narratives which positioned a middle-class, London-based WSPU at their centre. Liddington and Norris challenged the prominence of a middle-class WSPU by restoring working-class activists of the NUWSS to the historical agenda. The London-centredness of previous research was countered by focusing research on Lancashire. Their work did not break from the dichotomy of militant/constitutional suffrage.[7] However, the technique of using a local study spawned a variety of similar work.[8] We now know much more about how suffrage worked in many areas of Britain, and how nationally devised campaign tactics were translated into actions by the local branches of many organizations. These local studies point us towards the creation of a fresh national history of suffrage. This new history can be truly national, drawing on information from all over Britain and taking full account of the many regional differences and variations, fluctuations in class and style and standards of living, which have previously been submerged. New local studies have offered evidence to uphold the suggestion of Liz Stanley and Ann Morley that:

> At the level of individual feminist women and their political actions and allegiances, the organisational divisions and sharp ideological differences that most accounts of Edwardian feminism have seized upon are, at best, only a small part of the total picture.[9]

It is with this question of the 'total picture' – correcting it, challenging it, upholding it or overturning it – that local suffrage history is most concerned. Local studies create fresh narratives which immediately alter the perspectives of national suffrage histories by placing new protagonists at the centre. National figures retire to the margins, diminished in stature, or do not appear at all.

A simple story will illustrate this point. On Saturday 5 September 1908, Miss Alice E. Burton, a 50-year-old comic actress, attended an open-air suffrage demonstration in front of St George's Hall, Liverpool.[10] It was a decision which was to have far-reaching effects for her life over the next six years. The demonstration was organized by the local Men's League for Women's Suffrage (MLWS) and its main platform speakers came from that organization. Other platforms featured speakers from a variety of other interested parties – reforming clergymen, local academics, and women from the NUWSS and the WSPU – invited by the MLWS. Alice, 'a lifelong rebel against the idea of women's intellectual inferiority', found herself drawn to the WSPU platform.[11] Here she heard Mrs Nellie Martel, an Australian woman voter, describe 'the practical effects of Women's Enfranchisement ... both social and political'.[12] The facts Mrs Martel presented, and her advocacy of militancy, struck a chord with Alice, particularly the idea that suffrage could bring social equality. Since retiring from the stage in 1893 Alice had eked out a living for herself teaching shorthand and elocution, so was well acquainted both with low levels of female pay and with the low status of much of women's paid work.[13] Eschewing the more moderate messages presented by other societies at the demonstration, she immediately joined the WSPU and was soon immersed in the life of the local branch, reporting on local meetings for *Votes for Women* and undertaking administrative work.[14]

Alice chose to join the WSPU because of its militant message, which stressed a variety of direct actions rather than the tactics of gentle persuasion favoured by local constitutional suffragists.[15] She took the first opportunity to join in more high-profile direct action in March 1909, when Mrs Pankhurst came to speak in Liverpool and asked for delegates to attend the next 'Women's Parliament' at Caxton Hall, London, at the end of that month.[16] Alice volunteered and, along with Mrs Bessie Morris, Miss Ada Broughton, Miss Patricia Woodlock and Miss Cecilia Hilton, formed 'the Liverpool contingent' to the Women's Parliament.[17] During the subsequent procession to Westminster all five women were arrested and sent to Holloway, convicted on charges of obstruction and assault. Imprisonments were a good source of publicity to the WSPU, and the Liverpool branch began a campaign of 'indignation' meetings to capitalize on its heroines. Through their arrest and the subsequent campaign around them, a collective identity was forged for these five women, based both on their identification with militancy and on their local links.[18] Miss Burton and three of the other four 'Liverpool Prisoners' were released in April after each serving one month in Holloway Prison. (Patricia Woodlock had received a heavier sentence of three months, this being her fourth imprisonment.) They were feted, first at the Albert Hall where they all received silver Holloway brooches and made speeches, Miss Burton drawing on her former stage career to adapt a quotation from *Macbeth*: 'I dare do all that may become a woman; who dares do more is none.'[19] The former prisoners then returned home to Liverpool to another large welcome meeting at which they received bouquets from Miss Bertha Elam, a recent recruit who had joined the WSPU after having been inspired by the efforts of the fifth prisoner, Patricia Woodlock. Two months later, in June 1909, Bertha Elam and Alice Burton were able to develop their acquaintance when both were arrested and subsequently imprisoned during another suffrage demonstration in London.[20]

The stories of Alice and Bertha, and others like them, serve several purposes for historians of suffrage. At a basic level, they restore to the historical narrative significant individuals who have long been 'hidden from history'. In so doing, they also emphasize the strong connections and networks which existed between suffrage activists within local branches. Moreover, as Sandra Holton has recently pointed out, new narratives which place marginal figures at their centre can significantly alter the emphasis of what was previously thought to be the whole story.[21] The figures of the Pankhursts, so often presented as the personification of the WSPU, are almost invisible in the suffrage narrative of Alice Burton. An Australian, Nellie Martel, brought her into the WSPU. Alice then became a 'Liverpool Prisoner', and it was the collective inspiration of this group of women which was instrumental in recruiting Bertha Elam to the cause. Both Alice and Bertha went on to play a significant part in the Liverpool WSPU and are major figures in the history of suffrage on Merseyside. Their own activism was often played out on a national stage, but firmly located by them within local boundaries. They never held national office in the WSPU, and are missing from even the fullest national accounts.[22]

Yet even these fresh stories are only a small part of the entire narrative of suffrage on Merseyside. They tell us something about the concerns and actions of militant suffragettes, but have little to say about those who rejected the militant message. At the large demonstration at which Alice Burton was converted to militancy, other organizations presented different messages to which she did not respond. The measured words of the Liverpool Women's Suffrage Society (LWSS) articulated by Eleanor Rathbone, who warned against 'starting a sort of battle between the sexes', struck no chord with Alice.[23] So although her decision to stand in front of St George's Hall that day plunged her into a close local network of militant suffragettes, it can also be read as the point at which another rich female network, the one surrounding the LWSS, was closed to her. Reclaiming Alice and Bertha as subjects helps our understanding of the history of the WSPU, but simultaneously diverts us from other, equally under-researched areas of local women's activities.

A more holistic picture emerges through the inter-organizational relationships of Merseyside's suffrage groups, which allow the origins of differences in policy and tactics to be examined as well as occasions when they were circumnavigated. Without diverging too much into the broader historiography of the region, it is helpful to point out that much of the history of women's suffrage movements on Merseyside mirrors the broader tendency towards exceptionalism noted in other areas of local political life.[24] In other words, as Merseyside so frequently provides historians with the exception to a national picture, so it offers alternatives to the national suffrage 'norm'. Obviously, taking a particular provincial district and placing it at the centre of the narrative immediately moves the focus away from London and, by implication, a national leadership, both of which have dominated suffrage historiography.[25]

There is also a richness of suffrage activity at a local level which it is simply not possible for the historian to convey on a national scale. Rather than simply contemplating any existent national pictures and the extent to which local studies confirm or deny them, I wish to demonstrate how a local study can also have many other uses. The remainder of this chapter will provide a close focus which is, for want of a better word, manageable enough to allow the complexity of relationships within and between suffrage organizations to be explored in detail. Of course, it is impossible to ignore altogether my earlier point about a national model, and much of what I have to say about inter-organizational relationships will also relate to this. However, in my exploration of these relationships I am more concerned with different issues surrounding the choices individual women made about their suffrage activity. What was it that made particular organizations appeal to some women more than others, such as was the case when Alice Burton chose the WSPU over the LWSS? And why, having opted to join one organization, did some suffrage activists then locate their activities across a variety of organizations while others remained in one group alone? Why was a multiplicity of identities essential to many of those who would be suffrage activists, but seemingly irrelevant to others?

Some of these questions can be answered by looking at the way that the characters of particular suffrage organizations developed in a district. By 1914, nine suffrage organizations had functioning Merseyside branches. The Liverpool Women's Suffrage Society (LWSS, the local branch of the NUWSS) and the Liverpool WSPU were the two largest local groups. They were joined, in order of establishment, by the WFL, the MLWS, the Conservative and Unionist Women's Franchise Association (CUWFA), the Church League for Women's Suffrage (CLWS), the Votes for Women Fellowship (VFWF), the United Suffragists (US) and the Catholic Women's Suffrage Society (CWSS). The US was slightly different as its local branch did not form until after the outbreak of the First World War, when many other societies had become less active. The MLWS is also less relevant as although it at some point worked with all the other suffrage groups on an individual basis, its *membership* was, of course, restricted to men, who were debarred from full membership of many women's suffrage bodies.[26] So, at the height of suffrage campaigning on Merseyside, between 1909 and 1914, female activists had a choice of seven different organizations, and it is mainly the relationships between these bodies that will now be discussed.

The most interesting and colourful inter-organizational suffrage relationship on Merseyside was enjoyed by the NUWSS and the WSPU. The rivalry between these two bodies was deep and embittered, and has enjoyed a remarkable degree of longevity. Indeed, as recently as 1994 the daughter of a leading LWSS member began a public lecture on her mother's activities by explaining that she (her mother) 'did not throw stones' and was not 'silly, lawless or militant', but was a 'law-abiding' suffrage campaigner.[27] Such tactical divisions lay at the heart of the differences between the two organizations. Liverpool's WSPU members enthusiastically participated in every imaginable form of militancy both within the city and at national events. The LWSS remained committed to law-abiding methods of campaigning. These were often criticized locally for demonstrating a discretion verging on anonymity.[28] However, there were further divisions of class and politics between the two bodies which are more difficult to appreciate if one concentrates only on national trends. Constitutional suffrage had been a popular cause among many espoused by the radical elite of Merseyside society since the days of Josephine Butler.[29] The attendance at meetings of the LWSS frequently resembled a guest list from one of the area's fashionable parties.[30] In 1906 the *Liverpool Weekly Mercury*, a Saturday digest paper with a heavy content of light literature and social news and gossip, ran a series of portraits of prominent local society ladies on its front pages. The featured ladies were associated with a broad range of philanthropic concerns favoured by the radical elite, including anti-vivisection and the University Settlement. Most of them also claimed some involvement with the local constitutional suffrage society. A founder member of the branch was Mrs Allan Bright, the 'most womanly of women', who was married to a wealthy Liberal MP.[31] An early branch secretary was Eleanor Rathbone, daughter of the dynastic Rathbone family and heir to her father's philanthropic work. Mrs Alfred Booth, 'one of the most useful and practical ladies in Liverpool' and wife of one of Liverpool's richest shipping magnates, was another keen supporter, as was Miss Japp, the Lady Mayoress in 1906.[32] Mrs Nessie Stewart-Brown, wife of a prominent local barrister, whose father was the first Pro-Chancellor of Liverpool University, also played a key role. They were joined in the LWSS by the wives, sisters and daughters of other prominent local families, including the Bowrings, who endowed Bowring Park for the city, and the Pictons, who were responsible for the magnificent, round, eponymous Picton Library. Small wonder, then, that when the young Jane Colquitt threw in her lot with the NUWSS at the age of 17, her family had no concern about such youthful political activism as they were aware that she was with 'nice ladies'.[33]

The LWSS also had a distinct political identity which largely matched that of the class from which it drew most of its membership. Although a few of the ladies featured in the *Weekly Mercury* were Conservatives, as a rule progressive Liberalism was the main political creed of the LWSS. Miss Japp 'worked strenuously for the revival of Liberalism in East Toxteth' and was President of its local Women's Liberal Federation (WLF) as well as representing the Liberal Party on the local Board of Guardians. Mrs Bright and Mrs Stewart-Brown retained important roles in the local branches of the WLF during their years in the LWSS, and were also active in the WLF at national level. Although Eleanor Rathbone joined no political party, her parents and siblings were active Liberals. In fact, to a large extent the leading personnel of the LWSS and Liverpool WLF branches were interchangeable.

Notable by their absence were the large numbers of socialist and trade union women whom Jill Liddington and Jill Norris found to be so active in the greater Lancashire region, of which much of Merseyside was then still part.[34] They were to be found solidly within the WSPU in Liverpool. Militant suffragism was not popular among local society. This was partly for political reasons. Many suffragette attacks were aimed at the Liberal government, a target close to the heart of most LWSS members. As the WSPU was so antagonistic to the prominent political creed of the local radical elite, it boasted few wealthy members in Liverpool. However, such attitudes did ensure that the Liverpool WSPU recruited and retained a strong base of support among working-class women. Militant suffrage also achieved popularity among Liverpool's more avant-garde community, and the WSPU recruited several actresses and artists to its ranks.[35] This bohemian element would not sit comfortably in the drawing rooms of local society. The methods of the local WSPU also attracted women from the thriving socialist culture on Merseyside. Indeed, the branch owed its existence in part to the efforts of Mrs Alice Morrissey, a central figure in the local Independent Labour Party (ILP). Alice joined the LWSS in 1904 but left the following year, stating at the annual general meeting that she found the organization undemocratic and far too restricted to ladies of a particular class.[36] Her next venture into suffrage was via the WSPU, alongside her fellow socialist activist Miss Labouchere, the Union's first local contact.[37] This gulf of opinion, between forcing public attention through active militant political campaigning and more subtle constitutional attempts to persuade and educate an audience, characterized the relationship between the WSPU and NUWSS on Merseyside for the remainder of their coexistence.

In examining relations between local branches of the two largest organizations, then, we find, first, that the local picture overturns the national model. That is, the radical suffragists identified so usefully by Liddington and Norris as forming the backbone of the Lancashire suffrage campaign through their shared allegiances with the NUWSS, ILP, trade unions and Women's Co-operative Guild (WCG) never featured in the political life of south-west Lancashire. What emerges for this region is an opposite model where socialist militancy and suffrage militancy combined, and women moved happily between the ILP, WCG and WSPU. The LWSS, virtually indistinguishable in personnel from the WLF, displayed a consistent distaste for anything resembling socialist or radical militancy. Part of this aversion was due to the fact that much suffrage militancy was aimed at the LWSS's own party. Mrs Stewart-Brown constantly urged local Liberal women not to damage their party but to 'plead for the suffrage in a quiet and peaceable manner as many who would otherwise be on [our] side are now being alienated by the extreme measures used by the militant suffragettes'.[38] Indeed, the LWSS was so anti-socialist that it distanced itself from the National Union's Election Fighting Fund when the latter withdrew support from Liberal candidates. This division came out nationally through Eleanor Rathbone's very public dissent, which led to her resignation from the NUWSS executive in April 1914.[39] Locally it had deeper organizational repercussions when Eleanor formed a Municipal Women's Association in October 1911 in response to what she saw as the leftward drift of constitutional suffrage. The Municipal Women's Association attempted to educate women in the duties of citizenship, including such practicalities as how to fill in ballot forms. It also helped move the focus of local constitutional suffrage away from any association with socialism by immersing its members in a much broader and non-party campaign for female citizenship.[40]

Studying party loyalties at the grass roots of suffrage activism also challenges the perspective that all suffragettes happily complied with the Pankhursts' insistence that they cease from all personal party-political involvement until the vote was achieved. Alice Morrissey, for example, was ILP delegate to the Liverpool Labour Representation Committee for 1908–9, and District Secretary of the WCG in 1911. She and her husband completed a propaganda tour in the south of England on behalf of the ILP shortly before her sudden death in 1912. Yet she combined socialism with a high level of activity in the WSPU, including a spell as local secretary in 1910, despite the official prohibition on such dual activities. Further instances of simultaneous suffrage and socialist activity reflect similar determination by local socialist women to continue their party political allegiances.[41] As well as illuminating the reality of suffrage politics at a local level, this fact also provides an interesting contribution to the recent discussion regarding the stance of the ILP within debates on equal or adult suffrage. On this issue, the local picture upholds the findings of Ian Bullock and Logie Barrow that the ILP was more inclined towards support for equal than adult suffrage.[42] 'The adult suffrage swindle' was how a leading ILP member, John Edwards, described the latter position at the local Clarion Club in 1907. WSPU speakers continued to be featured at ILP meetings, the WSPU sometimes met at socialist venues, and the two groups even united to host a joint demonstration in 1912.[43] Moreover, such examples also demonstrate that the allegedly painful choices between the two positions were avoided by individual women, who simply altered their priorities as the need arose.[44]

So the complex relationship between the LWSS and Liverpool WSPU, with all its undercurrents of class and party-political identities, problematizes our understanding of an existing national model, emphasizing the fact that the local study is often seen as a reflection of the national whole. However, the friction between these two organizations, which was frequently expressed publicly within the local press, also provides an interesting framework within which my second point about choices and identities can be explored.

It is clear that there was mutual antagonism between the LWSS and

Liverpool WSPU, rooted firmly in differences of class and party politics between their membership. So great was this that although LWSS and WSPU members could happily work with other organizations to gain publicity, they only managed to co-operate in organizing one joint public demonstration during the nine years of their coexistence. This event, in November 1911, also involved the CUWFA, which was the only participating body to name all three co-organizing societies in later reports. The WSPU gave the LWSS only a passing mention, while the LWSS accounts avoided any reference to WSPU speakers.[45] This situation provided well for women who were politically active before they became involved in suffrage. Women socialists on Merseyside would nearly always gravitate towards the WSPU whereas women in the Liberal Party who became interested in the parliamentary franchise would have prior knowledge of friendship networks which would incline them towards the LWSS.[46] Fashionable society similarly gravitated towards the LWSS, while the WSPU contained many artists and several working-class women. However, this tells us very little about the choices available to women who did not fit these categories, or to those who also may have felt torn by dual allegiances in their suffrage activities, but not by those of the narrow party-political world of Liberal versus socialist. It is the inter-organizational relationships between the smaller organizations that tell us much more about these broader areas, and about the choices regarding priorities made by many suffrage campaigners on an almost daily basis. Within these fluid categories it is possible to begin to grasp something of the whole picture for a short period of localized time – a few snapshots rather than a film, if you like – which begins to speak to us of the richness, breadth and diversity of suffrage politics.

An interesting example of this appears in the activities of the two religious suffrage organizations on Merseyside. Sectarianism has long been a byword for Liverpool politics. Priests, ministers and other religious leaders are frequently credited by historians as holding more influence over the voting behaviour of the electorate than party spin doctors.[47] Here, in a district torn apart by sectarian violence on a regular basis, we find the opposite of the militant–constitutionalist divide, with its emphasis on separating women along the lines of class, party or suffrage tactics. There are two equally interesting if opposite sides to the religious suffrage story. First, there was no antagonism between the Catholic Women's Suffrage Society (CWSS) and the Anglican body, the Church League for Women's Suffrage (CLWS). Indeed, rather than sectarian sniping between the two bodies, we find occasional joint ventures.[48] These may be few and far between, but are remarkable for their very existence at a time when most of the public relations between Catholic and Protestant women involved fists and knives, especially in the marching season.[49]

A deeper analysis of the women involved in both the religious societies on Merseyside provides crucial evidence for the individual religious affiliation of many WSPU and NUWSS members. Looking at such evidence, it is clear that religious sectarianism simply was not an issue within women's politics. Despite the rarity of official joint ventures between the two religious suffrage bodies, it becomes clear that both the WSPU and the LWSS simultaneously united Catholic and Protestant women together in one campaign. Furthermore, this was not restricted to the level of ordinary membership. Some of the more prominent leaders of both militant and constitutional suffrage branches also possessed clear religious affiliations. The WSPU had a number of prominent Catholic women among its leading members: Alice Morrissey was a devout and observant Catholic, and was proud of having a priest for a brother; Patricia Woodlock, while not quite so publicly identified with her religion, was quick to involve herself in the CWSS when a local branch was formed. Florence Barry, a WSPU member in Birkenhead, even went on to lead the CWSS nationally.[50] Yet these prominent Catholic women worked happily alongside active Protestant suffragettes such as Hattie Mahood, who was also heavily involved in Liverpool's Nonconformist Pembroke Chapel, and Phyllis Lovell, a WSPU member who founded the Southport CLWS. Thus, when read in conjunction with the broader political history of Liverpool, suffrage becomes unique as the one political campaign to remain above sectarianism.

The other side to this transcendence of religious sectarianism was the ability of local religious suffrage groups to bridge the seemingly impossible divide between militant and constitutional suffrage activism on Merseyside. As I have indicated, this divide was not merely due to policy differences at national level. Locally, it had very firm roots in class and party politics. However, the variety of public affiliations provided through religious bodies allowed the gap to diminish as different priorities were selected by members. So just as the WSPU and LWSS were able to unite women of different religions, so the smaller religious suffrage groups were open to, and used by, militants and constitutionalists. Eleanor Rathbone was always one of the most outspoken opponents of militancy both locally and nationally. Nevertheless, when working under the banner of the CLWS, she was able to side-step this and bring herself to share a platform with Mr Bernard, a WSPU supporter, at a time when local WSPU–LWSS relations were at an all-time low.[51]

Although there were some early attempts to ban WSPU members who had actually participated in violence from the local CLWS, these were vigorously opposed. Predictably, opposition came from militant suffrage activists who wished also to participate in the new society. However, there were also constitutional suffragists who had been outspoken opponents of militancy but were willing to support the right of other Anglican women to identify with the CLWS whatever their external political views might have been. Cicely Leadley-Brown, a leading LWSS member, summed up this view at the first AGM of the Liverpool CLWS with her proposal that the organization should have 'the support of all church suffragists'. She declared herself happy to work within its ranks alongside WSPU members classed as 'militants on active service': that is, arsonists and window-smashers.[52] The situation in the CWSS was identical. The branch was formed by WSPU activist Florence Barry, but was supported and joined by women from across the militant–constitutional divide. The key to this plethora of shifting positions appears to lie in the concept of identity, and how individual suffrage activists perceived themselves at different times. In other words, it appears to have been crucial to certain women that they could publicly declare themselves as militants or constitutionalists when they so wished, but that they were also able to move into the identity of Catholic or Anglican on other occasions.

A similar blurring of identities, whether previous or simultaneously held, surrounded the US, which met on Merseyside throughout the First World War. By the time of the US's formation in 1915 the local WSPU branch had dissolved, without participating in Emmeline and Christabel Pankhurst's jingoistic pro-war campaign.[53] The LWSS continued to meet, although the main focus of its activity was now relief work rather than suffrage campaigning. Within relief work, suffragists from militant and constitutional organizations worked comfortably together. The US allowed those who wished to do something more an opportunity to preserve a public identity for themselves as suffrage campaigners, and to continue this single-issue campaign throughout the war. For many, the US provided another organization rather than a substitute. Phyllis Lovell, who was involved in forming the US branch, had been in the WSPU prior to the war. She was now in the forefront of the local campaign for women police as well as co-ordinating a large relief organization, the Home Service Corps. Dr Alice Ker, another US activist with an ex-WSPU background, was simultaneously running first-aid classes at the War Service Bureau co-ordinated by the LWSS. Therefore it cannot be said that the US simply filled a gap in their spare time. Varieties of war work more than amply filled their days, and the US appears to have met a very real need on the part of women to retain an extra identity as suffrage campaigners at this time. This role perhaps becomes clearer when the position of campaigners who were only active within the US and did not participate in relief work is considered. Many ex-WSPU activists found a niche within the US, including Helah Criddle and Ada Broughton, who had been two of the Liverpool WSPU's earliest speakers. Such examples serve to illustrate the adaptability and flexibility of Edwardian feminism.

There remains one final category of suffrage campaigner which ought to be explored if successful conclusions as to the nature of suffrage on Merseyside are to be drawn. The evidence I have presented up to this point speaks of the multifaceted layers of suffrage identity, and of women whose activities spanned two or three organizations at once. While they represent a proportion of the membership of all local suffrage organizations, it must be remembered that each organization also recruited a separate and distinct membership which was unique to them and not shared with other bodies. Sometimes this membership can be clearly identified as part of a larger organization within which an interest in suffrage played a small part. This is most evident within the religious suffrage societies, where, alongside the prominent members of the WSPU and LWSS mentioned above, there was another very active layer of individuals who appear not to have been involved in any secular suffrage society. These were churchwomen who felt strongly enough about the vote as Anglicans to join the CLWS, or as Catholics to enrol in the CWSS. Having done this, they felt no need to take any further steps into the secular suffrage organizations. Although it was important to them to publicly declare themselves as pro-suffrage within the context of their Christian activities, they did not step beyond this context into the lay world of suffrage politics. An identical situation can be seen in the CUWFA. Although some of its members were also very involved in the LWSS, the majority were in no suffrage organization other than the CUWFA, presenting themselves as 'Conservative suffragists' rather than 'Conservative' and 'suffragist'. Within the larger suffrage organizations too, there was a distinct layer of women on Merseyside who joined only one, the WSPU, LWSS or occasionally WFL.[54] For them, the vote alone appears to have been ample motivation. This may help to explain why many extremely active suffrage campaigners disappeared from public life once the vote was won. Campaigners who placed their suffrage work within the context of other activities simply returned to what had been their concurrent concerns during their 'suffrage days'. This can be seen in the later public work of some of the women discussed in this chapter. Nessie Stewart-Brown, who had always balanced constitutional suffrage with Liberalism, turned to the latter as a city councillor and prospective Parliamentary candidate. Helah Criddle of the ILP and WSPU continued her socialist activities and Florence Barry remained at the forefront of the St Joan's Alliance – as the CWSS became. Other women, including Alice Burton, simply cannot be seen in public life once their suffrage activities end. The one consistent factor I have been able to draw out is that of diversity; there appear to have been almost as many motivations for suffrage campaigning as there were suffrage campaigners, and almost as many foci and priorities within these campaigns.

Where, then, does this leave local suffrage studies as part of a larger national suffrage history? Are they simply useful as parts of a greater whole, or do they have something unique to offer which differs significantly from histories with a larger perspective? The answer to both questions has to be 'yes'. A very important part of the local study comes from its role as a chapter in the national picture, and from what it can bring to this in terms of regional variations. However, there is another side to this which should not be overlooked, which is its potential to recreate the entire whole, at least for one particular geographical area. One of the most rewarding things in doing local suffrage history has been the way in which it has been possible to reconstruct the entire spectrum of suffrage activity, at least for Merseyside women. It is this work of reclaiming and restoring to history those who were, for want of a better phrase, hidden from it that much of the work we call 'doing women's history' is still about.

Notes

1. S. Stanley Holton, *Suffrage Days: Stories from the Women's Suffrage Movement*, London, Routledge, 1996, p. 244.
2. Books which utilize recently discovered collections include L. Stanley with A. Morley, *The Life and Death of Emily Wilding Davison*, London, Women's Press, 1988; Holton, *Suffrage Days*. Fresh perspectives include M. Joannou and J. Purvis (eds), *The Women's Suffrage Movement: New Feminist Perspectives*, Manchester, Manchester University Press, 1998; S. Kingsley Kent, *Sex and Suffrage in Britain, 1860–1914*, London, Routledge, 1987, which has reassessed suffrage in terms of its contemporary sexual politics; L. Garner, *Stepping Stones to Women's Liberty: Feminist Ideas in the Women's Suffrage Movement, 1900–1918*, London, Hutchinson, 1984, which concentrates on varying ideologies; and L. Tickner, *The Spectacle of Women: Imagery of the Suffrage Campaign*, London, Chatto and Windus, 1987, which reminds us of the tremendous visual impact of the campaign.
3. R. Strachey, *The Cause: A Short History of the Women's Movement in Great Britain*, London, Virago, 1978 (first published 1928); R. Fulford, *Votes for Women: The Story of a Struggle*, London, Faber and Faber, 1957; A. Rosen, *Rise up Women! The Militant Campaign of the Women's Social and Political Union, 1903–14*, London, Routledge and Kegan Paul, 1974; L. Hume, *The National Union of Women's Suffrage Societies, 1897–1914*, New York, Garland, 1982.
4. Aspects of the history of the Women's Freedom League can be found in S. Newsome, *The Women's Freedom League, 1907–57*, London, Women's Freedom League Pamphlet, 1957; C. L. Eustance, ' "Daring to be free": the evolution of women's political identities in the Women's Freedom League, 1907–30', unpublished DPhil thesis, University of York, 1993; L. E. Nym Mayhall, 'Dare to be free: The Women's Freedom League 1907–18', unpublished PhD thesis, Stanford University, 1993; H. Frances, 'Our job is to be free: the sexual politics of four educated feminists, c. 1910–35', unpublished DPhil thesis, University of York, 1996.
5. N. Stewart Parnell, *The History of St Joan's Social and Political Alliance, Formerly the Catholic Women's Suffrage Society, 1911–61*,

London, St Joan's Alliance, 1961; N. Stewart Parnell, *The Way of Florence Barry, 1885-1965*, London, St Joan's Alliance, 1966; L. Walker, 'Party political women: a comparative study of Liberal women and the Primrose League', in J. Rendall (ed.), *Equal or Different? Women's Politics 1800-1914*, Oxford, Basil Blackwell, 1987; C. Hirshfield, 'Fractured faith: Liberal Party women and the suffrage issue in Britain, 1892-1914', *Gender and History*, Vol. 2, No. 2, 1990, pp. 173-97; K. Cowman, 'A party between revolution and peaceful persuasion: a fresh look at the United Suffragists', in Joannou and Purvis (eds), *The Women's Suffrage Movement*.

6. J. Liddington, and J. Norris, *One Hand Tied Behind Us: The Rise of the Women's Suffrage Movement*, London, Virago, 1978.

7. This dichotomy was so deeply entrenched within the actual organizations that it has proved almost impossible for historians to circumnavigate. See, for example, J. Purvis, 'Researching the lives of women in the suffrage movement', in J. Purvis and M. Maynard, *Researching Women's Lives from a Feminist Perspective*, London, Taylor and Francis, 1994, p. 169.

8. See, for example, S. Peacock, *Votes for Women: The Women's Fight in Portsmouth*, Portsmouth, Portsmouth City Council, 1983; I. Dove, *'Yours in the Cause': A Brief Account of Suffragettes in Lewisham, Greenwich and Woolwich*, London, Lewisham Library Service and Greenwich Libraries, 1988; L. Leneman, *A Guid Cause: The Women's Suffrage Movement in Scotland*, Aberdeen, Aberdeen University Press, 1991; R. Taylor, *In Letters of Gold: The Story of Sylvia Pankhurst and the East London Federation of the Suffragettes in Bow*, London, Stepney Books, 1993; A. V. John, '"Run like blazes"; the suffragettes and Welshness', *Llafur*, Vol. 6, No. 3, 1994, pp. 29-43; G. Hawtin, *Votes for Wimbledon Women*, London, privately published, 1994.

9. Stanley and Morley, *The Life and Death of Emily Wilding Davison*, p. 183.

10. Statement by Alice E. Burton, *Votes for Women*, 2 April 1909.

11. *Ibid*.

12. *Women's Franchise*, 10 September 1908.

13. Alice E. Burton, *Votes for Women*, 2 July 1909.

14. *Votes for Women*, 5 November 1908; 2 July 1909.

15. I discuss more fully how 'militancy' was defined by the Liverpool WSPU in my article '"The stonethrowing has been forced upon us": the function of militancy within the Liverpool Women's Social and Political Union 1906-14', *Transactions of the Historical Society of Lancashire and Cheshire*, Vol. 145, 1996 for 1995, pp. 171-92.

16. For details of this particular Women's Parliament see *The Times*, 29 March 1909.

17. *Liverpool Courier*, 7 March 1909.

18. For example, 'Liverpool ladies locked up', *Liverpool Courier*, 31 March 1909.

19. *Votes for Women*, 7 May 1909.
20. *Votes for Women*, 29 June 1909.
21. Holton, *Suffrage Days*, p. 245.
22. For example, E. S. Pankhurst, *The Suffragette*, London, Gay and Hancock, 1911; Fulford, *Votes for Women*; A. Raeburn, *The Militant Suffragettes*, London, Michael Joseph, 1973.
23. *Liverpool Courier*, 7 September 1908.
24. For a further discussion of this see J. Belchem, 'Introduction: the peculiarities of Liverpool', in J. Belchem, *Popular Politics, Riot and Labour: Essays in Liverpool History, 1790–1940*, Liverpool, Liverpool University Press, 1992.
25. London- and leadership-based accounts of suffrage include: Rosen, *Rise Up Women!*; Fulford, *Votes for Women*; Raeburn, *The Militant Suffragettes*; Hume, *The National Union of Women's Suffrage Societies*; Strachey, *The Cause*; D. Mitchell, *The Fighting Pankhursts: A Study in Tenacity*, London, Jonathan Cape, 1967. For a more recent overview which follows this trend see B. Caine, *English Feminism, 1780–1980*, Oxford, Oxford University Press, 1997, especially chapter 4.
26. See A. V. John and C. Eustance (eds), *The Men's Share? Masculinities, Male Support and Women's Suffrage in Britain, 1890–1920*, London, Routledge, 1997.
27. Unpublished paper, 'Mother walked to London', delivered by Mrs Paula Francombe, Liverpool, 12 July 1993.
28. See, for example, *Liverpool Daily Post*, 25 July 1895.
29. *Women's Suffrage Journal*, 1 March 1870.
30. Parties were a serious business in Liverpool. Sir William Nott Bower, the city's Chief Constable, recalled that there was a 'season' in Liverpool which rivalled that of London. See W. Nott Bower, *Fifty-Two Years a Policeman*, London, Arnold, 1926, pp. 101–2.
31. S. Tooley, 'The ladies of Liverpool', paper reprinted from *The Woman at Home*, n.d. (c. 1895), Liverpool Record Office; *Liverpool Weekly Mercury*, 7 July 1906.
32. Tooley, 'The ladies of Liverpool'.
33. Personal interview with Mrs Paula Francombe, daughter of Jane Colquitt, 1 December 1993.
34. Liddington and Norris, *One Hand Tied Behind Us*.
35. Alice Burton, for example, and also the artists Mary Palethorpe, Jessica Walker, Ethel Frimstone and Patricia Woodlock. For more detail see K. Cowman, *Mrs Brown Is a Man and a Brother! Women in Political Organisations on Merseyside, 1890–1920*, Liverpool, Liverpool University Press, forthcoming.
36. *Liverpool Daily Post*, 13 April 1905.
37. Women's Social and Political Union, first annual report, 1907.
38. *Liverpool Daily Post*, 2 March 1909.
39. J. Alberti, *Eleanor Rathbone*, London, Sage Publications, 1996.

40. The full agenda behind the formation of the Municipal Women's Association is discussed in K. Cowman, 'Engendering citizenship: women in political organizations on Merseyside 1890-1920', unpublished DPhil thesis, University of York, 1994.

41. See, for example, the career of Helah Criddle, a WSPU prisoner in March 1907 who continued public work for both the WSPU and Wallasey ILP at least until 1913.

42. L. Barrow and I. Bullock, *Democratic Ideas in the British Labour Movement, 1880-1914*, Cambridge, Cambridge University Press, 1996, p. 157.

43. *Liverpool Forward*, 22 June 1912.

44. The historical view that such choices were painful and difficult is well put by L. Garner, 'Suffragism and socialism: Sylvia Pankhurst 1903-14', in I. Bullock and R. Pankhurst (eds), *Sylvia Pankhurst: From Artist to Anti-fascist*, London, Macmillan, 1992.

45. *Votes for Women*, 8 December 1911; *Conservative and Unionist Women's Franchise Review*, January 1912.

46. Despite almost exhaustive research only one woman, Clare Stallybrass, has emerged as a socialist within the LWSS, and I have found no local WSPU members who declared themselves to be Liberals.

47. See P. J. Waller, *Democracy and Sectarianism: A Political and Social History of Liverpool, 1868-1939*, Liverpool, Liverpool University Press, 1981; F. Neal, *Sectarian Violence in Liverpool, 1819-1914: An Aspect of Anglo-Irish History*, Manchester, Manchester University Press, 1988.

48. Both groups co-operated together in a suffrage club during the First World War and participated in some joint meetings, such as in July 1916.

49. *Liverpool Weekly Mercury*, 26 June 1909, illustrates how prominent suffrage events, in this case the release celebrations for Patricia Woodlock, provided less attractive copy than violent clashes between women of different religious persuasions.

50. Parnell, *The Way of Florence Barry*.

51. *Church League for Women's Suffrage Monthly Paper*, January 1914.

52. *Ibid.*, March 1914.

53. See *Votes for Women*, February-March 1915, for accounts of early United Suffragists meetings.

54. The WFL did organize in the city on a sporadic basis, occasionally co-operating with the LWSS and sometimes hosting WSPU speakers. However, I have found no evidence of joint membership between the WFL and other organizations. Claire Eustance has suggested that this may be due to the geographical location of local WFL branches – in the north of the district where they were not competing with the WSPU, a suggestion with which I am happy to agree.

3 'Suffragettes Are Splendid for Any Work': The Blathwayt Diaries as a Source for Suffrage History[1]

June Hannam

On 28 June 1908, when the British suffrage movement was at its height, Emily Blathwayt wrote in her diary that 'so much is going on in life now it seems impossible to put anything into a diary. I always find it is so when there is much to record.' Fortunately for the historian, the increased pressures felt by Emily, and by her daughter Mary, who were both active supporters of the suffrage campaign in the immediate pre-war years, did not prevent them from writing personal diaries, which they continued to do for most of their lives. Their diaries provide an insight into the private and public activities of two provincial women from a comfortable middle-class background in the late nineteenth and early twentieth centuries, and also into the changing 'contexts in which they fulfilled their various roles'.[2] This chapter, however, will focus on the suffrage years. It will explore the ways in which the Blathwayt diaries can be used as a source for suffrage history and will argue that they can provide fresh insights into many of the new questions which are currently being raised by historians.

The family moved to live in Eagle House, Batheaston, a village on the outskirts of Bath, in 1882 when Colonel Linley Blathwayt retired from service in India. They were related to a substantial landowning family in the district who owned the nearby estate of Dyrham Park. Colonel Linley and his wife Emily had two children: Mary, who was born in 1879, and William, who was two years younger. Mary never married and does not appear to have taken on any paid employment. Her diaries often make reference to dividends on stocks and shares which, with an allowance from her parents, provided her with an independent living. William trained as an electrical engineer and then for a number of years taught English in Germany, returning home on the eve of the First World War. The family was a close-knit one and spent many hours together, walking, cycling, visiting friends and attending lectures and concerts.[3]

The Blathwayts provide an interesting example of those who became active in the women's cause only when the suffrage movement began to gain more publicity after 1906. Unlike many of the well-known leaders of the women's movement they were not involved in a range of other campaigns before this period and took little part in politics more generally. And yet they gave a great deal of time to the movement after 1907 and their house became one of the main centres of suffrage activity in the district. They were most closely associated with the Women's Social and Political Union (WSPU), but at different times members of the family also belonged to other suffrage organizations. Their activities are recorded in considerable detail in the diaries of Mary and Emily Blathwayt. Colonel Linley Blathwayt also kept a diary for much of his life, but the crucial years from 1907 to 1911 are missing. After that the entries are few and far between, possibly because his arthritis made writing difficult.[4]

Historians of the suffrage movement have made extensive use of personal material, including diaries, letters and autobiographies, to explore new questions such as the meaning of the vote for women, the way in which participation in the suffrage struggle transformed their lives and the relationship between personal and formal politics.[5] They have drawn attention to the importance of friendship networks in sustaining the movement and to the need to examine these questions at a local as well as at a national level.[6] This change in emphasis and approach, away from a concentration on formal parliamentary politics, has led to a re-interpretation of many aspects of the pre-war suffrage campaign, including the definition and nature of militancy, the boundaries between different suffrage groups and the relationship between the national leadership and the rank and file.[7]

On one level, autobiographies and diaries should not be seen as too distinct from each other. It has been suggested, for example, that diaries are a good example of the autobiographical process at work and that they form part of an autobiographical corpus of writing.[8] Far from being spontaneous outpourings or, as Virginia Woolf suggested, 'a capacious hold-all in which one flings a mass of odds & ends', diaries are highly selective, even if the author is not necessarily conscious of the structuring which is taking place.[9] Nonetheless, there are crucial differences between diaries and autobiographies as a source. Diarists cannot foresee the outcome of events; their choice of what to record and what to emphasize, therefore, is based on more immediate concerns than those of the autobiographer, who, from a retrospective perspective, structures a conscious, often unified narrative of her life which can be affected as much by her present interests as by events in the past.[10] Autobiographers tend to comment on earlier events which are woven into an overall story, whereas diarists are less coherent and tend to be more repetitive, recording similar material each week.[11]

The way in which historians can use diaries as a source for suffrage history depends largely on their style and content, for 'diaries have as many faces as those who hold pens'.[12] Emily and Mary Blathwayt provided a chronicle of everyday life, storing up memories of what seemed important to them. Mary wrote up to a page a day in a purpose-made diary in which she listed the activities of herself and her parents, noting visits to friends, leisure pursuits and the details of domestic life. She also showed considerable interest in the health of family members and their numerous visits to the doctor and the dentist. She was fond of cataloguing 'facts', such as train times and the price of clothing, and gave detailed accounts of the plots of books, but rarely provided an insight into her thoughts and feelings. The style of the diary may reflect Mary's personality and the need she felt to bring order and meaning to her daily life. As a member of the Bath Ladies' Microscopical Society she showed a similar preoccupation with classifying data, and her diaries contain numerous lists of grubs and insects.

Emily Blathwayt wrote in a more free-flowing style in a notebook which did not restrict the length of her entries; these could be very short or last for several pages. She covered similar topics to Mary but was less inclined to give lists of 'facts' and was far more willing to express her opinions. It is important to read the diaries in conjunction with each other since they provide an alternative perspective on what are essentially overlapping worlds, and there are interconnections between the texts.[13] Emily refers constantly in her diaries to what Mary is doing. She uses letters from her daughter, or conversations that they had had, to comment about how Mary viewed events – an insight which is not provided in Mary's own diaries. In July 1909, for example, Mary was involved in suffrage propaganda in Plymouth and merely noted in her own diary that she had chaired a meeting. Emily's diary, however, quoted from one of Mary's letters which gave more information: 'the crowd actually clapped after my small speech. I did not speak for more than two & a half minutes, but they seem to have liked what I said.'[14]

The style of their diaries did not change as Mary and Emily became involved in the suffrage campaign; instead, details of suffrage work were included alongside their other interests and, at different times, came to form the major item in their selection of what was recorded. Mary's diary provides valuable information for anyone interested in local suffrage history. She records the names and addresses of suffrage campaigners in Bath and Bristol and gives details about the meetings held, the preparations beforehand and the reaction of the crowds. Such accounts can 'give us a sense of what it must have felt like to be there at the time when the women's movement was emerging'.[15] It is the small, unusual details which bring the movement alive. The frequent references to the suffragette colours, for instance, show their importance in providing a sense of identity. In August 1908, for example, Colonel Linley gave Annie Kenney, a former textile worker who was one of the best-known WSPU speakers, white and purple sweet peas in a green vase.[16] During self-denial week Mary's friend Aethel Tollemache put a collecting tin around the neck of her dog and wrote on his collar in green and purple letters, 'please give Baloo something to help the women's movement. Votes for Women'.[17]

The more mundane preoccupations of daily life are often juxtaposed with details of the suffrage struggle, demonstrating that even at the height of campaigning political activity had to be fitted in 'alongside other more everyday aspects of being a woman'.[18] After giving details of a day full of suffrage activities Mary would note, for example, that she had paid 8d to have Annie's stockings mended or that a young speaker needed to borrow a nightgown when she stayed for the night. The Blathwayt diaries are also full of references to Annie Kenney's health problems, which included toothache, loss of voice and extreme tiredness. This gives a useful reminder of how exhausting the life of suffrage activists could be.

What the diaries can provide, which is very rare, is a consistent day-by-day account of the contribution of one particular family to the suffrage cause and, to a lesser degree, the contributions of other female activists in a particular local context. Mary's diaries show a complex rhythm of involvement which changes over time. The reasons for this are a mixture of her own personal preferences and responses to the development of new tactics as well as pressures from other members of the movement. Mary was the family member who took the most active, public role in the suffrage campaign. Her most intense period of activity was between May 1908 and October 1909, when she moved to Bristol to share lodgings with Annie Kenney and to help in her work as WSPU organizer for the West of England. Mary carried out organizing and propaganda work all over the West Country, frequently staying for up to a week in other towns. Suffrage work was now all-consuming and she no longer attended meetings of other societies to which she belonged. In the same month in which she moved to Bristol Mary wrote to the secretary of the Secular Society to say that she could not give him any money that year because she wanted it all for the WSPU: 'When women have votes, I shall be very pleased to subscribe again.'[19]

Mary returned to Batheaston in October 1909 because she was exhausted and suffering from problems with her eyes. She now concentrated on propaganda work in Bath; this involved regular commitments which were noted every week, such as helping to run the suffrage shop, and more intermittent work which included preparations for public meetings to be addressed by the leaders of the WSPU. Mary still visited Bristol frequently and remained closely involved with Annie Kenney until the latter left the district in 1911. Mary then found more time to take up older interests such as the Ladies' Microscopical Society, swimming and cookery lessons. As members of the WSPU became increasingly involved in large-scale destruction of property there was a noticeable tailing off of Mary's suffrage work and in May 1913 she finally resigned from the Union.

Although she attended public meetings and helped to distribute leaflets, Emily Blathwayt's contribution to the cause was more home-based. She organized numerous garden parties in the grounds of Eagle House in order to attract new members and to raise money, while Colonel Linley was in great demand to pick up suffragettes from the station in his motorcar, affectionately nicknamed Bodo. Annie Kenney's memoirs draw attention to the importance of those families who provided hospitality to speakers and she singled out the Blathwayts for special mention:

> There is just one [family] I should like to mention, that of the late Colonel Blathwayt. He and Mrs Blathwayt, of Eagle House Batheaston, treated me as though I were one of their own family. All my weekends I spent under their hospitable roof. They also gave hospitality to the numerous speakers who came to the centre. The question of hospitality was a serious one with organizers. It saved hotel bills.[20]

The extent and nature of the Blathwayts' involvement in the suffragette movement would have been far more difficult to determine, and might indeed have gone unnoticed, if they had not written so regularly and extensively in their diaries. Annie Kenney's memoirs, for instance, do not even mention the role played by Mary and cannot do justice in just a few lines to how much hospitality was provided. Almost all the leaders of the WSPU came to Eagle House, where they were given a meal or put up for the night, and they were encouraged to plant a tree in the part of the garden known as the 'suffragette field'. It is important, however, not to overestimate the importance of one family simply because their activities were recorded in diaries. Rather, insights provided by this source should encourage the historian to discover how widespread certain practices were. The Blathwayt diaries, for example, show that another local family, the Tollemaches, who were personal friends, played a similar role. Mrs Tollemache, the widow of a clergyman who had moved to Batheaston in 1894 after his retirement from service in the East, and her three daughters Grace, Aethel and Mrs Mary Everett, all gave support to the suffragettes. Speakers would often be shared between the two households; Henry Nevinson records in his own diary:

> To Batheaston beyond Bath & house called the Villa. Mrs Tollemache received me (lived 16 years Burma) – now courageous suffragette with 2 suff. daughters. Another married at Windsor. Meeting Guildhall. Mrs P again chair & AK platform ... fine old Colonel took Mrs P away![21]

Alongside details about the contribution of local activists who might otherwise have gone unnoticed, the diaries also provide insights into the character and role of the WSPU. Historians have been influenced in their judgements about the 'militant' campaign by the large number of autobiographies produced by former suffragettes, in particular in the inter-war years. Recent studies of these autobiographies have argued that they were concerned, in a highly self-conscious way, to shape a political identity for women in the pre-war years which was affected as much by the war and the difficulties facing the feminist movement in the 1920s and 1930s as it was by their lives in the militant movement.[22] Mayhall, for example, claims that they emphasized 'the "Suffragette Spirit" a heady combination of self sacrificing devotion to the Cause and to one's sisters in the movement', where the experience of hunger strikes and forcible feeding were crucial in forging a common identity.[23] She argues that this has had a long-lasting effect on the way in which historians have interpreted the pre-war suffrage movement, in particular in the distinctions drawn between militants and constitutionalists and in the equation of militancy with acts leading to imprisonment. Mayhall suggests that a critical reading of the texts reveals 'a more complex relationship between suffragettes' experiences and their representations of the same'.[24]

Diaries, which were usually compiled without the benefit of hindsight, can provide different and more immediate reactions to developments within the pre-war suffrage campaign. Nonetheless, the style of individual diaries and the purposes for which they were written can mean that many questions must remain unanswered. The Blathwayts did not use their writings to explore their innermost thoughts and feelings in a way that can be found in the diaries of some other suffrage activists.[25] They were silent, for example, about why they thought that it was important for women to gain the vote, making no mention of the extent to which the experience of sex inequalities in their own lives affected their attitudes towards the suffrage movement – a perspective which is far more common in autobiographies.[26]

On the other hand, the Blathwayt diaries do enable the historian to trace the process by which one family became involved in the suffrage campaign, the choices they made about which groups to join and the changes in their outlook over time. Emily and Mary first showed an interest in women's suffrage in 1906, when the campaign began to receive greater publicity in the press. Mary became a member of the national WSPU in July 1906 but, along with her mother, also joined the Bath Women's Suffrage Society (WSS) in May 1907. In the early months the Blathwayts carried out general propaganda work for women's suffrage which was closely tied up with their friendship networks in Bath. Mary's close friends Aethel and Grace Tollemache, and Inez Maskelyne, who lived nearby in Box, became involved at the same time. Mary and Emily tried to interest other friends by taking copies of the suffrage newspapers to which they subscribed, *Women's Franchise* and *Votes for Women*, whenever they made social calls, sometimes posting them to friends, and invited several generations of the same family to suffrage meetings in their home.

The process by which the Blathwayts became identified with the

WSPU was a complex one. It does not fit neatly into the narrative presented in many suffragette autobiographies, which emphasize that an initial encounter with a prominent suffragette led to conversion.[27] Mary first heard Emmeline Pethick-Lawrence, Annie Kenney and Christabel Pankhurst speak at a public meeting in Bristol in November 1907 which she attended with her parlourmaid and Aethel Tollemache. Emily recorded that Mary liked Emmeline and Annie very much, but there was no noticeable difference in Mary's general suffrage work for the next few months. Mary's attendance at public meetings of the WSPU did, however, increase her interest in the activities of the Union. In December 1907 she expressed irritation at being elected to the executive of the Bath WSS when 'I never said that I wished to be' and by February of the following year despaired because 'I don't see how I can work for two suffrage societies at the same time.'[28] A turning point came in March when she attended the Women's Parliament in London and marched with suffragettes to Holloway Prison. In April she finally resigned from the Bath WSS so that she could become treasurer of the newly formed Bath branch of the WSPU.

The Tollemache family and Inez Maskelyne also became active suffragettes, but other friends remained in the Bath WSS; Mary's fears that the group might collapse made her reluctant at first to resign, as did loyalty to the President, Lilias Ashworth Hallett, a pioneer of the nineteenth-century suffrage movement. However, Mary was put under pressure to resign by members of the Bristol WSPU, 'for they may soon have work for M'.[29] Lilias Ashworth Hallett was herself ambivalent in her loyalties in this period; she wore a 'Votes for Women' badge at meetings, attended WSPU demonstrations in London and was keen that the Bath WSS should help in the preparations for a large WSPU meeting planned for April 1908.

The most likely explanation for the Blathwayts' interest in the WSPU was their perception that it was the only group which was willing to take action. Emily made frequent references to the Union's 'inspiring leaders' and in April 1908 wrote that 'L is much impressed by the Society. They are in real earnest, different to the half hearted ones who would not suffer anything for the Cause.' Later she reported that 'this Society prospers at once but the other seemed hopeless, & M never felt her heart in it'.[30] Nonetheless, Emily continued as a member of the Bath WSS: 'The militant societies carry all before them now, but we still remain members of this as M says some of the Bristol ones are very good to them.'[31] Emily, Mary and other WSPU members also turned up to public meetings organized by the Bath WSS and retained personal friendships with many of the members.

Of all the 'inspiring leaders' of the WSPU it was Annie Kenney who had most influence on the Blathwayts, although she is given far less prominence in standard histories of the Union than Emmeline and

Christabel Pankhurst. In these accounts emphasis is given to the charismatic leadership of Christabel and the extent to which she was able to exercise 'autocratic control' of the WSPU because of the devotion she inspired in others.[32] Annie Kenney is portrayed as one of these faithful followers who 'worshipped' Christabel and rarely took any initiatives of her own; it is significant that the word 'childlike' is used most often by historians to describe her.[33] This impression is partly based on the assessment made by contemporaries in their autobiographies, including the one written by Annie Kenney in which she seems proud to describe herself as 'Christabel's blotting paper'.[34]

A very different view of Annie Kenney emerges from the Blathwayt diaries. She was the one who had the charismatic personality and who inspired the Blathwayt family and their immediate circle of Bath friends to give a more full-time commitment to the WSPU. Other leaders of the movement may have been admired, but in the pages of the diaries they come through as rather remote, whereas Annie Kenney was a more immediate, accessible figure. Mary was impressed by Annie as a speaker and it was after taking tea with her several times that she was persuaded to take a more public role in the Union and to put the suffrage struggle at the centre of her life. In this case it was the Blathwayts and their friends who were the devoted followers. They looked after Annie when she was ill and, in an interesting reversal of class roles, performed personal services for her such as mending and washing her clothes or cooking her supper so that nothing would interrupt her suffrage work. Annie Kenney may have been devoted to Christabel and ready to follow her lead, but in the diaries she comes over as strong-minded, capable of exercising initiative in her own right and as someone whose opinions were listened to. She was the one who edited articles before they were put in the local press and who gave advice about political tactics. When Emily left the WSPU she decided not to become active in the National Union of Women's Suffrage Societies (NUWSS), commenting that 'Annie does not like that Society as they always support the Liberal if favourable & work against the WSPU tactics.'[35]

In her study of suffragette autobiographies Joannou suggests that the self, although in some ways unique, can be seen to exist in a symbiotic relationship with the life of another whose importance for the autobiographical self is sometimes not diminished years after a formal separation.[36] Annie Kenney was clearly a 'significant other' for the Blathwayts in the immediate pre-war years. The extent to which their lives were intertwined is reflected in the central position that Annie Kenney's activities, health, opinions and needs assumed in the diary entries, in particular between 1908 and 1911. In later years there is still the occasional reminder in Mary's diary of how important Annie Kenney had been in her life. One poignant entry simply said, 'It is Annie Kenney's birthday today. She is 35. Today I have made soup & beef tea, chocolate shape & junket.'[37] The Blathwayt family continued to maintain a sporadic contact with Annie throughout the First World War and sent her a wedding present in 1920.

In recording those influences which seemed most important at the time, diaries can provide an alternative 'reading' of the role played by 'inspiring' leaders as compared with those to be found in texts written after the event. Diaries can also encourage a more complex view of the tactics and methods used by suffrage campaigners; the Blathwayt diaries, for instance, help to contribute to recent reassessments of militancy by shedding light on the extent to which militancy had a variety of meanings for contemporaries and how far these changed over time. At first the Blathwayt family seemed able to identify with militancy because it was equated with willingness to take energetic action rather than with violence and imprisonment. Linley and Emily sympathized with suffragettes who disrupted meetings, although they did not take such action themselves. When WSPU members shouted at Birrell, a Liberal Cabinet Minister, during a meeting in Bristol, Emily commented that 'our women are justified as they have no legal voice as men have'.[38]

It was possible for members of the WSPU to give support in varied ways which suited their personal circumstances. For Emily and Linley Blathwayt this took the form of extensive hospitality and quiet but persistent propaganda work among family and friends. For other local WSPU members, including Mary, it meant engaging in a range of activities which took them out into the street rather than remaining in the more familiar environment of the drawing room or small indoor meeting place. Mary had always led an active life outside the home, but apart from her participation in the local rifle club, which was unusual, she did not step outside the boundaries of what would be expected of a young woman of her class and generation. It was her involvement in the suffrage movement, however, which gradually increased Mary's confidence and her willingness to take action in public. After returning from the Women's Parliament in London in February 1908 she wore her WSPU badge for the first time in Bath and wrote 'Votes for Women' in chalk on a wall and on a letter box in the village. When she worked with Annie Kenney in Exeter she chalked pavements to advertise meetings and at one of these took the chair, 'the first time I have ever done such a thing'.[39] On numerous occasions she encountered violence from the crowd; at one meeting on Durdham Downs in Bristol 'the young boys sang songs & threw paper at us; and an apple which hit me on the head'. At Weston-super-Mare, when Annie Kenney and several other Bristol women spoke, the meeting became very rough: 'A man gave Mr Rodgers a black eye, because he stood up for us .... A crowd followed us back to Weston Station.'[40] While such meetings were frightening, they were also exhilarating; in May 1908 Emily exclaimed that 'I never knew M work so hard before' and again in June she noted that 'M is *very* busy & she *is* enjoying herself.'[41]

All the Blathwayts were uncomfortable, however, with acts of violence against people or property. As early as August 1908 Mary wrote to the editor of *Votes for Women* asking him not to print her name in telegrams from Bristol suffragettes to Miss New and Mrs Leigh when they came out of prison; they had broken Asquith's window with a stone. During 1909, when there were many more arrests and clashes with the police, Mary was sent a letter from the WSPU asking her to go to prison on the 29th. She recorded in her diary that 'Annie does not wish me to go', but in a reply next day to Mrs Pankhurst she claimed that she could not join the deputation 'as father would not like it'.[42] It is difficult to know whether Colonel Linley's opposition was the real reason for Mary's refusal, or whether she used this as an excuse for her own reluctance to become involved in this level of activity. Nonetheless, she did send £1 to the WSPU fund because she had not been to prison. Mary appears to have been shielded by Annie Kenney on many occasions from the possibility of violence; for example, Emily recorded with relief that

> Annie is always doing kind things without letting people know. M is convinced she sent her off to Swansea so as to be out of the row in Bristol for Mr Birrell's visit, when streets were barricaded against the women. She always promised us to take care of M.[43]

Annie also seems to have felt that she needed someone like Mary to manage the movement for her in Bristol if she were arrested.[44] The reaction of the Blathwayts to changing tactics and forms of militancy was shared by many others in the WSPU. The history of the organization is characterized by resignations, usually because of disagreements over the escalation of violence, although individuals differed in their views about what was unacceptable and in the timing of when they left the union. Emily made her decision to resign on 8 September 1909 after two 'young hooligans', Elsie Howey and Vera Wentworth, who had often stayed with the family, joined Jessie Kenney in accosting Asquith as he left Lympne Church. One of the women struck him repeatedly. Although Emily had approved of militant methods when she was first a member, since then 'there has been personal violence & stone throwing which might injure innocent people'.[45] She also, for the first time, expressed concern about what other people in the village might think. On the other hand, neither Emily nor Linley discouraged Mary from her continuing involvement with the WSPU and they still offered their support to the suffragettes. At the time of her resignation Emily wrote in her diary, 'I shall continue to do what I can to help, but I cannot conscientiously say now that "I approve the methods" used by several of the members.'[46] Emily and Linley tended to distinguish between the actions of different members of the Union; Emily recorded that the last time Elsie Howey and Vera Wentworth had left Eagle House she had 'promised myself they should never come again if it were only on account of the reckless destruction of other people's property'.[47] On the other hand, she saw Mary Phillips, an organizer for the WSPU in Scotland, as a different type of militant who disapproved of stone throwing and then just running away.[48]

Friendships which had developed in the WSPU were still important to the Blathwayts. When Emily and Linley joined the Conservative and Unionist Women's Franchise Association (CUWFA) because, in contrast to the NUWSS, it did not support Liberal candidates, they wrote to explain their reasons for leaving the WSPU, adding a rider that '[we] have lots of friends in it'.[49] Emily expressed concerns whenever friends such as Annie Kenney or Emmeline Pankhurst were force-fed and tended to excuse their actions on the grounds that they had been provoked by the government.

Although Mary remained active in the Bath WSPU she was clearly uncomfortable about the increase in attacks on property. After 1912 suffrage work took up far less of her time, but she did not formally resign from the WSPU until June 1913. Her diary merely records that she had sent a resignation letter to Grace Tollemache and that she had given no reason. It was left to Emily, as usual, to provide an explanation:

> I am glad to say Mary is writing to resign membership with the WSPU. Now they have begun burning houses in the neighbourhood I feel more than ever ashamed to be connected with them ... the other day Bath ladies went to Trowbridge to interrupt a Cabinet minister's meeting disguised as market women. People seeing this in the papers may think M was one of them, Miss Tollemache (AE) – only being mentioned by name, calling out 'I protest'. She was turned out.[50]

Emily claimed that many of their friends and acquaintances, including Lilias Ashworth Hallett, could no longer support the kind of militancy which involved wholesale destruction of property. Aethel and Grace Tollemache, however, never wavered from their commitment to the WSPU and were both imprisoned for actions which included pouring tar into postboxes and cutting telephone wires. Their mother took part in the Tax Resistance League and in 1912 her furniture was sold at the White Hart, Batheaston, where Mary held a banner saying 'No Vote, No Tax!'[51] It is difficult to explain why the Tollemaches remained supportive of militancy, although they were unusual among Mary's friends in taking an interest in labour and socialist politics. Even after her resignation Mary remained friendly with Grace and Aethel. She still met with them in the suffrage shop, but now played a more passive role, taking photographs of her friends as they carried out suffrage work and turning these into postcards to be sold to make money for the WSPU.

Despite her disapproval of the escalation of militancy, Emily was reluctant to be too critical of her former colleagues and saved her most astringent comments for Asquith. She blamed him for the violence because he had failed to keep his promises, and commented that 'one can but despise such a man'. She agreed to join the NUWSS in 1914 only because at last they were willing to go against the Liberals.[52] Histories and reminiscences written by NUWSS members tend to give the impression that militancy was judged to be ineffective and counter-productive by suffrage campaigners in the immediate pre-war years.[53] Emily Blathwayt, however, referred constantly to the fact that militancy had been effective in bringing suffrage into the limelight, even though she had resigned from the WSPU. She disputed the judgement of *The Times* that Asquith had received an NUWSS deputation because of its peaceful methods, commenting, 'but we know he would never have done it except for the militants'.[54] When the NUWSS Pilgrimage reached Hyde Park Emily noted again that 'they were received with enthusiasm thanks to the militants having changed public opinion about them'.[55] She resigned from the CUWFA in October 1913 because their MPs were half-hearted in the House: 'then we do not care for the way they are now doing business. At the meeting it was all more an abuse of the Militants than in favour of the suffrage.'[56]

The Blathwayt diaries, therefore, provide a complex view of shifting allegiances to groups and their tactics and suggest that, even if the methods used led individuals to resign on principle from specific organizations, this did not mean that personal relationships were damaged beyond repair or that they became critical of all aspects of the movement. They debated with themselves, and with others, about the effectiveness of different forms of militancy and did not necessarily see the more constitutionalist methods of the NUWSS or their political tactics as the best way forward. Emily, for example, often asserted that Bristol NUWSS members were like 'Liberal Primrose Dames', whereas the WSPU was open to all classes.

The diaries also raise questions about women's politicization. The Blathwayts appear to have been drawn into political activism for the first time by the suffrage campaign. Their involvement in the WSPU developed from a complicated interconnection between their attraction to individuals such as Annie Kenney and their support for the aims and objectives of the movement more generally. They were inspired by the suffragettes' willingness to take action and infuriated by the actions of the government, which made their own support more resolute. Nonetheless, the end of the pre-war suffrage campaign also brought an end to the Blathwayts' active engagement in political life. Mary continued to subscribe to a range of societies such as the Workers' Educational Association, the Royal Society for the Prevention of Cruelty to Animals and the Selborne Society, and helped the Red Cross during the war, but these interests reflected the kind of life she had led before 1906 and could not be compared with the upheavals of the suffrage campaign. Mary and Emily both showed an interest when the Reform Bill, which enfranchised some women aged over 30, was passed in 1918. Emily commented that she and her husband 'wondered how quietly this had come at last, but the war occupies all our thoughts'.[57]

The diaries themselves provide few clues to explain why the Blathwayts, in particular Mary, withdrew from political life. It can only be assumed that this middle-class, gentrified family were inspired to act by the suffrage campaign, but failed to connect this with any deeper sense of oppression in their own personal lives or with any wider political beliefs. As noted earlier, an absence of any extensive discussion about personal beliefs and feelings in their diaries makes it difficult for the historian to explore the motivations of the family and the development of their political identity.

The attitudes expressed by the family towards the WSPU and its actions are not always straightforward or consistent; part of the interest of the diaries, therefore, lies in the complex and varied layers of meaning which can be read into the wealth of information provided. It is important also to recognize that the diaries present a view of the suffrage struggle in a local context through the eyes of one particular family; it is tempting to speculate on how different this view would have been if the diaries had been written by the Tollemaches, who were committed to the WSPU and militancy up to the outbreak of war. Emily Blathwayt in particular was aware that she was being selective in what she wrote and perhaps the last word should be left to her. Writing in her diary in the month in which war was declared, she noted, 'I do not put about everything in the diary. There is so much & it will all be history.'[58]

Notes

1. Emily Blathwayt (EB), diary, 9 May 1909. The Blathwayt diaries are kept at Dyrham House, Dyrham, near Bath. I would like to thank the National Trust for permission to use them.

2. B. Kanner, 'Autobiographical writings: women in English social history, 1800-1914. A guide to research volume 3', *Gender and History*, Vol. 2, No. 1, 1990, p. 90.

3. Family details and extensive extracts from the diaries can be found in B. M. Wilmott Dobbie, *A Nest of Suffragettes in Somerset*, Batheaston, Batheaston Society, 1979.

4. Wilmott Dobbie, *Nest of Suffragettes*, p. 9.

5. T. Davis *et al.* have used autobiographies to 'get nearer to an understanding of the nature of feminist consciousness', in ' "The public face of feminism": early twentieth century writings on women's suffrage', in Centre for Contemporary Cultural Studies, *Making Histories*, London, Hutchinson, 1982, p. 307; see also J. Purvis, 'The prison experiences of the suffragettes in Edwardian Britain', *Women's History Review*, Vol. 4, No. 1, 1995, pp. 103-33.

6. L. Leneman, 'A truly national movement: the view from outside

London', in M. Joannou and J. Purvis (eds), *The Women's Suffrage Movement: New Feminist Perspectives*, Manchester, Manchester University Press, 1998; L. Stanley with A. Morley, *The Life and Death of Emily Wilding Davison*, London, The Women's Press, 1988.

7. For an overview of recent interpretations see S. S. Holton, 'Women and the vote', in J. Purvis (ed.), *Women's History: Britain, 1850-1945*, London, UCL Press, 1995; B. Caine, *English Feminism, 1780-1980*, Oxford, Oxford University Press, 1997.

8. J. Bottoms, 'Writing herself: the diary of Alice James', in J. Swindells (ed.), *The Uses of Autobiography*, London, Taylor & Francis, 1995, p. 112. See also T. Vannen, 'Introduction to special issue on auto/biography', *Gender and History*, Vol. 2, No. 1, 1990, p. 19.

9. V. Woolf, diary, 20 April 1919, quoted in H. Blodgett, *Centuries of Female Days: Englishwomen's Private Diaries*, Gloucester, Alan Sutton, 1989, p. 21. See also Bottoms, 'Writing herself', p. 110, and L. Stanley, 'Moments of writing: is there a feminist auto/biography?', *Gender and History*, Vol. 2, No. 1, 1990, p. 61.

10. Blodgett, *Centuries of Female Days*, p. 8. C. Sjoblad, 'The Lund Project on women's autobiographies and diaries in Sweden', *Gender and History*, Vol. 2, No. 1, 1990, p. 88.

11. Blodgett, *Centuries of Female Days*.

12. Sjoblad, 'The Lund Project', p. 87. For different types of diaries, see Blodgett, *Centuries of Female Days*, chapters 1 and 2.

13. For a discussion of the 'textual interconnections' between the diaries of Arthur Munby and Hannah Cullwick see Stanley, 'Moments of writing', p. 61.

14. EB, diary, 14 July 1908.

15. T. Thompson, *Dear Girl: The Diaries and Letters of Two Working Women, 1897-1917*, London, The Women's Press, 1987, p. 6.

16. Mary Blathwayt (MB), diary, 6 August 1908. For a discussion of suffrage colours see L. Tickner, *The Spectacle of Women: Imagery of the Suffrage Campaign, 1907-14*, London, Chatto and Windus, 1987, Appendix 6.

17. MB, diary, 3 May 1910.

18. S. S. Holton, 'The suffragist and the "average woman"', *Women's History Review*, Vol. 1, No. 1, 1992, p. 11.

19. MB, diary, 19 July 1908.

20. A. Kenney, *Memories of a Militant*, London, Edward Arnold, 1924, p. 120.

21. Diaries of H. W. Nevinson, 15 April 1910, Bodleian Library, Oxford. I am grateful to Angela John for this reference.

22. L. E. Nym Mayhall, 'Creating the "suffragette spirit": British feminism and the historical imagination', *Women's History Review*, Vol. 4, No. 3, 1995, p. 320; H. Kean, 'Searching for the past in present defeat: the construction of historical and political identity in British

feminism in the 1920s and 1930s', *Women's History Review*, Vol. 3, No. 1, 1994, pp. 57-80.
23. Mayhall, 'Creating the "suffragette spirit"', p. 320.
24. *Ibid.*, p. 319.
25. Thompson, *Dear Girl*.
26. Holton, 'The suffragist and the "average woman"'.
27. Kean, 'Searching for the past in present defeat', p. 69.
28. MB, diary, 13 December 1907 and 15 February 1908.
29. EB, diary, 3 April 1908.
30. EB, diary, 1 April 1908 and 23 May 1908.
31. EB, diary, 30 April 1909.
32. For example, see A. Rosen, *Rise up Women! The Militant Campaign of the Women's Social and Political Union, 1903-1914*, London, Routledge and Kegan Paul, 1974, p. 208; M. Ramelson, *The Petticoat Rebellion*, London, Lawrence and Wishart, 1972, p. 46. For a discussion of this literature and a different view of the Pankhursts see J. Purvis, 'A "pair of ... infernal queens"? A reassessment of the dominant representations of Emmeline and Christabel Pankhurst, first wave feminists in Edwardian Britain', *Women's History Review*, Vol. 5, No. 2, 1996.
33. Rosen, *Rise up Women!*, p. 208; J. Liddington and J. Norris, *One Hand Tied Behind Us: The Rise of the Women's Suffrage Movement*, London, Virago, 1978, p. 188.
34. Kenney, *Memories of a Militant*, p. 193. See also E. S. Pankhurst, *The Suffragette Movement*, London, Virago, 1977 (first published 1931), p. 186; E. Pethick-Lawrence, *My Part in a Changing World*, London, Victor Gollancz, 1938, p. 151.
35. EB, diary, 4 October 1909.
36. M. Joannou, 'She who would be politically free must strike the first blow: suffragette autobiography and suffragette militancy' in J. Swindells (ed.), *The Uses of Autobiography*, London, Taylor and Francis, 1995, p. 33.
37. MB, diary, 13 September 1914.
38. EB, diary, 2 May 1909.
39. MB, diary, 11 May 1908.
40. MB, diary, 6 August and 22 August 1908.
41. EB, diary, 26 May and 7 June 1908.
42. MB, diary, 15 and 16 June 1909.
43. EB, diary, 10 October 1909, quoted in Wilmott Dobbie, *Nest of Suffragettes*, p. 37.
44. EB, diary, 31 July 1909.
45. EB, diary, 8 September 1909.
46. EB, diary, 8 September 1909.
47. EB, diary, 14 September 1909.
48. EB, diary, 15 September 1909.
49. EB, diary, 4 October 1909.

50. EB, diary, 6 June 1913.
51. MB, diary, 6 March 1912.
52. EB, diary, 20 June 1914 and 3 January 1914.
53. For example, see R. Strachey, *The Cause: A Short History of the Women's Movement in Great Britain*, London, Virago, 1978 (first published 1928).
54. EB, diary, 9 August 1913.
55. EB, diary, 23 May 1914 and 28 July 1913.
56. EB, diary, 4 October 1913.
57. EB, diary, 7 February 1918, quoted in Wilmott Dobbie, *Nest of Suffragettes*, p. 59.
58. EB, diary, 6 August 1914.

4 Teetotal Feminists: Temperance Leadership and the Campaign for Women's Suffrage

Margaret Barrow

By the second half of the nineteenth century temperance work had become almost endemic among the Nonconformist middle classes, first as part of the broader Victorian philanthropic agenda and later as a political campaign.[1] For the 'true believers' there were temperance hotels, coffee taverns, drink-free concerts, temperance friendly societies, temperance insurance and funeral clubs. There were the long-established temperance families, including the Brights, Cadburys, Sturges, Hiltons. Many of these families were Quakers and so their concerns over excessive drinking were well established.[2] The publisher John Cassell, Thomas Cook and George Cruikshank were also temperance advocates. Cruikshank, the leading English caricaturist of his generation, who drank heavily while creating his famous cartoons, later converted to temperance, becoming a 'zealous advocate' for the cause.[3]

In contrast to studies of New Zealand, Australia and the United States, very little is known about the connections between the temperance movement and other campaigns undertaken by women in Britain.[4] This does not mean that British temperance women simply 'signed the pledge'; on the contrary, many actively participated in the movement and also linked their temperance work with the other causes they supported, including women's suffrage. This chapter traces the evolving and complex relationship between demands for temperance and women's suffrage through the experiences and policies of three presidents of the main British temperance society, the British Women's Temperance Association (BWTA), between 1876 and the years immediately prior to the First World War.

Women have in general been marginalized from much that has been written on temperance. Harrison's work makes little mention of women's activities and Shiman covers the topic only briefly.[5] However, women were active from the beginning of the temperance movement. They organized their own societies and associations in the 1830s and 1840s and incorporated temperance into their philanthropic activities. Early women temperance campaigners in Britain were active individually and collectively in the anti-slavery movement, participated in the demands for the Married Women's Property Acts, and supported Josephine Butler's campaign against the Contagious Diseases Acts. Indeed, Butler herself was both a supporter of the temperance movement and teetotal. Campaigners also actively supported the Anti-Corn Law campaign, the peace movement, higher education for women, social purity and women's suffrage.[6] Although the men's temperance movement consisted of many different organizations which had difficulty in unifying around a common philosophy, among women campaigners one organization dominated, the BWTA. This association was founded in 1876 and, while not the first female temperance organization, it was to become the most powerful. In its heyday at the turn of the century its president, Rosalind Howard, Countess of Carlisle, was to claim a membership of over 100,000.[7] Many of the women who joined the BWTA were middle-class evangelical women who had already gained organizational experience from their activities in Christian and philanthropic work. The organizational skills gained by BWTA members meant they were well placed to extend their philanthropic concerns into political activity.

In the early 1870s a great deal of temperance work was conducted within the philosophy of Christian temperance: the belief that temperance alone was not enough to 'save' individuals and had to be linked with conversion to a Christian way of life. Supporters of this philosophy received an impetus to widen their activities following reports of the 1873 'Women's Whisky Crusade' in the United States. This 'crusade' was a spontaneous movement that began in Ohio when women took to the streets, singing hymns, kneeling in the snow praying and even smashing bars.[8] Out of this movement, which spread chiefly through the north-eastern states, the Women's Christian Temperance Union (WCTU) was formed. This organization was to have a profound influence on the British women's temperance movement. There were reports of similar activities in Britain, for example in Liverpool and Scotland,[9] although these were not widespread, and the accounts of the 'crusade' in the British press were a contributory factor leading to the foundation of the BWTA in Newcastle in 1876. Links between British and American temperance women took a more direct form when Eliza Stewart, one of the leading members of the American campaign, met British temperance women at a meeting of the Independent Order of Good Templars (IOGT).[10]

The BWTA, a non-denominational organization, was, from its foundation up to the onset of the First World War, the most important national women's temperance organization in Britain. It acted as a centre for affiliated branches all over the country. Branches were grouped regionally, mainly by counties, giving members the opportunity to expand their contacts within a limited geographical area. The branches were able to organize themselves with a large degree of autonomy permitting individuals to espouse specific causes broadly within the remit of the BWTA. The BWTA had four presidents in the period up to the First World War. The first president, Clara Lucas Balfour, was a well-known temperance activist and author of many temperance novels and tracts. She suffered ill health for most of her short presidency and died in 1878.[11] The other three leaders, Margaret Bright Lucas, Lady Henry Somerset and Rosalind Howard, Countess of Carlisle, all had a significant influence on the association, and they brought to it very different experiences and styles of management. All three were actively involved in the campaign for women's suffrage, but as with their leadership styles, their approaches to suffrage and its relationship to the temperance movement varied significantly.

When Margaret Bright Lucas became president in 1878 she was already an experienced temperance worker and a member of the IOGT. She brought to the association her experience of the anti-slavery movement, the campaign against the Corn Laws and the Contagious Diseases Acts repeal campaign, in which she had worked with Josephine Butler.[12] Lucas subscribed to the London suffrage committee, which had drawn up the first women's suffrage petition in support of John Stuart Mill's attempts to pass a measure through Parliament. A supporter of Millicent Garrett Fawcett, she was emphatic in her belief in suffrage, stating, 'as long as I can work I shall strive to obtain complete equality between men and women before the law'.[13]

Lucas had impressive political connections through her brothers John and Jacob Bright and her brother-in-law Duncan McLaren, all of whom were MPs. More significantly, she was part of the extensive feminist network that built up around the Bright family, which included links to the women's suffrage movement in the United States.[14] Her sister, Priscilla Bright McLaren, was active in both temperance and the campaign for women's suffrage and was a key figure in the Edinburgh Society for Women's Suffrage.[15] Another family connection to the women's suffrage campaign existed through her sister-in-law, Ursula Bright, who was on the executive committee of the Manchester Women's Suffrage Society, and later of the Women's Franchise League. Lucas also had political connections in her own right, as president of the Bloomsbury branch of the Women's Liberal Association. Therefore, in addition to suffrage demands, temperance was also a part of the liberal politics of the exceptional women of the Bright family.[16]

Lucas's belief in, and support for, votes for women was also known in the temperance movement. In an article in 1875 published in *The Good Templar's Watchword*, the journal of the IOGT, she was described as an advocate of women's right to the suffrage. In the article she was quoted as 'believing that where women were ratepayers or otherwise equally qualified with men, their sex should not disqualify them to exercise the suffrage'.[17] In 1878, the same year in which she became president of the BWTA, she moved the following motion at a meeting of the IOGT:

> Believing that temperance legislation would be greatly aided by women who are ratepayers, having a vote for MPs as well as Town Councils, Poor Law Boards and School Boards, this conference of the IOGT urges members of the Order to give all support in their power to this movement.

The resolution was passed[18] and Lucas took advantage of the IOGT's at least theoretical commitment to providing women equal rights and opportunities within its structure by rising to the rank of Grand Worthy Vice Templar.[19]

Lucas encouraged the membership to consider the question of women's suffrage, pointing out the value of the vote in combating problems associated with drinking. She was not averse to drawing on arguments common to women's suffrage activists at the time, notably the rights of women taxpayers to vote. Writing in the BWTA annual report of 1883-4, she stated:

> I put it to you, has not the time come when it becomes a duty to claim the vote on the side of temperance? ... it is hard that intelligent women - taxpayers - who feel so deeply on this and moral questions would be left without a voice. I urge you, my sisters, to study this question with regard to its bearing on our work.[20]

In her capacity as president of the BWTA Lucas wrote to other temperance organizations in 1883, making the pleas that the Franchise Reform Bill then before Parliament should include women:

> We earnestly entreat the [temperance workers] to make common cause with us and to besiege members of parliament with letters and personal interviews asking them for the sake of right and for the sake of the highest welfare of the nation to vote for the admission of women householders into this household bill.[21]

This letter, which also appeared in a number of temperance newspapers, was written in collaboration with Isabella Tod, who shared Lucas's interests in temperance and suffrage. She was honorary secretary of the Belfast branch of the National Society for Women's Suffrage, a founder member of the Belfast Women's Temperance Association, and was active in the campaign against the Contagious Diseases Acts. She attended the Geneva meeting of the British, Continental and General Federation for the Abolition of Government Regulation of Prostitution in 1877, with Lucas and also with Josephine Butler.[22]

Despite the obvious sympathies of their president, in the early years of the BWTA the rank and file showed more interest in Christian philanthropic work than in politics. The exception to this lack of interest was in the North-East, where BWTA members were more politically active.[23] The views of the majority were probably responsible for Lucas's careful wording when addressing the issue of suffrage, and she was always careful to emphasize the advantage to the temperance cause rather than making a straightforward demand based on women's rights *per se*. Even so, Lucas provided the groundwork which enabled the BWTA to expand from its Christian temperance beginnings; it was through her presidency that the BWTA became more politically active. Lucas encouraged members to support the suffrage campaign by articulating the benefits this would bring to their temperance work and the opportunities it would provide for the furthering of their cause.

After Lucas's death in 1890, Lady Henry Somerset was elected to the presidency of the association, in part because the BWTA membership thought it beneficial to have a titled president. It was something of a coup for the BWTA to have secured Somerset as president, although the depth of her personal commitment to temperance has been the source of speculation; it is rumoured that she drank her last sherry before taking over her duties![24] Somerset quickly became extremely popular with both her executive committee and the branches and many of the affiliated societies, and was to remain so, at least with the latter two, despite what was to be a troubled presidency.

Following her election Somerset began to put her own stamp on the BWTA, changing and widening its structure. She wanted to modernize the association into one with a more political aware and effective membership, and in doing so she attempted to emulate the WCTU in the United States of America. Having taken on the role of a reforming president, Somerset accepted an invitation to visit the United States, arriving late in 1891. During her stay she visited both the WCTU and its international arm, the World WCTU.[25] Somerset had originally planned to stay for six weeks, but the visit became extended and she did not return to England until May the following year.[26] It was during this lengthy visit that Somerset met and was impressed by Frances Willard, the American president of the WCTU.

A powerful leader and speaker, Willard was to have a profound influence on both Somerset and the BWTA. She was renowned for her 'Do everything policy', which included many reform activities. Willard had linked the WCTU to the campaign for suffrage under the slogan of 'Home Protection', believing that a vote for prohibition would give women protection from drunken husbands. All petitions calling for women's suffrage from the WCTU in the United States called for a 'Home Protection bill'; Willard put forward the idea that the vote would give women security, particularly in the home, from the devastation caused by the 'legalized' traffic in strong drink.[27] The *Home Protection Manual* was the cornerstone of Willard's policy. It outlined the basis of temperance women's claim for the vote: 'We want that ballot because the liquor traffic is entrenched in law, and grows out of the will of the majorities, and the majorities [*sic*] of women are against the Liquor traffic.'[28] The demand here was not for equality or citizenship but for the defeat of the trade in alcohol. Willard's rhetorical style was aimed at emphasizing the moral consequences of not giving women the vote. She declared women's suffrage to be essential for women to enable them to vote for prohibition. Marilley describes this stance as a 'feminism of fear' and as an ideological campaign based not on equality but rather on reinforcing the moral standards of women and domesticity.[29] Lucy Bland's assertion that a rejection of male sexual violence – which must surely include alcohol-induced violence – underpinned much feminist activity in this period provides a rather more positive perspective on Willard's feminist credentials.[30]

During her visit to the United States, Somerset witnessed Willard's strategy of joining together the suffrage and temperance campaigns and believed that this was the way forward for the BWTA. An important difference between the two presidents was that Somerset did not appear to lay such emphasis on violence inflicted on women through male drinking. Instead, she saw the main result of the 'drink traffic' to be drunken women and the difficulty of their reclamation. Somerset believed that it was women themselves who needed to be directly protected from alcohol abuse.[31] Back in Britain, Frances Willard's aggressive entry into the suffrage debate in the United States was viewed with suspicion and her 'Do everything policy' did not cross the Atlantic successfully. The multiplicity of causes that Lady Henry Somerset tried to add to the BWTA's agenda caused great concern among sections of the membership. Despite the attempts to generate support for suffrage within the temperance movement first by Lucas and now by Somerset, some members still feared that any attempt to attach temperance to demands for women's suffrage worked to the detriment of the temperance campaign. Others, while supporting suffrage on a personal level, still wished the BWTA to remain an exclusively temperance society.

Somerset's long absence in America had led to her power and influence being diminished. She had expected the BWTA executive committee to follow her lead in all policy changes, but instead they resented the high-handed methods she had adopted while abroad. The committee, many of whom were of the opinion that the BWTA should not involve itself directly in suffrage agitation, were upset by the cabled instructions that branches should 'memorialize' in favour of Rollitt's women's suffrage bill.[32] In the event, despite their reservations, a whip was sent out to MPs requesting that they be present in the House and vote for the bill. Additionally, there was increasing confusion over the date of Somerset's return to Britain, which resulted in difficulties in organizing the BWTA's annual meeting.[33]

In spite of widespread reservations and uncertainty, the BWTA welcomed Somerset back to Britain with a large reception. In her opening speech the president made reference to Willard's work with the WCTU and discussed the linking of suffrage and temperance:

but what are politics by the great home government of the world? And if this is not women's work what is? We have tried moral suasion since we first began, and at this moment we are confronted with the fact that we are precisely where we were. ... Unless the women's voices are heard in legislation, the men will not be able to carry these changes ... by the woman's vote temperance reform will surely be secured.[34]

Somerset's return to Britain was soon followed by first a private visit by Willard in 1892, when she stayed at Reigate Manor (Somerset's home), and later an official visit.[35] It was during this second, official visit that Somerset began touring the country with Willard to canvas opinion about broadening the remit of the BWTA to include women's suffrage, social purity,[36] peace and arbitration and links to the organized labour movement. Although Bordin claims that problems within the BWTA pre-dated Willard's arrival, there is no doubt that the sight of the two women touring the British Isles caused consternation among some sections of the membership.[37] The association became polarized, and while Somerset's tour exacerbated the grievances of conservative members, it appears to have delighted her supporters. In January 1893 the Free Trade Hall in Manchester was filled with both men and women for a 'Great Temperance Demonstration'. Somerset gave a speech which underlined again the necessity of votes for women, arguing that only this could ensure 'great reform'.[38] The same month Somerset and Willard visited Liverpool, where, as well as attending BWTA meetings, they attended a meeting of the local Women's Liberal Association.[39] From the North-West the two women travelled to Scotland before returning to London for a final large meeting in the East End.[40] During the course of the tour they had firmly linked their demands for temperance and women's suffrage.

The majority of the executive committee were unsettled and felt aggrieved at Somerset's demand that they include new elements into their work; not only suffrage, but also social purity, peace and arbitration, the opium question and the labour question.[41] Opinion among the majority of members of the BWTA executive continued to favour a single-issue organization as the road to total abstinence. They believed that under Somerset's plans temperance work would become secondary to the work for women's suffrage. At the root of this trouble lay disagreements over tactics and a reluctance to overstretch the association and thereby reduce its temperance campaigning potential.

The local branches of the association were also becoming more divided into two camps, those who believed that suffrage was a part of their temperance work and those who supported a single-issue approach. Some branches brought suffrage to the attention of their members through discussion meetings. In 1892, for example, the Mansfield branch discussed the 'topic of suffrage' and on a show of hands 'not one was held up against the principle'.[42] In the same year the Stoke Newington,

Rectory Road branch in London passed a resolution in favour of women's suffrage and sent a petition to Sir Albert Rollitt.[43] These BWTA members claimed the vote as a right, knowing that it would enable them to vote for temperance but that it would also give them political power. The members who favoured the continuation of a single-issue approach had the same concerns as members of the executive committee: that temperance would become neglected and also that suffrage campaigning could be best addressed by the suffrage societies.

Concerns over the future of the association boiled over at the 1892 annual council meeting, held soon after Somerset's return from the United States. Her speech, like many of her major speeches, was long and covered many issues including, unsurprisingly, the role of the suffrage campaign in the association. Worrying for some of the membership was her stated intention to establish a department within the BWTA for purity campaigning. Worst of all in the eyes of her strongest critics was the part of her long speech which dealt with the situation in the United States and the work of the WCTU and its international organization, the World WCTU.[44] Somerset and Willard had organized for the next world convention to be held in London in the following June, and this too was perceived by some as a threat to the BWTA. The gulf between the rival factions widened as the supporters of a single-issue body became increasingly alarmed at what they believed to be the 'Americanization' of the association.

Supporters of the single-issue approach were in a majority on the executive committee and were led by Mary Docwra, a founding member of the BWTA, and Louisa Stewart, who had worked with Margaret Bright Lucas. It was the single-issue 'dissenters' who had control of the journal of the BWTA, *Wings*, and they used it to put forward their views. Criticism of Somerset's ambitions was published both openly and by innuendo in the journal. The monthly feature 'British women at home', for example, focused on the traditional activities of temperance women. The February issue contained a statement on the 'progressive policy advocated by the majority of the executive committee';[45] it stressed the necessity of working exclusively for temperance reform and affirmed the belief that 'a diffusion of energy at this time, an abstraction of strength from our ranks will weaken our chance'. Also, believing that Somerset's support was London-based, her opponents proposed that a consultative committee should be formed of country members.[46] The association was in a state of crisis.

Somerset responded by putting out a strong statement that the association would not be changed into an organization with a 'Do everything policy'.[47] However, her attempts at reconciliation did not appease the majority of her executive committees. This was because Somerset also proposed that the association should be run in the period between half-yearly national meetings by a subcommittee made up of herself, a treasurer, recording secretary, assistant recording secretary and only eight other members of the executive committee.[48] It was feared that by these means Somerset would gain a stranglehold on the association, to its detriment. Somerset was perceived at best to have become 'Americanized' and at worst mesmerized by Frances Willard.[49]

Even so, it was not until Somerset bypassed the executive committee and circulated her 'Outline of policy of the BWTA' that they became particularly alienated. The actual wording of the 'Outline' was to cause much debate, and yet the version published in *Wings* was innocuous enough: of the seventeen items on their programme of work, the vast majority referred to straightforward temperance issues.[50] The only possible bone of contention was the section 'Work among municipal women'. This department of the BWTA's work centred on encouraging women with a local franchise to use their vote to influence decisions relating to temperance. The purpose of this department was to persuade temperance women to become Poor Law Guardians and to sit on school boards, and this policy was gradually encouraging members to become politically active.

In the event it was not these watered-down proposals but the affection of branch members that won Somerset the vote when the issue was debated at the next BWTA annual meeting. And yet, while the vote was claimed as a splendid victory, a sizeable minority of the membership did not support Somerset; she achieved a majority of 69 votes, which meant that 193 out of a total 455 had been cast against her.[51] Following the outcome of the vote, a majority of her executive committee walked out and went on to form the Women's Total Abstinence Union (WTAU). The BWTA was left with Somerset and the members who had backed their president, but had lost many long-standing and devoted temperance activists. Ironically, many of those who joined the WTAU were to continue actively to support the campaign for suffrage, but as individuals, leaving the new organization to campaign on the single issue of total abstinence.[52] (Members of the two societies did not reunite until 1926.)

Even after the departure of the dissatisfied members, the BWTA's policy on suffrage did not necessarily become any clearer.[53] Somerset had succeeded in the main not because of her perceived stance on suffrage, although undoubtedly some members hoped that she would pursue the suffrage cause vigorously, but because the branches wanted her to remain as their president. The conflict had been concentrated among the national leaders, but the rank-and-file members had had the ultimate say.

Somerset continued as president of the BWTA, working closely with Frances Willard until the latter's death in 1898, but her presidency was not without further controversy. Somerset made a grave error of judgement by appearing to support the implementation of the Cantonment Acts (which proposed the introduction of the Contagious Diseases Acts into India) and weakened her position as a result.[54] Somerset also continued to support the suffrage campaign and to expand the remit of the BWTA, but she began to compromise her total abstinence stance. While giving evidence to the Royal Commission on the Liquor Licensing Laws in 1897-98, Somerset stated that she did not believe that drinking in itself was wrong, and that she was not entirely opposed to public houses.[55] Not surprisingly, she became increasingly marginalized within a temperance movement whose aim was prohibition in the form of the local veto.[56]

Somerset recognized the importance of continuing to communicate directly to the BWTA membership and sought another mouthpiece after the association's paper, *Wings*, was taken over by the WTAU. In 1893 Somerset began publishing the *Woman's Herald* (which had taken over from the *Woman's Penny Paper*). The situation was not ideal since the paper was also the official organ of the World WCTU, although the activities of other organizations were reported, including the Women's Liberal Federation (WLF) and the Central National Society for Women's Suffrage.[57] The affinity with the World WCTU did not benefit the BWTA, nor was the paper a financial success. It needed a firm editorial policy, and temperance news on its own was not interesting or stimulating enough, particularly for Somerset's more radical readers. Somerset continued with the arrangement until January 1894 when Florence Fenwick Miller took over the publication; it was renamed *Woman's Signal*, and she intended it to be a feminist newspaper.[58] Fenwick Miller agreed that the BWTA's news would be included in the third issue of the month; however, this arrangement was not a success and Somerset, as corresponding editor, again exerted her influence and attempted, unsuccessfully, to gain control of the journal on behalf of the association.

It is clear that Somerset, in spite of a somewhat chequered presidency, inspired some women to support the campaign for women's suffrage. Members of the Manchester Women's Christian Temperance Association (WCTA), which for many years had been traditional in its approach to temperance activity (it did not even join the BWTA until 1886), were enthusiastic about her approach. The branch also admired Frances Willard and closely followed her speeches during the 1892 tour of Britain. In 1894 a mass meeting at the Free Trade Hall, organized by the Manchester National Society for Women's Suffrage, was supported by a number of organizations, including the Manchester WCTA. Temperance women were present at the same venue during the first militant protest of the WSPU, when Annie Kenney and Christabel Pankhurst tried to question Sir Edward Grey in 1905, resulting in their ejection from the hall and subsequent arrest. The Manchester members of the WCTA appear to have admired the forthright outburst; indeed, according to a report by BWTA member Bertha Mason, Christabel was likened to Frances Willard[59] in the sense that both were seen as radicals who supported women's suffrage and who were fearless in their approach.

It is difficult to ascertain how deep Somerset's commitment to women's suffrage actually went. Was she just captivated by the WCTU approach to reform? She may have envisaged herself as a major leader of the women's movement, as Willard was in the United States. However, it was not the question of suffrage which was to finally turn the membership of the BWTA against Somerset, but her handling of the proposed introduction of the Contagious Diseases Acts into India. Somerset resigned the presidency, but was persuaded to return and survived the crisis – but only just. Her subsequent support of disinterested management rather than the direct veto caused her final and permanent resignation in 1903.

Somerset had taken her lead from Frances Willard, and yet even with Willard's help it is unlikely that she could have made the BWTA membership part of the mainstream suffrage movement; the BWTA was too broad a church. Nor did Somerset have the political skills, stature or reputation of other suffrage leaders. It is possible to speculate that Somerset's presidency might have been more successful had she been able to convince more of her membership of the necessity of making women's suffrage a central plank of the BWTA's programme. And yet, she could hardly have picked a more difficult time, given the widespread lack of confidence among British suffrage campaigners in the 1890s generally.[60] Alternatively, she could have followed the example of Bertha Mason and many others and continued to pursue the two agendas separately: temperance through the BWTA and suffrage through an organization like the WLF. After Somerset's resignation it was those women who were active in both movements, women like Bertha Mason, Eva McLaren, Florence Balgarnie and Laura Ormiston Chant, who were left to build upon their commitment to temperance and suffrage. They were joined by the next president of the BWTA, Rosalind Howard, Countess of Carlisle.

Rosalind Howard, who became president of the BWTA in 1903, was probably one of the most difficult women to espouse the causes both of temperance and of women's suffrage.[61] Howard was the daughter of Henrietta Maria, Lady Stanley of Alderley, who was involved in the campaign for women's education and was one of the founders of Girton College. Both were strong women, and mother and daughter were to clash over the issue of Home Rule for Ireland.[62] On becoming Countess of Carlisle in 1889, Rosalind personally managed the two Howard estates at Naworth and Castle Howard. Autocratic, Carlisle was feared by many and was described by her daughter as having a dominating character and impetuous temperament. Her son-in-law, who greatly admired her, admitted that she had 'her human imperfections, notably a vehement temper which does not seem to have given trouble in the first half of her life, but which in later years at times got beyond her control'.[63] Carlisle differed from her two predecessors in that her loyalties were clearly spread over different organizations and causes. What is more, she put a great deal of effort into integrating the concerns of each of the societies of which she was a prominent member: the WLF, the BWTA and the constitutional section of the twentieth-century women's suffrage movement. An ardent suffragist and staunch Liberal, she put the latter loyalty first, remaining committed to the Liberal Party despite what she considered to be its treachery over women's suffrage, the local veto and Home Rule. She came to lead not only the WLF but, from 1903, the BWTA.

When the WLF was founded under the presidency of Mrs Gladstone, Carlisle at first declined to join, feeling that the dominance of the wives of prominent Liberals would prevent effective pressure for women's suffrage. When she eventually joined in 1890 she initiated her suffrage and temperance agenda within the federation when she founded the Carlisle Women's Liberal Association. Carlisle made a lengthy speech at the inaugural meeting in which she discussed not only women's suffrage, but also what she considered to be the successes of the Liberal Party in a number of other areas - including temperance.[64] The following year she spoke at the Longtown Women's Liberal Association, stating that temperance should be considered a woman's issue and encouraging women who had the qualifications to vote in municipal elections to exercise their right in support of the Liberal Party.[65] She tried to get the WLF to put women's suffrage on the national agenda from 1891, and when in 1893 she succeeded, the federation split as a consequence.[66] Subsequently suffrage became a central plank of the WLF programme and eventually, after much debate, the organization decided to refuse to support all anti-suffrage candidates. Carlisle's support for suffrage was to bring criticism from within her own family, particularly from her son Michael, who was strongly opposed to women's suffrage.[67]

Carlisle had been able to take control of the WLF by a meticulously planned campaign in which she organized her daughters Mary and Dorothy, Eva McLaren and Bertha Mason to canvas local associations for support. In 1891 she travelled around WLF local associations trying to gather support for her suffrage stance. Where necessary she was prepared to establish new branches of the WLF in areas where none existed, or where existing branches were opposed to suffrage. Carlisle supported Liberal women, who agreed to back her suffrage agenda within the federation. She agonized long over 'problem' constituencies which would not support her pro-suffrage stance and used many tactics - including bullying - to convert waverers to her cause.[68] And being in awe of her status, in many instances they gave in.

Carlisle's support for temperance is thought to have originated in 1881 when, together with her husband, she became teetotal.[69] They were in agreement on temperance and they made their Cumberland estate the centre of their temperance activities. Brewing was discontinued at Castle

Howard and temperance was made a condition of becoming a tenant on the Howard estates. Public houses were closed on both estates and replaced by reading rooms. The expansion of the railway gave Carlisle the opportunity to buy up coaching inns which had been bypassed by the railways and close them. Even so, she was to continue to serve wine at her table until she became president of the BWTA.[70]

Carlisle's considerable organizing ability enabled her to combine her fight for both the suffrage and the temperance cause. She built around her a team of women who lectured and promoted both temperance and suffrage. Their role was to do the groundwork for her. Bertha Mason was a prime example: a Liberal, a temperance worker and a supporter of women's suffrage, she organized branches of the WLF and ran the BWTA Lancashire and Cheshire Union. Carlisle considered both these organizations to be a part of her power base.[71] Mason was also able to assure Carlisle of the support of Ashton-under-Lyne and she continually visited associations in both Lancashire and Cheshire throughout 1891, believing that the federation should 'openly advocate and work for the enfranchisement of women', although she did not 'approve of the suffrage being made a test question at elections'.[72] Great emphasis was placed on the local WLF associations in the North-West, and the McLarens, Bertha Mason and Rosalind Carlisle all visited the region in the summer and autumn of 1891 to gather support for the inclusion of suffrage and local prohibition in the WLF's remit. On her election as president of the WLF, Carlisle brought a new and directly party political approach to the management of the federation. Mason continued to work with her and in 1897 was touring Lancashire branches, canvassing for support for women's suffrage and reporting her findings to Carlisle: the Oldham Liberal Party had a 'considerable majority against an extension of the parliamentary franchise to women'; Bury was considered 'an almost impossible place for suffrage work'; 'Burnley is more hopeful'.[73] By 1899 it was reported that conditions were more hopeful in Aston-under-Lyne after the male Liberal Association had allowed a deputation of women to give their point of view on the suffrage question. As a result a suffrage resolution was passed 'after 12 years of opposition'.[74]

Whereas Somerset had frequently been absent from BWTA executive meetings, Carlisle was a regular attendee of committee meetings.[75] She radically restructured the association after becoming president, reassessing its scope, departments and the range of causes it supported. Changes were swift and there was a clear and rapid shift of emphasis from the all-embracing association developed under Somerset, in imitation of Willard, to a highly focused political temperance society. Carlisle established a BWTA political department that included suffrage within its remit, and generally the slimmed-down organization became more effective. She also ensured that temperance became a primary focus in the WLF and she fought hard for the introduction of the local veto following the Liberal victory in the general election of 1906. During the election campaign Carlisle had exhorted her membership to ensure that parliamentary candidates were pledged to support the reversal of the Licensing Act of 1904, as well as supporting other temperance legislation.[76]

Carlisle's leading role in both the WLF and the BWTA made it easier for her to encourage temperance women to support the suffrage campaign and Liberal women to embrace suffrage. Such was her success in rallying her temperance troops to the suffrage cause that she wrote of the progressives having 'more temperance reformers than the other side'.[77]

It was Carlisle's attention to detail that enabled her to manage her political campaigns – as well as her overwhelming personality. She continued to support temperance and to use the BWTA as a power base for her temperance politics; she ensured that the BWTA both backed her view of prohibition in the form of the local veto and continued to support the suffrage campaign. However, Carlisle did manage to alienate many Liberal women and some of the Liberal temperance advocates by refusing, out of loyalty to the Liberal Party, to make suffrage a test question. In spite of these occasional moments of conflict, Carlisle's control over the BWTA was complete and she ensured that the membership followed her lead.

As president of the BWTA Carlisle enjoyed links with other temperance organizations and she was vice-president of the United Kingdom Alliance (UKA), a strongly prohibitionist society. And while she used her numerous other contacts to further the cause of temperance she did not neglect suffrage during her presidency of the BWTA; a good number among the 100,000 membership were suffragists and it remained an issue close to Carlisle's heart.[78] She kept the membership aware of the work still to be done! Annual council meetings were an ideal forum for her ideas, and resolutions in favour of women's suffrage were regularly passed. As the suffrage struggle reached a climax in Britain, Carlisle repeatedly refused to have any contact with the militant wing of the women's suffrage movement and extended this stance across the organizations of which she was president. She believed that militant tactics alienated many potential supporters, particularly MPs. The resolution passed at the BWTA 1909 council stated her position directly. She highlighted the long-standing commitment of the membership of the BWTA to suffrage and noted, in what was a distinct exaggeration, that the Association had 'for many years striven to win the franchise for women', but left no doubt as to her opinions of the militants:

> The British women plead with those who have hitherto been supporters of justice to the disenfranchised, not to swerve from their course because of the lawless misconduct of a section of 'militant' women suffragists, whose unconstitutional, violent and dangerous methods are repudiated with indignation and grief by the vast majority of the women and men who are

strenuously working for women's suffrage, and for the truest and highest emancipation of the womanhood of their country.[79]

Carlisle was not to waver either in her stance on women's suffrage or in her refusal to have any contact with the Women's Social and Political Union (WSPU) or other militants. This stance was in tune with the views of the majority of the BWTA membership, although some did take up militancy. Where others might be pragmatists she remained firm in her convictions. To Carlisle the vote should be gained by legal political means, specifically by the lobbying of MPs. Despite this, there is little doubt that she felt betrayed by the Liberal Party over the lack of achievement for both temperance and women's suffrage legislation.

Carlisle established herself as part of the suffragist movement and considered herself to be at the heart of the constitutional struggle. She managed a rota of lecturers, numbering about twenty, whom she could call upon when required. It included Florence Balgarnie, Laura Ormiston Chant, Agnes Slack and her daughter Lady Cecilia. Carlisle's stance was not without its contradictions, for in spite of her reluctance to be associated with the militants from the earliest days of the WSPU, Sylvia Pankhurst recalled that 'Lady Carlisle made a pet of this mill girl [Annie Kenney]'.[80] Carlisle rejected the call to enfranchise women on the same terms as men believing that equal suffrage would enfranchise only women with property. This, she felt, would provide the Conservative Party with more support, to the disadvantage of the Liberals. And yet in spite of her loyalty to the Liberal Party she believed that Liberal women were better off working together in the WLF than with men.[81]

Carlisle was certainly an extraordinary woman. Millicent Garrett Fawcett considered that she was 'worth at least 20 votes in the division', adding that she had been 'nobbling these men ... romping around Harcourt, Asquith and Bryce, cajoling and threatening by turn' for the Faithful Begg bill back in 1897.[82] Despite the onset of ill health at the turn of the twentieth century, Carlisle remained as president of the BWTA – lobbying, organizing and campaigning for temperance legislation and women's suffrage – up to the First World War. She was a charismatic leader but as her views became increasingly fixed she became alienated from other suffrage leaders and her constitutional work was overshadowed by militant tactics. Nevertheless, Carlisle was an exceptional leader of the British women's temperance movement and a dedicated supporter of the suffrage campaign; never as well known as the Pankhursts or Millicent Garrett Fawcett, she was a strong and determined advocate of women's rights.

The differing personalities of the three BWTA presidents and their styles of management provide an alternative account of changing attitudes towards women's suffrage in the period 1876–1914. Although suffrage was not the primary concern of the rank and file of the BWTA, the entire membership could not avoid being influenced and affected by the ideas of and developments in the women's suffrage campaign and the women's movements of Britain and the United States. The temperance-suffrage link was clearly a powerful one; it had a rationale, which many women could accept, of claiming the vote so that women could vote for prohibition. Women's involvement in the temperance movement has similarities to other, more clearly political campaigns adopted by women in this period. It enabled them to acquire political skills and for some members it served as a route on to school boards and to service as Poor Law Guardians. Relative to the suffrage, temperance was a 'safe' cause to espouse, but, through its national network of branches, it provided women with a route into the network of women's organizations which was to become the twentieth-century women's movement.

Notes

1. Temperance, total abstinence and teetotalism are for the purpose of this chapter gathered together under the general shorthand term of temperance except where a distinction between the various aspects of the movement is essential.

2. The yearly meeting of 1857 expressed its concern in the following words: 'This meeting had been brought under deep concern in view of the fearful amount of sin and misery existing in our land through the prevailing use of intoxicating liquors. Whilst we would carefully avoid interfering with the Christian liberty of our dear Friends we would encourage them seriously to consider what may be their individual duty in relation to this important subject.' The Religious Society of Friends, *Christian Faith and Practice in the Experience of the Society of Friends*, London, Society of Friends, 1972, p. 560.

3. B. Harrison, *Dictionary of British Temperance Biography*, Coventry, Society for the Study of Labour History, 1973, p. 37.

4. New Zealand, the first country to achieve the enfranchisement of women, is an interesting case; see R. Dalziel, 'Representing the enfranchisement of New Zealand women abroad', in C. Daley and M. Nolan (eds), *Suffrage and Beyond: International Feminist Perspectives*, Auckland, Auckland University Press, 1994, and A. R. Gregg, 'Prohibition and women: the preservation of an ideal and a myth', *New Zealand Journal of History*, Vol. 17, 1983, pp. 144-65.

5. B. Harrison, *Drink and the Victorians*, 2nd edition, Keele, Keele University Press, 1996. L. L. Shiman, *Crusade against Drink in Victorian England*, London, Macmillan, 1988.

6. M. G. Fawcett and E. M. Turner, *Josephine Butler: Her Work and Principles and Their Meaning for the Twentieth Century*, London, Association for Moral and Social Hygiene, 1927; G. W. Johnson and

L. A. Johnson, *Josephine Butler: An Autobiographical Memoir*, Bristol, J. W. Arrowsmith, 1913.

7. Finance, salaries statistics and staff 1904-1919, Castle Howard Archives (CHA), J23/150; Membership statistics, CHA, J23/151.

8. J. Blocker, *'Give to the Winds Thy Fears': The Women's Temperance Crusade, 1873-74*, Westpoint, CT, Greenwood Press, 1985, provides the fullest account of the Women's Crusade, but see also R. Bordin, *Women and Temperance: The Quest for Power and Liberty, 1873-1900*, New Brunswick, NJ, Rutgers University Press, 1990, pp. 15-33.

9. *Englishwomen's Review of Social and Industrial Questions*, October 1873, p. 286. E. King, *Scotland Sober and Free: The Temperance Movement 1829-1979*, Glasgow, Glasgow Museums and Art Galleries, 1979, p. 17.

10. *The Good Templar's Watchword*, Vol. 3, No. 104, p. 33. The IOGT was a fraternal organization established in the United States in 1851-2. It became one of the world's largest temperance organizations. It organized its members into communities by the use of rituals and regalia. From its earliest days women had equal rights to vote and to stand for office, even though they were charged lower dues. The equality granted women was unique in temperance societies and a third of the membership was female. Despite the ritual and regalia, many Quaker women became members. Women were encouraged to write in the journal *The Watchword* and as a result were able to campaign for, and to publicize, the women's temperance movement and its activities.

11. In common with many women temperance advocates, Clara Lucas Balfour has been largely ignored and there is no biography. The main sources of information about her life and work are *Dictionary of National Biography*, London, Smith Elder, 1885, Vol. 3, pp. 49-50; *Temperance Record*, 11 July 1878, pp. 439-40; D. Burns, *The Late Mrs C. L. Balfour: The Memorial Discourse*, London, S.W. Partridge, 1878.

12. Information on Margaret Bright Lucas is sparse; the memorial published by the BWTA focuses on her temperance work but refers to her links with the Anti-Corn Law movement. L. Stewart and J. A. Fowler, *Memoirs of Margaret Bright Lucas, President of the British Women's Temperance Association*, London, BWTA, 1890. For her work on the Contagious Diseases Acts see Fawcett and Turner, *Josephine Butler*, p. 52; Johnson and Johnson, *Josephine Butler*, pp. 96, 161.

13. *Women's Penny Paper*, 8 February 1890, p. 175.

14. S. S. Holton, 'From anti-slavery to suffrage militancy: the Bright circle, Elizabeth Cady Stanton and the British women's movement', in Daley and Nolan (eds), *Suffrage and Beyond*, p. 221.

15. *Women's Signal*, 2 January 1896, pp. 1, 221-5. Issues of the *Englishwoman's Review* in the 1880s contain information on the suffrage activities of the Edinburgh branch of the National Women's Suffrage Society.

16. See also S. S. Holton, *Suffrage Days: Stories from the Women's Suffrage Movement*, London, Routledge, 1996.
17. *The Good Templar's Watchword*, Vol. 2, No. 89, 6 October 1875.
18. *Englishwoman's Review*, 15 January 1878, p. 30.
19. *The Good Templar's Watchword*, Vol. 2, No. 89, 6 October 1875.
20. British Women's Temperance Association, Annual Report 1883-4, BWTA, 1884.
21. *Englishwoman's Review*, 16 June 1884, p. 259.
22. Johnson and Johnson, *Josephine Butler*, p. 161.
23. *The National British Women's Temperance Association: Its Origin and Progress. A Jubilee Sketch*, London, NWBTA, 1926, pp. 12-14.
24. This was brought to my attention by Dr David Fahey of Miami University, Oxford, Ohio. For more information on Somerset's views on alcohol consumption, see her evidence to the Royal Commission on Liquor Licensing Laws, 1897-9, 34-8, Cmnd 8355-6, 8963, 8821-2, 9075-6, 9379-81, minutes of Vol. 3, pp. 164-84 (hereafter Royal Commission, Vol. 3) and I. Tyrrell, *Woman's World, Woman's Empire: The Women's Christian Temperance Union in International Perspective, 1880-1930*, Chapel Hill, University of North Carolina Press, 1986, pp. 264-6.
25. The World WCTU began sending its missionaries abroad in 1884. The first missionary was Mary Clement Leavitt, who set out on a reconnaissance tour. It was this first mission that established branches of the WCTU in Australia and New Zealand. Often the evangelical temperance missionaries revitalized existing branches rather than establishing new societies.
26. R. Bordin, *Frances Willard: A Biography*, Chapel Hill, University of North Carolina Press, 1986, pp. 197-200. A fuller account of the visit exists in the WCTU Archives, WCTU National Headquarters Historical Files (Joint Ohio Historical Society/WCTU), microfilm edition (hereafter WCTU Historical Files), scrapbook 56 Lady Henry Somerset, personal scrapbook, United States, 1891-2.
27. F. E. Willard, *Home Protection Manual, Containing an Argument for the Temperance Ballot for Women and How to Obtain It as a Means of Home Protection, also Constitution and Plan of Work for State and Local WCTUs*, New York, 1879, p. 9.
28. *Ibid.*, p. 4.
29. S. M. Marilley, *Woman Suffrage and the Origins of Liberal Feminism in the United States*, Cambridge, MA, Harvard University Press, 1996.
30. L. Bland, *Banishing the Beast: English Feminism and Sexual Morality, 1885-1914*, London, Penguin, 1995, pp. 95-123, 311.
31. Royal Commission, Vol. 3, in particular questions 31,296-31,304 and 31,509.
32. *Wings*, Vol. 11, No. 4, 1893, p. 188. This was despite the fact that many of the committee were also members of suffrage societies.

33. *Ibid.*
34. *British Women's Temperance Journal*, Vol. 10, No. 6, June 1892, pp. 61-2.
35. Bordin, *Frances Willard*, p. 225.
36. The phrase 'social purity' encompassed a wide range of moral feminist issues including prostitution, and the reintroduction of the Contagious Diseases Act in India. The BWTA did not, in the majority of branches, address these major issues but frequently addressed more local issues. These included lectures on purity to young women, on the temptations caused by drink and, for barmaids, on the need for chastity.
37. Bordin, *Frances Willard*, pp. 202-3. WCTU files on Willard's stay indicate the travel undertaken by Somerset and Willard and are in sharp contrast to the BWTA organ, *Wings*, which generally ignored them. See WCTU Historical Files, scrapbooks 60-65; Frances Willard in England, 1892-4.
38. *Manchester Courier*, 24 January 1893; *Manchester Guardian*, 25 January 1893.
39. WCTU Historical Files, scrapbook 57.
40. *Ibid.*
41. *Wings*, 1 June 1893, pp. 211-13.
42. *British Women's Temperance Journal*, Vol. 10, No. 7, July 1892, p. 76.
43. *Ibid.*
44. Presidential Address of Lady Henry Somerset delivered before the Council of the British Women's Temperance Association, May 1892 [1893].
45. *Wings*, February 1893, p. 161.
46. *Ibid.*
47. *Wings*, March 1893, pp. 176-7.
48. *Ibid.*
49. Charges of Americanization appeared in a number of temperance newspapers and were reprinted in the *Temperance Record*, 9 February 1893, pp. 86-7. See also K. Fitzpatrick, *Lady Henry Somerset*, London, Jonathan Cape, 1923, pp. 171-6.
50. *Wings*, March 1893, p. 176.
51. L. L. Shiman, *Women and Leadership in Nineteenth Century England*, London, Macmillan, 1992, p. 165.
52. Mrs Charlotte Wilson, Mrs Louisa Stewart, Mrs Blakely and Mrs Massingham were suffrage supporters but joined the WTAU.
53. For clarity this chapter uses the abbreviation 'BWTA' throughout, even though the BWTA changed its name to the National British Women's Temperance Association following the split in 1893.
54. Somerset wrote a letter to *The Times*, 21 April 1897. The outcry following this letter can be seen in issues of *The Shield* throughout 1897. See Fitzpatrick, *Lady Henry Somerset*, pp. 181-5.

55. Royal Commission, Vol. 3, p. 177.

56. Local veto was originally introduced in the Local Veto Bills of 1893 and 1895. The fundamental provision was that if a tenth of the municipal electors requested it, a poll could be taken on the prohibition and the issuing and renewing of licences. A two-thirds majority was needed for a 'no licence' policy.

57. *Woman's Herald*, 1893.

58. Florence Fenwick Miller was the editor of the *Woman's Signal* from 1894 to 1899. She had trained at the Female Medical Society and became a midwife at Endell Street Hospital. She had many connections with the women's movement and lectured on both temperance and suffrage. She became a founder member of the London School Board, campaigned against the Contagious Diseases Acts and was a founder member of the Women's Franchise League in 1889.

59. Letters from Bertha Mason, CHA J23/445.

60. J. Lewis, *Before the Vote Was Won: Arguments for and against Women's Suffrage 1864–1896*, London, Routledge and Kegan Paul, 1987.

61. See D. Henley, *Rosalind Carlisle*, London, Hogarth Press, 1958, pp. 80–94.

62. R. Strachey, *Millicent Garrett Fawcett*, London, John Murray, 1931, pp. 128–9.

63. C. Roberts, *The Radical Countess: The History of the Life of Rosalind, Countess of Carlisle*, Carlisle, Steele Bros, 1962, p. 160; Henley, *Rosalind Carlisle*, p. 25.

64. Roberts, *The Radical Countess*, pp. 182–95.

65. *Ibid.*, pp. 166–81.

66. O. Banks, *The Biographical Dictionary of British Feminists*. Vol. 2, *A Supplement, 1900–1945*, New York, New York University Press, 1990, pp. 102–5.

67. *Ibid.*

68. Henley, *Rosalind Howard*; Castle Howard Archives, J23/445: letters from Bertha Mason, J23/443: letters from Walter and Ena McLaren, J23/361: the struggle between the progressives and anti-suffragists in the WLF, 1891–3.

69. D. Fahey, 'Rosalind Howard, Countess of Carlisle', in J. O. Baylen and N. J. Gossman (eds), *Dictionary of British Radicals*, Vol. 3 (1870–1914), pp. 458–63.

70. Henley, *Rosalind Howard*, p. 109.

71. Bertha Mason was Lancashire County president and superintendent of the Department for Women Voters of the BWTA. She was also treasurer of a branch of the National Union of Women's Suffrage Societies (NUWSS), a member of the executive committee of the Women's Liberal Federation and author of a history of the women's suffrage campaign. She was the daughter of Hugh Mason, who took up the leadership of the 1881 suffrage bill.

72. B. Mason, *The Story of the Women's Suffrage Movement*, London, Sherritt and Hughes, 1912; letters from Bertha Mason, CHA J23/445.
73. Letters from Bertha Mason, CHA J23/445.
74. *Ibid.*
75. NBWTA, minutes of the subcommittee 1903-4, NBWTA, 1904.
76. NBWTA, annual report 1904-5, NBWTA, 1905.
77. Letters relating to the struggle by the progressives, CHA J23/361.
78. Membership statistics, CHA J23/1904-1919.
79. BWTA, Annual Report 1909-10, p. 36.
80. S. Pankhurst, *The Suffragette Movement*, London, Longmans, Green, 1931, p. 200.
81. Speech by Lady Carlisle in support of a Women's Liberal Association in Longtown, in Roberts, *The Radical Countess*, pp. 166-81.
82. Strachey, *Millicent Garrett Fawcett*, p. 174.

5 'Doing Justice to the Real Girl': The Women Writers' Suffrage League

Sowon S. Park

I

In 1908 Britain saw the formation of the first professional organization of women writers: the Women Writers' Suffrage League (WWSL). The league attracted some of the most distinguished writers of the day, but its membership was not restricted to them. That it was a *writers'* group and not a *literary* society may indicate how it differed in nature and scope from other contemporary groups such as the Imagists (1910–18) and the Vorticists (1912–15). Whereas *literary* societies were founded upon the idea of a text as the expression of a highly gifted individual and conceived of themselves as an exclusive collective of authors, or poets in the high Romantic sense, the WWSL welcomed writers of every ideal and level; it defined a writer simply as one who had sold a text.[1] That women writers formed a group is perhaps not so remarkable, for the idea of a women writer was nothing new. But a writers' group comprising women of all classes, against the background of the class-riven Edwardian society and, more pertinently, an increasingly 'high' literary culture, offers a fresh perspective on the early twentieth-century literary landscape, which is too often dominated by Modernism.[2]

The formation of the WWSL marks a significant point in the process of the professionalization of British women writers, but it was by no means through sheer chance that the suffrage movement led to the league's organization.[3] The suffrage movement had politicized thousands of women of all classes and women's organizations proliferated nation-wide in many professions and along regional and political lines. Goaded by anti-suffragism as well as carried forth by the spirit of activism, women artists developed a new degree of professionalism through organizations

---

* This chapter was previously published under the title 'The first professionals: the Women Writers' Suffrage League', in *Modern Language Quarterly*, Vol. 57, no. 2, June 1997, pp. 1–16. Copyright 1997 University of Washington. Reprinted by permission of Duke University Press.

such as the Artists' Suffrage League (1907) and the Suffrage Atelier (1909). The thousand-member Actresses' Franchise League, a 'happy marriage' of the theatre and the suffrage movement, effected a dramatic improvement in actresses' working conditions.[4] Just as it spurred women in the theatre to action, the suffrage movement prompted women to write, publish and read. The Women Writers' Suffrage League provided a base within which women writers could raise issues, bring isolated problems to collective awareness, and construct a sense of female agency by giving public voice to communal problems.

Amid widespread suffrage agitation, Cicely Hamilton, already a well-established author and playwright, with *How the Vote Was Won* and *Marriage as a Trade* behind her, formed the league.[5] Hamilton, who felt that transforming the public interest aroused by the spectacular suffragette campaigns into feminist commitment needed more effective media than ephemeral speeches, now sought strategic ways to raise the public's consciousness of political gender inequality. Encouraged by the journalist and playwright Bessie Hatton, Hamilton announced that the WWSL's aim was an equal franchise and its method would be the one 'proper to writers – the use of the pen'. Its members would produce suffrage literature to 'ensure ventilation of the subject in such ways as are open to them – by writing articles, taking part in newspaper correspondence'.[6] They would focus on journalistic work to steer quickly changing public opinion: the emerging popular newspapers had already shown the potential of mass communication, and an article on a force-fed suffragette could be front-page national news. Elizabeth Robins, the league's first president, observed in 1911:

> The permeation of journalism, as well as of the less evanescent forms of literature, by Suffragist views has been an element in the propaganda so quiet as to find a way unchallenged into many Anti strongholds, yet so steady as to show its widespread result only in the retrospect.[7]

The repudiation of 'androcentrism' – repeated in similar fashion in the second-wave feminism of the 1960s and the 1970s – was a staple of suffrage writing. The bulk of it was revisions of well-known poems, sections from plays, novels and familiar narratives, such as fairy tales. Suffrage writers also parodied conventional myths and re-read famous anti-feminist works.

The political, class, gender and literary diversity of the league's members made their writing admissible to different circles. Along with contributing to the more obvious publications such as the *Vote*, *The Common Cause*, *The Suffragette*, *Votes for Women*, *Women's Suffrage News*, *Women's Suffrage Journal*, *Women's Suffrage*, *Women's Franchise*, *Women's Dreadnought* and *The Independent Suffragette*, they attempted to reach the unconverted by engaging in public debate in conservative newspapers which were unmistakably anti-suffrage in their editorial tone.

Robins became famous for her defence of the cause against the arch-antisuffragist Mrs Humphry Ward in *The Times*. Many WWSL publications were quick responses to widely read newspaper articles. For example, May Sinclair's *Feminism* appeared on 31 March 1912 as a refutation of a three-column letter published in *The Times* three days earlier by the influential Sir Almroth Wright, who claimed that the suffragettes suffered from the 'hysteria bacillus', a symptom of spinsters. Rudyard Kipling's poem 'The Female of the Species', which appeared in the *Morning Post* of 20 October 1911, elicited a succession of poems and essays in reply, including one by Christabel Pankhurst. One poem, 'A Species of the Female', which appeared in *The Standard* three days later, carried the satiric inscription 'suggested by Mr. Rudyard Kipling's delicate tribute to "The Female of the Species"'.[8]

The whetstone of anti-suffragism such as Kipling's sharpened the rhetoric of suffrage. But the WWSL did more than repudiate anti-feminist men writers. In conjunction with the Actresses' Franchise League, it gave innumerable matinées of plays and pageants, some to pay tribute to Shakespeare for portraying the varied qualities of women. In *Shakespeare's Dreams*, an arrangement by Beatrice Harraden and Bessie Hatton, Portia, Viola, Perdita, Lady Macbeth, Rosalind, Kate, Beatrice, Puck, Ariel and Cleopatra each appear before the sleeping poet, saluting him, offering flowers, and reciting their best-known lines.[9]

The WWSL's most outstanding feature was its inclusiveness: provided that they were pro-suffrage, writers not only of every class and literary ideal but of both genders and every political persuasion were welcome. Debates as to where to draw the line were frequent. For example, Marie Belloc Lowndes, a vice-president of the League, expressed strong doubts about the admission of the writer of *Letters from a Flapper at the Durber* and other 'pornographic' novels: 'Any woman who has disgraced herself professionally should not be asked by us.'[10] But the principle of exclusion, by which most societies worked, was usually defeated, inasmuch as the league sought to harness literary activity to political and social change and therefore to have as immediate and widespread an influence as possible. League membership ranged from the 'New Woman', such as Sarah Grand (1854-1943) and Olive Schreiner (1855-1920), to 'popular' writers such as the previously mentioned Marie Belloc Lowndes (1868-1947) and Margaret Woods (1856-1945), to 'experimental' writers such as May Sinclair (1863-1946). The mystical poet Alice Meynell (1847-1922); the novelist and 'society hostess' Violet Hunt (1866-1943); Evelyn Sharp (1868-1955), a writer for the *Yellow Book* and a hunger-striking militant; and Ivy Compton-Burnett (1884-1969), a Dame Commander of the British Empire now regarded more as a post-war novelist, were members also. The categories into which all these writers are placed today held little significance at the height of the suffrage campaign when they were united, albeit temporarily. Their camaraderie is difficult to conceive in the late twentieth century when feminism itself is variegated but their intense affinity for one another comes through strongly in most of their autobiographical writing.[11]

The active participation of men, as honorary associates of the league, also differentiates the WWSL from late twentieth-century feminist groups. H. N. Brailsford, Laurence Housman, John Masefield and Ramsay MacDonald, then household names, frequently gave speeches and produced suffrage literature as members. Other well-known men who spoke and appeared at the WWSL meetings and congresses and wrote for the cause included Joseph Clayton, the Reverend C. Hinscliffe, Frederick Pethick-Lawrence, Saleeby Read, Pett Ridge, Richard Whiteing and Israel Zangwill. More than half the contributions to the 'Woman's Platform' pages of *The Standard* were penned by men.[12]

As for the WWSL's tolerance of political difference, Robins recorded in 1911 that the members embraced

> Conservatives, Liberals, and Socialists, women of Leisure and women who toil for their daily bread, members who are militant and members who are non-militant. The League therefore did not and could not, as a body, take part in the more active political demonstrations. Its members expected to be left free, and were left free, to serve the Cause in whatever way individual opinion and opportunity made fitting and practicable.[13]

The diversity of membership and work contradicts frequent descriptions of the WWSL as 'an auxiliary of the National Union of Women's Suffrage Societies' (NUWSS), since many prominent members were affiliated with the militant WSPU and Women's Freedom League (WFL).[14] As stated in the launch pamphlet, the WWSL was 'entirely independent of any other suffrage society; at the same time it was formed with the intention of assisting every other suffrage society by the methods proper to writers'.[15] The WWSL's method may have been 'the use of the pen', but its strategies, like those of other suffrage organizations, included the full drama of marches and public protests. The 'Great Demonstration' organized by the WSPU on 21 June 1908 was watched by a quarter to half a million people.[16] *The Times* describes an exuberant contingent of more than a hundred WWSL members, all wearing scarlet and white badges transfixed with quills.[17] Marching behind a dramatically appliquéd black, cream and gold velvet WWSL banner designed by Mary Lowndes were the league's leading figures: Olive Schreiner, Sarah Grand, Gertrude Warden, Alice Meynell, May Sinclair, Flora Annie Steel, Edith Zangwill and Mrs Havelock Ellis. It is interesting to see the women the WWSL chose to celebrate as role models in the elaborately embroidered banners, for time has little changed the preferences: Maria Edgeworth, Jane Austen, Elizabeth Barrett Browning, Charlotte and Emily Brontë, Fanny Burney, George Eliot and Mary Wollstonecraft.[18] The WWSL also participated in the suffrage processions of June 1910 and June 1911, when the contingent walked under a new banner designed by a staunch male supporter, W. H. Margetson.[19]

The WWSL sent delegates to various conferences held jointly with other suffrage organizations and hosted separate drawing-room 'at homes', in hotels and offices as well as members' homes, at which the league's literary positions and aspirations were articulated and discussed. It provided speakers and sold suffrage literature at public meetings. There were also author's readings, exhibitions and book fairs, costume balls and sales of cakes and sweets. The WWSL's fund-raising, advertising and marketing were remarkably sophisticated and successful. One bookstall at the WSPU women's exhibition at the Prince's Skating Rink in Knightsbridge, where autographed books donated by such suffrage sympathizers as John Galsworthy were sold, made £70, the equivalent of over £3000 in 1999. The league also held literary contests for the best suffrage fiction and plays (mostly, though not exclusively, open to first-time writers), awarded prizes and recruited women to write, as well as providing the means for publishing.[20]

Suffrage literature – fiction, sketches, plays, poems – was intended mainly to entertain the common reader. But its writers also meant to exploit its potential to bring about social change. To many writers steeped in the language of popular culture, it was the most natural form of literary production. Therefore the documentary-like naturalism that the suffrage writers employed was at once a political choice, directed at their conative aim, and a market-dependent one.

With the advent of the First World War the focus of the WWSL changed. Like most other suffragist organizations it turned its attention to aiding the nation on the home front. An obvious form of service was to provide reading material for wounded soldiers, and Elizabeth Robins, Bessie Hatton and Beatrice Harraden set up a library in a military hospital in Endell Street, London. Reflecting the inclusiveness of its membership, the league circulated all types of fiction, the popular and the sensational. Harraden, after surveying the wounded soldiers in 1917, wrote of her thoughts on their 'popular' tastes:

> Our wounded warriors have surely earned the right to amuse themselves with the books that please them most, and to be free from the kind of officious pedantry that would seek to thrust upon them literature of a class and type for which they have, as they themselves would say, 'no use'.[21]

Popular literature spoke a language meaningful to a far wider cultural stratum than literature 'of a class and type'. League members who had been writing plays for the Actresses' Franchise League (AFL) continued to produce them for the Pioneer Players.[22]

The WWSL was formally dissolved on 24 January 1919, within a year of the passing of the 1918 Representation of the People Act, which enfranchised around $8\frac{1}{2}$ million women. Although the league had not realized an equal franchise, its work was substantially done, and its members moved on to make feminist contributions to other organizations.

II

Although the WWSL is here distinguished as a writers' group, as opposed to a literary society, it did not disavow the principle of talented individuals producing exceptional literary texts. On the contrary, it made good use of celebrated names to promote itself; moreover, many of its members had their own aspirations and achieved admirable standards. But as a writers' group the WWSL had a far wider scope than any society centred on particular literary values. A writer's prestige or distinction had to have a use for gender politics if she or he were to contribute to the league. In this sense suffrage literature, if it can be said to constitute a discourse, was unlike the literature of other early twentieth-century movements, whose members, according to Dennis Brown, 'virtually "canonised" each other, as prophets of the New'.[23] Elitist notions of cultural aristocracy were burgeoning among the Modernists and the idea of the supremely achieved individual was reaching new heights. The uniquely particular was the aim of many a Modernist – T. S. Eliot, D. H. Lawrence and W. B. Yeats, to name but a few. Paradoxically, the same authors sought cosmic forces beyond the individual and tended towards the 'impersonal' in their literary ideals. In contrast, the WWSL writers had little interest in individual prestige and distinction through their suffrage literature.[24] Yet despite their belief in collective expression and their practice of collaboration and anonymous publication, many suffrage writers, conversely, placed great importance on achieving authentic individuality, as the vast amount of suffrage autobiographies attest. Just when the 'cultural aristocrats' eschewed the personal, the suffragists seemed to embrace it. But the 'social' has no place in the Modernist desire for the impersonal, which for them did not imply a *collective* – especially not a *specific* collective as mundane as disfranchised women. The individuals celebrated by suffragists, on the other hand, formed a very specific group, held up as role models for all women.

Nor did the WWSL writers take the 'literariness' of a suffrage text as its aim, unlike the modernists, who elevated ideas of authorship and to whom creative processes were normative ideals.[25] To use Roman Jakobson's paradigm of six elements in communication, suffrage writing, for the WWSL members, was less of an 'emotive' act, i.e. an expression of a selected author, or a 'poetic' act, i.e. focusing on the language rather than what is said, than a 'conative' one, i.e. concentrating on effect.[26] Thus it was interventionist and pragmatic in using whatever tools were at hand.

The WWSL's concern that society should appropriate its texts helps explain the suffrage writers' relative indifference about individual ownership of them. Rhetoric mattered more than authorship and style. As Robins observed in 1911, 'a vast amount of the most effective work done by the Writers has been anonymous'.[27] Some of the suffrage articles and sketches produced by the WWSL were even marked 'specially not copyrighted'. The writers' detachment is rooted also in the history of bourgeois individualism. In a market economy, where married women could not own property until 1882, and indeed functioned *as* property, the social persona of an author, a proprietor, and its psychological underpinnings, may have involved special difficulties for first-time women writers from non-literary backgrounds.

In addition, anonymity, though not so frequently resorted to as in the nineteenth century, provided cover from the still unfavourable social implications of authorship. Many women writers, most notably Cicely Hamilton, had written anonymously for the same reasons that the Brontës had written under pseudonyms in the previous century. As she stated in her autobiography, stage managers warned her that it was advisable for a woman playwright to conceal her sex 'until after the notices were out, as plays which were known to be written by women were apt to get bad reviews'.[28] Elizabeth Robins is seen by Jane Marcus as having faced similar problems:

> [She] did not kill the angel but directed the angel's energies into a service of a cause. It was easier to see oneself as a vessel of historical consciousness than to deal with the guilt aroused by declaring oneself as an artist. Self expression was social sin.[29]

Suffrage writing did not force one to assume the persona of an artist; thus it presented fewer psychological barriers to the women who were beginning as writers. Margaret Homans speculates that the strong Romantic tradition of the Poet, which is clearly male, made it difficult for the aspiring woman poet or author to ignore her sexual identity in the process of writing.[30] The WWSL, being unrestrained by such notions, provided a different site for women to consolidate and to affirm in writing their otherwise isolated and haphazard sense of reality.

The work of the WWSL might be defined, in Antonio Gramsci's words, as 'functional literature': literature based on a plan or on a pre-established social course.[31] Robins characterized the function as 'educational'.[32] The WWSL's aims, like those of the suffrage movement, went beyond equal franchise. While the movement contested the ideology of femininity, the league sought to demystify the production of literature, opposed its 'androcentricity', and tried to use it to raise the public's consciousness of gender inequality. By holding up role models like Jane Austen and George Eliot the WWSL hoped to open up writing for all women.

With the thrill of discovery, Robins told the WWSL membership in 1911, 'there she stands – the Real Girl! – waiting for you to do her justice'.[33] This idea of the 'Real Girl' as an objective reality, 'waiting' to be truly depicted, expresses the central tenet of the league's approach to literature.[34] Although its members held diverse views about how to depict the 'Real Girl', they were united in their belief that the medium of language, as a separate and instrumental entity of the existing world, could reflect, and ultimately change, reality. One of the WWSL's most prolific exponents, Robins conveyed the tremendous excitement of standing at the portals of an untouched field of 'true femininity'. 'Fellow-members of the League,' she began,

> you have such a field as never writers had before. An almost virgin field. You are, in respect of life described fearlessly from the woman's standpoint – you are in that position for which Chaucer has been envied by his brother-poets, when they say he found the English language with the dew upon it. You find woman at the dawn.[35]

Robins's note of exhilaration indicates not so much women's actual silence in literary history as a perceived silence, as various studies in women's writing have shown.[36] It is ironic that literature by women who urged the importance and necessity of the visibility and accessibility of women's writing became subject to the process of silencing and has itself been forgotten.[37] Robins, like many of her contemporaries, bemoaned the scarceness of literature on women's experience, personal or professional. By the same token, Robins said of suffrage fictions that 'these [books], and books like them, are a foretaste of that library that waits to be written'. May Sinclair, a vice-president of the WWSL, expressed similar convictions. In an article entitled 'How it strikes a mere novelist' that appeared in *Votes for Women* on Christmas Eve 1908, she wrote, 'the coming generation will, I believe, witness a finer art, a more splendid literature than has been seen since the Elizabethan Age'.[38] Sinclair gives as the reason for her conviction the 'spiritual certainty of women' which will 'come through the coming revolution, by the release of long captive forces, by the breathing in among us of the Spirit of Life, the genius of enfranchised womanhood'. Cicely Hamilton, the founder of the WWSL, agreed:

> It sometimes seems to me ... the women who write or paint will have an enormous pull for a generation or two over the men who write or paint, for the men will have only the old ideas to work on but they will be every one of them new to us.[39]

Similar ideas were later discussed by Woolf in what is now considered to be the founding text of feminist criticism, *A Room of One's Own*: 'For if Chloe likes Olivia and Mary Carmichael knows how to express it she will light a torch in that vast chamber where nobody has yet been.'[40] Indeed, all the strands of feminist literary theory found in *A Room of One's Own* (1929) or in the more radical *Three Guineas* (1938) are readily found in the suffrage writings of the decade(s) before. Hamilton's materialist theory of literary production in her best-selling *Marriage as a Trade* (1909) corresponds to Woolf's more famous question as to why there has been no woman Shakespeare. The patriarchal origins of militarism revealed in *Three Guineas* were explicated by suffragists Mary Sargent Florence and G. K. Ogden in *Militarism and Feminism* in 1915.[41] Articles published in *Jus Suffragii*, edited by Mary Sheepshanks, put forward the thesis that militarism implied the subservience of women.[42] The point is not whether Woolf was directly influenced by her predecessors' preoccupations in her polemical texts, but rather that the socio-cultural conditions of the early twentieth century were conducive to such questioning and that these feminist ideas were very much in the air owing to the wide suffrage debate.

The suffrage activists shared the Edwardian fascination for selfhood and believed in a 'true' self that could be found if the false 'role' of femininity could be discarded.[43] Concomitant to the belief in the true depiction of women was the conviction that textual practice had, and should have, immediate and significant influence on society. In the 1909 prospectus Hamilton had stated, 'a body of writers working for a common object cannot fail to influence public opinion'. Similarly, Robins recalled, 'we must have known that one of the most important, most indispensable services to Social Reform would have to be undertaken by the Writers'.[44]

The firm belief of these women in the power of the written word could be seen as a reflection of the fact that they had themselves been strongly affected by texts. That 20 per cent of suffrage activists listed in the 1913 *Suffrage Annual and Women's Who's Who* were university educated is a disproportionate percentage considering that only 0.2 per cent of the female population in the age group 20 to 24 would have had university education at that time.[45] Olive Banks, in *The Making of a Feminist*, claims that 62 per cent of active 'feminists' born between 1872 and 1892 had higher education.[46] Even taking into account the fact that the education available to middle-class girls in the last decade of the nineteenth century had greatly improved, and suffrage activists were predominantly of middle-class origins, suffrage activists were unusually well educated for their time and class. Thus it is perhaps natural that suffrage writing would be imbued with this educative, conative aim.

However, since suffrage activists of all classes professed themselves particularly subject to literary influences, the importance that they attributed to textual influence need not solely be based on their background. In many suffragette autobiographies and memoirs, women testify to the part that texts played in their conversion to the cause.[47] The case of Emmeline Pethick-Lawrence, treasurer of the WSPU and co-editor of *Votes for Women*, is a good example. In her autobiographical writing she emphasizes the process of reading, and subsequent identification with literary models, that led her to political activism. In a WSPU pamphlet titled 'Why I went to prison' she credits the novels of George Eliot, Irving's *Faust* and Sir Walter Besant's *Children of Gideon* with having formed and confirmed her vocation, and concludes by stating that she went to prison for the suffrage cause as she had 'made a passionate resolve that when I grew up I would put myself between the helpless and the wronged and the wicked and cruel world'.[48] Cicely Hamilton provides another example: she wrote in her autobiography, *Life Errant*, that from 'very early in life my real interest was the written word'.[49] The belief in realism and the anticipation of a new women's literature which would have a direct social effect might also, in part, reflect the experience of the core members of the WWSL; they were in their forties and fifties, and had lived through and indeed had written the 'woman question' novels in the 1890s, which had had considerable and immediate impact.[50] The emphasis on 'truth to life' and 'realistic' portrayals of women was linked to the questioning of the social conditioning of women, the problematization of women's textual representation, and attempts to redefine patriarchal language. Elizabeth Robins explicitly argued that gender bias is instituted by and in language; she redefined history as the 'record of the deeds of heroes – of men who fought against the great obstacles and overcame them' and society as 'a place not only where all the great deeds are done by men – but a place where all the great qualities are said to be masculine'.[51] With regard to such mis(re)presentation, and the ideology that arises from it, she declared that 'it is the business (the business as well as the high privilege) of men and women writers to correct the false ideas about women which many writers of the past have fostered'.[52] The solution she offered was the 'practically limitless power of suggestion', which

> has been pressed into the service of the education of men. From the time a boy is old enough to follow a fairy-tale, he is told how Jack killed the Giant. ... When the boy is older he begins to take from history, from the classics, and from literature in general, the incentives and the cue for action. ... The world will never know how much power to serve it has been killed in women's hearts by that old phrase, 'only a girl'. ... Which, of all these books, tells about a girl's courage, good temper, wit, resourcefulness, endurance? Not one. ... they had to wait for women to celebrate them.[53]

III

The WWSL recognized writing as a profession and attempted to organize women writers to form a collective voice. Though it is indisputable that the core of the league was made up of established authors, women without links to a literary coterie and educational benefits were actively encouraged to participate in the WWSL's literary workshops, 'at home' discussions, literature contests and public meetings. Writing became a more accessible profession for many women, prompted by the fervour of suffrage, for whom the WWSL provided a cohesive and potent base for collective identification and mobilization.

Nonetheless, it is a lamentable fact, not unrepresentative of feminism in general, that many suffragists expressed identical ideas in isolation and remained unaware of having a strong *tradition* of rebellion. Though they revered previous women authors, the celebration often stopped short at honouring their successes. The literary theory laboured by the suffrage novelists would have benefited greatly from the opportunity, largely missed, of studying and observing the feminist feats the eighteenth-century women accomplished in writing.[54] Nor did the second-wave feminists of this century express an awareness of, or make use of, the tradition of feminist struggle. Their belief in the newness of their protest at every point in feminist history assures us that they must have also believed themselves isolated from the mainstream of history. Combating this unjustified feeling of isolation is one of feminism's fundamental challenges. Despite immense changes, the first- and second-wave feminisms, and yet still, present-day feminism, have many points of common struggle, and only through a sense of feminist tradition can there be any appreciation of progress.

Notes

1. The WWSL prospectus (1909) stated the criteria of membership as 'the publication or production of a book, article, story, poem, or play for which the author has received payment'. Subscription to the League cost 2s 6d, which in 1908 had the purchasing power of a popular novel, or two suffrage booklets; in 1992, it would have been equivalent to around £4.10. See A. J. R., *The Suffrage Annual and Women's Who's Who*, London, Stanley Paul, 1913, pp. 34–7.

2. Many women from the aristocracy wrote before the seventeenth century, like the Duchess of Newcastle and Lady Winchilsea; and many middle-class women were earning their living through writing in the nineteenth century. However, writing was a profession little practised by working-class women before the twentieth century.

3. The Society of Authors, founded in 1884 by Walter Besant, with Lord Tennyson as the first president, to promote the interests of authors and to defend their rights, was another *writers'* society. Members have included Shaw, Galsworthy, Hardy, Wells, Masefield, Forster, T. S. Eliot and A. P. Herbert. The establishment of the Society of Authors and that of the Publishers' Association and the Booksellers' Association in the 1880s and the 1890s mark the key moments in the professionalization and specialization of the overall writing industry in Britain.

4. S. Stowell, *A Stage of Their Own: Feminist Playwrights of the Suffrage Era*, Manchester, Manchester University Press, 1992, p. 42.

5. The constitution of the WWSL was drawn up by Hamilton early in 1909: the first presidency was taken by Elizabeth Robins, and the chair of the committee was Cicely Hamilton. Robins was re-elected president on 15 October 1917 and held office until 24 January 1919 when, having realized the aims for which it had been founded, the WWSL was formally dissolved.

6. E. Robins, *Way Stations*, London, Hodder and Stoughton, 1913, pp. 106-7.

7. Robins, 'Time table', in *Way Stations*, p. 225.

8. *The Standard*, 23 October 1911.

9. *Shakespeare's Dreams* was performed on 9 February 1912 at the New Prince's Theatre in Oxford Street, London.

10. S. Lowndes, *Diaries and Letters of Marie Belloc Lowndes 1911-1947*, London, Chatto and Windus, 1971, p. 35.

11. Other committee members included Alice Abadam, Lena Ashwell, Elizabeth Banks, Nina Boyle, Mrs Havelock Ellis, Mrs E. Rentoul Esler, Elizabeth Gibson, Bessie Hatton, Margaret Hope, Mrs Darent Little, Annesley Kenealy, Dr Arabella Kenealy, Mrs Waldemar Leverton, Mrs Eileen Mitchell, Mrs H. W. Nevinson, Alice Perrin, Mrs C. Romanne-James, Mrs Archibald Little, Madeline Lucette Ryley, Mrs Baillie Reynolds, Lilian Sauter, George Paston Symonds, E. M. Tait, Dr Margaret Todd, Sarah Tooley, Edith Waldermar Leverton, Gertrude Warden, Peggy Webling and Edith Zangwill. Over 400 other members were actively writing for the league.

12. The 'Woman's Platform' began as a daily two-page section dedicated solely to suffrage news, but was increased to three and at times four pages by popular demand. It provided detailed reports of meetings and deputations, as well as debates, articles and letters on the suffrage question. The advertisement launching the 'Woman's Platform' stated that it was 'for a ventilation of all women's interests. It is open to all men and all women in the land, of every class and party, and all shades of opinion, who desire to help the interests of women.' Advertisements had been running daily for a week preceding the launch of the 'Woman's Platform' section. *The Standard*, 2 October 1911.

13. Robins, *Way Stations*, p. 225.

14. For example, E. Showalter, *A Literature of Their Own: British Women Novelists from Brontë to Lessing*, Princeton, NJ, Princeton University Press, 1977, p. 218; C. M. Tylee, *The Great War and Women's Consciousness: Images of Militarism and Womanhood in Women's Writings, 1914-64*, Iowa City, University of Iowa Press, 1990, p. 135.

15. Robins, 'Time table', in *Way Stations*, p. 106.

16. Estimated by *The Times*, 23 June 1910. The beauty of the banners and the impact of the march were reported in the *Standard*, the *Daily News*, the *Daily Express* and the *Daily Chronicle*, 23 June 1910.

17. *The Times*, 22 June 1910. The colour schemes of the suffrage movement, in which individual organizations had their own colours,

were very successful. The various combinations were as follows: the NUWSS – red, white and green; the WFL – green, gold and white; the Artists League – blue and silver; the Suffrage Atelier – blue and orange; the WSPU – purple, green and white. That only purple, green and white caught on nationally, appearing in advertisements for merchandise as diverse as bicycles and soap, and that it appeared as the colour scheme of the whole suffrage movement, illustrates the powerful impact that the WSPU had on the movement.

18. Other distinguished figures in the arts and society were commemorated: Vashti, Boadicea, Black Agnes of Dunbar, Queen Elizabeth I and Queen Victoria, as well as two astronomers, Caroline Herschel and Mary Somerville, and, representing music and drama, Jenny Lind and Sarah Siddons. Two living persons were honoured: Florence Nightingale and Marie Curie.

19. The design had 'WRITERS' across the top, a black crow with a quill above it in the centre, and 'LITERA SCRIPTA MANET' below. Described by L. Tickner as 'the most striking of all suffrage banners', it was carried in turn by Cicely Hamilton, Evelyn Sharp, Sarah Grand and Beatrice Harraden: see L. Tickner, *The Spectacle of Women: Imagery of the Suffrage Campaign, 1907–1914*, London, Chatto and Windus, 1987, p. 260.

20. For instance, Violet Pearn was awarded a £10 prize by the WWSL for her 'The will and the power' on 7 December 1911: see *The Vote*, 9 December 1911.

21. The favourite authors of the wounded soldiers were Nat Gould, Charles Garvice and E. Philips Oppenheim. See B. Harraden, *Life of Florence Barclay*, London, G. P. Putnam's Sons, 1921, p. 251.

22. The Pioneer Players was founded by Edith Craig, a suffragist and the daughter of Ellen Terry, on 8 May 1911 to promote a political theatre. In its ten-year lifespan, Craig produced 150 plays.

23. See D. Brown, *Intertexual Dynamics within the Literary Group: Joyce, Lewis, Pound and Eliot – the Men of 1914*, Basingstoke, Macmillan, 1990, p. 5.

24. Needless to say this does not apply to other non-political texts that the members were writing, or went on to write.

25. Modernism, an omnibus term, denotes a literary movement from 1890 to 1930 which included the Imagists and the Vorticists.

26. R. Jakobson, *Poetry of Grammar and Grammar of Poetry*, Vol. 3 of *Selected Writings*, The Hague, Mouton, 1981, p. iii.

27. Robins, *Way Stations*, p. 225.

28. C. Hamilton, *Life Errant*, London, J. M. Dent, 1935, p. 60.

29. J. Marcus, *Art and Anger: Reading Like a Woman*, Columbus, Ohio State University Press, 1988, p. 129.

30. See M. Homans, *Women Writers and Poetic Identity: Dorothy Wordsworth, Emily Brontë and Emily Dickinson*, Princeton, NJ, Princeton University Press, 1980.

31. A. Gramsci, 'Functional literature' in D. Forgacs and G. Nowell-Smith (eds), *Selections from Cultural Writings*, Cambridge, MA, Harvard University Press, 1985, p. 129.

32. Robins, 'Time table', in *Way Stations*, p. 225.

33. Robins, 'The women writers', in *Way Stations*, p. 236. A speech given to the members of the WWSL at the Criterion, 23 May 1911.

34. The literary theory of the WWSL has been traced through a number of exemplary comments on writing by individual members. This approach is a limited one as it presupposes that the recorded authorial intentions explain the theory within which they were working, but it provides a point for research with which to start. Thus these comments will be taken as evidence but handled circumspectly.

35. Robins, *Way Stations*, pp. 235-6.

36. As the number of entries for early writers in V. Blain, P. Clements and I. Grundy, *The Feminist Companion to Literature in English*, London, Batsford, 1990, shows, there were many women writing before the twentieth century.

37. Moreover, it is not only their writing that has been forgotten; suffrage activists themselves, who were at one point in history ubiquitous, vanished without a trace. The difficulty in piecing together the history of the WWSL was in the lack of preserved information, attributable not only to accidents or carelessness but also, to an extent, to the reticence of many suffrage activists, who, writing in the anti-feminist atmosphere of the post-war era, greatly underplayed their suffrage involvement in their memoirs and autobiographies. Cicely Hamilton's memoir *Life Errant* is a typical case in point.

38. *Votes for Women*, 24 December 1908, p. 211.

39. *The Vote*, 14 January 1911.

40. V. Woolf, *A Room of One's Own*, London, Hogarth, 1978 (first published 1929), p. 88.

41. [M. Florence and C. K. Ogden], *Militarism and Feminism*, London, Allen and Unwin, 1915, was published as an anonymous pamphlet. It was widely reviewed, as in the *TLS*.

42. Catherine Marshall was among the most persistent in voicing the link to what she called 'the profound enmity between militarism and feminism'. See *Common Cause: The Organ of the National Union of Women's Suffrage Societies*, Vol. 6, No. 308, February 1915, p. 747, and Vol. 6, No. 311, March 1915, p. 779. See also the *Labour Year Book* for 1916.

43. See C. Hamilton, *Marriage as a Trade*, London, Chapman and Hall, 1909, pp. 195, 204; and Robins, *Way Stations*, p. 7: see the section on 'woman's instinct for the mask'.

44. Robins, 'To the women writers', in *Way Stations*, p. 110. A speech given to the members of the WWSL at the Waldorf Hotel, 4 May 1909.

45. J. Park, 'The British suffrage activists of 1913: an analysis', *Past and Present*, No. 120, 1988, pp. 147-62.

46. O. Banks, *Becoming a Feminist: The Social Origins of 'First Wave' Feminism*, Athens, University of Georgia Press, 1987, p. 13.

47. For a more detailed analysis see K. Flint, *The Woman Reader 1837–1914*, Oxford, Clarendon Press, 1993, pp. 234–48.

48. E. Pethick-Lawrence, *Why I Went to Prison*, London, The Women's Press, n.d. (Suffragette Fellowship Collection, Museum of London).

49. Hamilton, *Life Errant*, p. 3.

50. In the founding year of the WWSL, 1909, the ages of the committee members were as follows: Alice Meynell, 61; Sarah Grand, 54; Olive Schreiner, 53; Elizabeth Robins, 45; May Sinclair, 45; Beatrice Harraden, 44; Violet Hunt, 42; Marie Belloc Lowndes, 40; Evelyn Sharp, 39; and Cicely Hamilton, 36.

51. Robins, 'The woman writers', in *Way Stations*, p. 231.

52. *Ibid.*, p. 110.

53. *Ibid.*, p. 231.

54. Dale Spender has written of the process by which women's writing is banished to the periphery within a short space of time, and subsequently consigned to oblivion because women's theory does not become general public knowledge. On the cyclical repetition of women's 'new-found rebellion' see D. Spender, *Feminist Theorists: Three Centuries of Key Women Thinkers*, New York, Pantheon, 1983.

6 Suffragette Experience Through the Filter of Fascism

Julie Gottlieb

In the political diaspora from the militant suffrage movement some former activists settled into the seemingly infertile territory of British fascism during the 1930s. Mary Richardson, Norah Elam (Mrs Dacre Fox) and Mary Allen each sought refuge and renewal in Sir Oswald Mosley's British Union of Fascists (BUF), importing with them the legacy of their militant feminist struggle in the pre-war period and their disillusionment with the post-war condition of the women's movement in the aftermath of female enfranchisement. These fascist women evoked the extra-parliamentary methods and militancy of their earlier suffragette struggle, while deciding at the same time that the vote was an 'empty vessel' and democracy a sinking ship. While the masculine spirit of British fascism might well have been hostile to the enlistment of militant women, it was the irony in this case that the former suffragettes were welcomed amid much favourable publicity, held posts of prominence and trust in the movement's Women's Section, and found a forum in which to express their revisionary feminism. They were ideologically accommodated by the development of a BUF historiography in which the suffragette struggle was claimed as a precedent for fascist dissent.

At first glance the membership of the ex-suffragettes in the BUF appears curious, owing to the overwhelming impression of fascism as a masculine movement, inherently opposed to the furtherance of women's emancipation and underlined by an ideology of gender complementarity which took for granted that woman's place was in the home. Evidence to support this appraisal of British fascism is certainly available. In the BUF's manifesto, *The Greater Britain* (1932), Mosley inaugurated a hierarchical vision of gender bifurcation and female subordination when he prescribed that 'the part of women in our future organization will be important, but different from that of men; *we want men who are men and women who are women*'.[1] A. K. Chesterton, one of the BUF's chief propagandists, went even further towards articulating fascism's misogyny, its anticipated purge of feminine influence, and the movement's revolt against the rule of 'old women' in government when he commanded, 'let us smash the matriarchal principle and return to the grand object of manhood'.[2] Chesterton spoke of fascism's construction of the man of action, and located the nascent spirit of fascist endeavour in the life work of Shakespeare, Beethoven and Velázquez. Paradoxically, the heritage of the last of these cultural heroes had been literally and figuratively assaulted by Mary Richardson in 1914, when she slashed the 'Rokeby Venus' in protest against the imprisonment of Mrs Pankhurst.

Contrary to this image of overt masculine supremacy, the fascist movement in Britain welcomed and accommodated the support of women during the 1930s. It is estimated that women accounted for 30 per cent of Mosley's supporters; available statistics on the composition of fascist meetings and marches suggest that women represented 28 per cent of participants; and between 1940 and 1945 of the 747 BUF members detained under Defence Regulation 18B, 100 were women.[3] Women's work in the movement consisted principally of canvassing, organizing fund-raising events, selling literature, attending physical fitness and speakers' classes, and holding their own meetings. Dressed in their black blouses and grey skirts, they filled the ranks of marching columns and thereby served as mascots of British fascism's liberality towards women's political participation. As a further challenge to the common apprehension that fascism would divest women of their role in public life, corps of women were trained for defensive and offensive violence. Members of the Women's Propaganda Patrol held the St John Ambulance certificate and were instructed in ju-jitsu, precautions 'made necessary by the behaviour of communist women at some of our rougher meetings, who turned to their own advantage the fact that our men are not allowed to eject a woman'.[4]

The BUF claimed on numerous occasions that it adhered to the principle of the equality of the sexes; that women would be granted unprecedented political representation in the promised corporate state, and that fascism was the ideal home for the patriotic but independent and active woman. The BUF denied that its model for organizing women was based on continental fascism or Nazism, and in striving to differentiate the treatment of women in his movement from the German example, Mosley claimed:

> We have a higher percentage of women candidates than any other party in this country and they play a part of basic equality. We are pledged to complete sex equality. The German attitude towards women has always been different from the British, and my movement has been largely built up by the fanaticism of women; they hold ideals with tremendous passion. Without the women I could not have got a quarter of the way.[5]

Mosley's statement had an eerie resemblance to Hitler's declaration upon coming to power in 1933. Hitler had been recorded as saying, 'I can only confess that without the endurance and really loving devotion of the women to the movement I could have never led the party to victory'.[6] While a superficial similarity is discernible, what was striking was the extent to which Mosley's BUF distanced itself from the foreign models for the role and treatment of women by developing a culture of *feminine fascism* which took as its point of departure the approbation of the militant suffrage movement.

While the pre-war activities of the BUF's suffragette recruits have been recorded in histories of the Women's Social and Political Union (WSPU) and in the BUF press, the story of their fascist activities is somewhat more obscure. It must be pieced together from public records, personal memoirs and the women's own self-representation in the movement's publications.

After the First World War Norah Elam (then going by the surname of her first husband, Dacre Fox, born *c.* 1878), eager to taste the fruits of the Representation of the People Act, stood unsuccessfully as an Independent candidate for Richmond, Surrey. From the vantage point of the 1930s, she explained how in 1918 'my own distrust of Party politics made me chary of turning in this direction, and I preferred to stand as an Independent, going down with all the other women candidates on this occasion, save one'.[7] Subsequently, apparently putting aside her revulsion for party politics, she became a member of the Conservative Party, and she and her second husband, Dudley Elam, defected from the Conservatives to join the BUF in 1934. Dudley Elam had been chair of the Chichester Conservatives, was a retired civil servant from the Ministry of Health, and worked as an unpaid receptionist at the BUF's national headquarters. Norah Elam became the BUF County Women's Officer for West Sussex and a prospective parliamentary candidate for the British Union in 1936, and she was a frequent contributor to BUF publications from 1935 to 1940.

Elam's status in the BUF and the sensitive tasks with which she was entrusted offer some substance to the BUF's claim to respect sexual equality. In principle the movement was segregated by gender, and women in positions of leadership were meant to have authority only over other women, but Elam was clearly admitted to Mosley's inner circle. Mosley explained to inquisitive detectives from the Special Branch that, owing to fears that the headquarters might be bombed and even that he might be assassinated by an angry mob, Mrs Elam 'took charge of part of our funds for a short period before and after the declaration of war. There was nothing illegal or improper about this.'[8] Further evidence of the high esteem with which Mosley regarded her emerged when the police raided Elam's offices of the London and Provincial Anti-Vivisection Society on 18 December 1939. The police found Elam in possession of a list containing the names of eight members of the BUF, 'together with a letter from Oswald Mosley, stating that Mrs Elam had his full confidence, and was entitled to do what she thought fit in the interest of the movement on her own responsibility'.[9]

Norah Elam was the only ex-suffragette to be interned in Britain under Defence Regulation 18B; her second foray into anti-government activity landed her back in Holloway Prison, this time as an indisputable 'political prisoner'. (During her previous spells in prison, she, along with other suffrage prisoners, had been refused that status.) Elam was interned in May 1940, and was among the first BUF officials arrested. She was somewhat exceptional for never making an appeal before the 18B Advisory Committee; nevertheless Diana Mosley strongly advocated her release.[10] In 1943, she was among the very few former members of the British Union to be granted a visit with the 'Leader' and Lady Mosley when the couple were interned together in Holloway Prison. At the same time it was reported that Unity Mitford was staying with the Elams at their London home in Logan Place.[11] Elam was also active in the furtherance of the aims of the 18B Detainees (British) Aid Fund, and thereby had the opportunity to reapply the tactics she had used during suffrage days when she had agitated for the release of her fellow activists.

Although her road to fascism was much less coherent than either Elam's or Mary Allen's, Mary Richardson (1883-1961) rose to the highest position in the women's hierarchy of the BUF. It was rumoured in fascist circles that prior to the First World War, when she was breaking windows on the WSPU's behalf, she had known Benito Mussolini, at that time the editor of the socialist journal *Avanti!* She opposed the fascist movement from its Italian inception in 1922 and wrote Mussolini a scathing letter after his March on Rome in which she accused him of betraying his socialist principles. In reply, he sent her a prophetic telegram with the words 'Some day, perhaps, your eyes will be opened.'[12] In 1916, Richardson became a member of the Labour Party and stood as a candidate for Parliament three times, losing to the Conservative incumbent on each occasion: she contested Acton, Middlesex, in 1922 as a Labour candidate, the same constituency in 1924 for the Independent Labour Party, and fought Aldershot, Hampshire, in 1931, again for Labour. In December 1933 it was announced that Mussolini's prophecy had been fulfilled when Richardson joined the Blackshirts. She explained that she was attracted to the BUF because 'its policy of Imperialism, and action combined with discipline raise the movement above comparison with the present party system'.[13] By January 1934 she had been made assistant to Esther Makgill, leader of the BUF's Women's Section, and by May she had taken over as Chief Organizer of the Women's Section, when Lady Makgill was forced to resign after being caught embezzling funds. On 24 April 1934 Richardson opened a National Club for Fascist Women at 12 Lower Grosvenor Place, the headquarters of the Women's Section.

The integration and status of the Women's Section within the BUF's hierarchy was exemplified by the extent to which women leaders were involved in the factionalism and scandals at national headquarters. In

January 1935, Richardson was appointed to take charge of the Lancashire area for the BUF, which spawned vehement opposition from F. M. Box, Controller of Organization, and also from Mosley's mother, Maud Lady Mosley, the Director of Organization of the Women's Section. In February 1935 'Ma' Mosley complained to her son about Richardson's 'dishonest efficiency [and] ... sullen opposition to me. I was a stumbling block to collaring the machine and all its resources.'[14] In this atmosphere of inner-party strife, Richardson had defected from the movement by 1936.[15]

Of the three BUF ex-suffragettes, although Mary Allen (1878–1964) was a card-carrying member for the shortest time, her association with the fascist movement can be traced back the farthest. Allen is best remembered for her pioneering work with women police, her mannish attire and preference to be addressed as 'Sir' at her headquarters,[16] her obsession with women in uniform, and her moral alarmism directed at all branches of the 'vice racket'. She spent the First World War as Margaret Damer Dawson's subcommandant in the Women's Police Force, received the OBE in 1917 for her war service, and became commandant upon Damer Dawson's death in 1920. The war over, she was not prepared to obey the Metropolitan Police Commissioner's instructions that her Women Police should disband, and founded her own 'unofficial' Women's Police Reserve, which in 1923 was renamed the Women's Auxiliary Service. Her political ambitions undeterred by public and official censure, in 1922 she stood as a Liberal candidate for the St George's Division of Westminster, focusing her campaign on women police and the importance of the uniformed officer. Not surprisingly perhaps, she came bottom of the poll with only 6.5 per cent of the votes. She spent most of the inter-war years globe-trotting to promote women police, and visited Germany, Spain, France, Brazil, Poland and Egypt in her capacity as 'Commandant'. Again without official backing, in November 1933 she formed the Women's Reserve to enrol women to serve in the event of a national emergency.

Her open admiration for, and collaboration with, fascism both at home and abroad and her virulent anti-communism can be traced back to 1926, the year of the General Strike. In that year she mobilized her women against the strikers and accepted recruits to her Women's Auxiliary Service from the British Fascists. Also in 1926, while attending the International Police Congress in Berlin, she met General O'Duffy, the leader of the Irish Blueshirt movement, by whom she was much impressed. In 1933, with her Women's Auxiliary Service, she visited the British Fascists, and in April 1934 she addressed a meeting of the BUF's January Club. In January 1934, shortly after the Reichstag fire, she visited Germany 'to learn about the truth of the position of German womanhood'[17] and to encourage the Führer to re-establish women police in the new Reich. She was given an audience with Hitler and Goering, and she was very impressed by Hitler, entranced by his oratory and spellbound by his visionary eyes. She 'recognised in him an enduring blood-brother of the ordinary decent people of Europe, whatever their nationalities, who want peace for their trade and safety for their children'.[18] Indeed, in her autobiography, *Lady in Blue* (1936), Allen devoted more space to her interview with Hitler and to her tour of the exhibition of communist weapons at the secret police headquarters in Berlin than to any other episode in her proud career as a crusader for 'women in blue'. In 1936 she visited Spain as General Franco's guest, where, it was alleged, she preached the doctrine of a Fascist International and 'had made complete arrangements with the British Fascist party and its sympathizers to stage meetings of protest, if and when the British Government showed any symptoms of sympathy for the Republicans'.[19]

Allen's 'coming out' as a member of the British Union was untimely, as she joined soon after the declaration of war in the autumn of 1939. She occupied a seat of honour at a luncheon for the movement's London administration in March 1940, and she spoke at a BUF Women's Peace meeting at Friends' House on 13 April 1940. Special Branch also maintained that in March, April and May 1940 she attended secret meetings convened by leaders of Britain's pro-Nazi and anti-Semitic organizations to prepare plans for a fascist *coup d'état*.[20] She claimed that she had joined the BUF because she agreed with its policy for peace and its concentration on the interests of the British Empire. She also testified that she had become associated with the fascist movement through her friendship with Norah Elam, whom she had known since her days as a member of the WSPU.[21]

An order under Defence Regulation 18B(1A) was made against Allen and served on 16 June 1940, and, while she was never interned, her activities were restricted under 18B(2). At her appeal before the Advisory Committee she revealed her deep resentment against a government which had never paid her due credit: 'I believe I have earned more than I have been given. ... There are always people who live to found movement after movement but nothing is done for them.'[22] Looking back upon her life's work, mourning the absence of official recognition, and suffering from the 'grave injustice' of the Defence Regulations imposed by the Home Secretary, perhaps she took some small comfort in the fact that she had broken the windows of the Home Office in 1909! Such considerations aside, a final indignity was imposed on Allen's martial patriotism when five Metropolitan Women Police were placed in charge of alien and fascist internees on the Isle of Man.

Elam, Richardson and Allen shared more than pride at their ordeals as pre-war WSPU activists, and certain similarities in their post-suffrage experiences offer clues to the type of militant woman who was susceptible to the lure of revolutionary (fringe) fascism. The BUF's ex-suffragettes had all been unsuccessful in their bids to be elected to Parliament, and felt at first hand the disappointment that arose from the failure of any former suffragette to benefit from the democratic right they had fought for so tirelessly. Elam spoke with deep regret in 1936 when she recalled how the first woman to be elected to the House of Commons was the Sinn Feiner Constance Markievicz, and the first to take her seat was the American-born Nancy Astor, the presence of both 'outsiders' being an affront to her nationalist feminism. All three ex-suffragettes had made some attempt at accommodation with the very parties which had treated militant women 'with such unprecedented contempt';[23] they were all members of one of the main political parties before they opted for the abolition of the entire 'decadent' party system and the overthrow of 'financial democracy'. While none had been active in a feminist organization during the inter-war period, each identified the fulfilment of her own national service-oriented feminist principles in fascism. From a psychological perspective, with varying degrees of intensity each believed that she was owed more than she had received for her dedication to the women's struggle for citizenship, and that this inheritance had remained wanting. In their ultimate rejection of liberal democracy, each in her political life personified one extreme of the disillusionment and the disappointed hopes of politicized women in post-suffrage Britain.

The seemingly anomalous membership of the ex-suffragettes in the BUF either is generally evaluated as an accident of history and the eccentricity of personality, or elicits a disturbed reaction from those who see in their political allegiance a treachery to feminism. However, links between pre-war suffrage activists and the British right emerged as soon as the 'votes for women' banners were lowered. Richardson's, Elam's and Allen's eventual conversion to fascism does not seem such an aberration when we examine the post-suffrage routes taken by a number of their WSPU heroines, and when we remember how some of their revered WSPU leaders turned decisively towards vigilant nationalism from the outbreak of the First World War. Christabel Pankhurst recalled how 'war was the only course for our country to take. This was national militancy. As Suffragettes we could not be pacifists at any price.'[24] The BUF's former suffragettes each remembered supporting the Pankhursts' decision to transfer the energy exerted on anti-government militancy to loyal and patriotic service in war. Mrs Dacre Fox's conversion from the suffrage cause to nationalism was clear from the very beginning of the war, and at a Brighton meeting on 21 September 1914 she urged 'the young men of the nation to answer Lord Kitchener's call for fresh reinforcements'.[25] After her release and pardon in the summer of 1914, Richardson reminisced how Mrs Pankhurst 'pleaded with us to be loyal to the Government and to the country. Some of us felt a little bewildered. But her eloquence did much to persuade us she was right.'[26] Similarly disconcerted but loyal, Allen obeyed the Pankhursts' message to 'cease fire'. She described how we were to drop our private struggle with those in power, and offer ourselves as the first volunteers to help the Government in its dark hour. I won't pretend we liked it! We were heart and soul in our fight to gain recognition for women.[27]

Allen's experience of suffrage militancy convinced her that she was overqualified to enlist for more staid auxiliary work. Instead of taking up a post offered to her at the Needlework Guild, she was among the first to enrol in Margaret Damer Dawson's Women Police, because, as she wrote later, 'I wanted action'.[28]

A rightward turn among some suffragettes became even more definite as the First World War progressed. Pandering to nationalist fervour, the WSPU's *The Suffragette* was renamed *Britannia* on 15 October 1915. In late 1917 and 1918 Emmeline and Christabel Pankhurst and Flora Drummond preached against communism and wartime strikes by workers in south Wales, the Midlands and on Clydeside. They were accompanied on these expeditions by Norah Elam, who was later credited by the BUF with placing 'her services at the disposal of the Government (at the outbreak of war). Mrs Elam had a distinguished war record – recruiting in "Red" South Wales, working in a munitions factory, and was a member of several Government Committees.'[29] In 1918, together with Annie Kenney and Flora Drummond, Christabel Pankhurst formed the Women's Party; their campaign propaganda borrowed freely from the agenda of the right as Christabel championed heavy German reparation payments, expressed opposition to Irish Home Rule and to trade unionism, and confined the feminist content of her platform to the advocacy of improved housing.[30] Christabel failed narrowly to win the Smethwick seat, the very seat which Oswald Mosley was to hold for Labour in 1926 and again in 1929.

During the General Strike of 1926, Emmeline Pankhurst, one-time member of the Independent Labour Party, took a firm stand against trade union agitation, told Lady Astor that she wished to organize relief work, and finally pledged her support to one of her former Edinburgh WSPU organizers, Mary Allen. On 1 May 1926, 'Commandant' Mary Allen picked up the telephone at the temporary headquarters of her Women's Auxiliary Service at Rochester Row only to hear

> the voice of Mrs Emmeline Pankhurst, my own former Suffragette leader, putting her services entirely at my disposal. During the strike she organised meetings and concerts in slum areas where the wives and children of strikers, open as they were to subversive propaganda and likely to feel the pinch of hunger, provided a dangerous explosive material ready for the first agitator match.[31]

In 1927 Emmeline Pankhurst was adopted as the Conservative candidate for Whitechapel and St George's, by which time, according to Brian Harrison, 'her concern for empire, her distaste for socialism and her support for Baldwin had displaced feminism from her list of priorities'.[32] Although Mrs Pankhurst died before she could contest the seat, Christabel predicted that 'she might well have been elected to Parliament by acclamation and agreement between voters of all parties and no party, as a sign of political reconciliation between men and women, between the post-war and pre-war eras'.[33] Christabel's hopes for the form of her mother's success were reminiscent of that paradoxical absence of regard for the democratic process, constitutionalism, and the exercise of the vote increasingly in evidence within the WSPU's pre-war internal government.[34] In striking contrast to the political sympathies and activities of the socialist anti-fascist Sylvia Pankhurst, Adela Pankhurst Walsh was a founding member of the Australia First movement and was interned in March 1942 under Regulation 26 of the National Security Act, in circumstances parallel to the detention of suspected Fifth Columnists in Britain.[35] In their radically varied political choices during the inter-war period, the dispersal of the Pankhurst women over the political spectrum bore many resemblances to another notorious family of distinguished women which was similarly splintered by extremist politics, the Mitford sisters.

Nor were reactionary responses to inter-war politics among former suffragettes confined to members of the Pankhurst family. In April 1926 Flora Drummond, the 'General' of the WSPU, organized a march of thousands of women which demanded an end to strikes, and in 1928 she formed the anti-communist Women's Guild of Empire, which 'pioneered the idea that women should be mobilized against the trade unions'.[36] In light of the political experiences of these leading figures of the WSPU, Richardson, Elam and Allen could each convince herself that she was remaining faithful to her suffragette mentors in her own rightward journey across the political landscape.

The cross-fertilization between feminine militancy and British fascist politics was a persistent feature throughout the inter-war period and pre-dated the formation of the BUF. The first fascist organization in Britain was founded in May 1923 by a woman, Miss Rotha Lintorn-Orman (1895–1935). It was telling that New Scotland Yard wrongly took this eccentric ultra-patriotic ex-servicewoman to be 'an ex-suffragette' who ran her organization 'with the assistance of some very "harmful" lunatics'.[37] The perception was that Edwardian suffrage militancy had been effortlessly metamorphosed into post-war nationalist chauvinism. While there is no evidence to suggest that Lintorn-Orman herself had been a suffragette (she had been occupied leading Girl Scout (later Girl Guide) troops in Bournemouth since 1909), female members of her British Fascists did volunteer for service with Mary Allen's Women's Special Police during the General Strike of May 1926,[38] when they worked alongside Allen's most notable recruit, Mrs Pankhurst.

Traces of proto-fascism have been identified in the suffragette movement, and the Pankhursts' rule over WSPU has been characterized as a dictatorship. Cicely Hamilton argued that the WSPU was 'the first indication of the dictatorship movements which are by way of thrusting democracy out of the European Continent'; and Emmeline Pankhurst 'was a forerunner of Lenin, Hitler and Mussolini – the leader whose fiat must go unquestioned, the leader who could do no wrong'.[39] In 1938 Emmeline Pethick-Lawrence admitted with some regret that developments in the WSPU 'bore a certain resemblance to the dictatorship so common in the world to-day. ... It is so-called upholders of democracy who create, when they are false in their principles, and when they attempt to crush their opponents, dictatorships.'[40] Both movements have depended to differing degrees on the leadership principle, hero worship, quasi-spiritual inspiration, palingenetic imagery and Romantic longings for national regeneration; both encouraged the development of women's skills for self-defence, and gave vent to female aggression and rebelliousness; and both were accused by rivals of criminality, lunacy, fanaticism and tyranny. When Winifred Holtby noticed a young woman donning a black blouse walking sturdily towards BUF headquarters, she recalled how 'that enviable sense of exaltation is not the exclusive property of the Blackshirt movement. It has been observed in Catholic converts, Salvation Army recruits, militant suffragettes, communists, Jacobites, jingoes and pacifists alike.'[41] In *Wigs on the Green*, Nancy Mitford mocked the militant spirit that animated suffragette and woman fascist alike, and satirized the humourless devotion to a charismatic leader which drove otherwise idle women to become earnest and ridiculous. Eugenia Malmains (Unity Mitford), member of the Union Jackshirts (BUF), mounted her soap-box to preach, '"The country must be purged of petty vice before it can be fit to rule the world." ... "That's a fine girl", said Jasper. "If she had been born 20 years sooner she would have been a Suffragette."'[42]

On a more serious note, it was indicative how the suffragette struggle was claimed as a precedent for dissent by fascists and anti-fascists alike. Anti-fascist hecklers who were attacked mercilessly by Blackshirts at the Olympia rally of 7 June 1934 were figured as latter-day suffragettes. One writer to the editor of *The Times* observed that 'organised interruption provokes organised terrorism as we saw during the Suffragette campaign, when women were treated by Liberal stewards almost as badly as the Fascists treated their hecklers'.[43] Similarly, an Independent Labour Party witness to the Olympia rally noted how

> twenty years ago the women Suffragists interrupted Cabinet Ministers to arouse public attention to their demand for the right to vote. To-day, Socialists and Communists are interrupting the leader of the Fascist movement to arouse public attention to the character of Fascism.[44]

From the fascist camp, *Action*'s radio critic, commenting on Flora

Drummond's appearance on the BBC production *I Saw the Start*, commended her for bringing to light 'two occasions in which women were thrown out and brutally assaulted at meetings of the Liberal Party, the Party which nowadays turns pale pink at what it is pleased to call "Blackshirt brutality"'.[45] Rights to the suffrage legacy were fiercely contested in the heated atmosphere of extremist politics during the 1930s.

While the majority of inter-war feminists lamented the resemblances and fought against fascism at home and abroad,[46] Richardson, Elam and Allen relished the thought of continuity between their militant feminism and fascism, and went to great lengths to prove the benefits of this relationship. In 1934 Mary Richardson engaged in a press polemic over the treatment of women under fascism with her former sister-in-arms Sylvia Pankhurst. Richardson counted on the endurance of her own and Sylvia Pankhurst's shared memories, pointing out that they had been close associates in the WSPU, had worked together in Bow and were confined to Holloway at the same time. However, she was still at pains to convince Pankhurst that the two movements resembled one another in activity and in the public responses they elicited. She implored Sylvia to 'remember' the indignities of forcible feeding; the shame of the actions of the mob on Black Friday; the militants' proud use of 'force and bludgeons, of dog whips, truncheons (carried and used by Mrs Pankhurst's bodyguard), stones in their multitude, and bricks and hammers'; and that when suffragettes were attacked they had no other choice than to offer violent but valiant resistance. Richardson explained how

> I was first attracted to the Blackshirts because I saw in them the courage, the action, the loyalty, the gift of service, and the ability to serve which I had known in the suffrage movement. When later I discovered that Blackshirts were attacked for no visible cause or reason, I admired them the more when they hit back, and hit hard.[47]

Familiar with the inner workings of both movements, the BUF's ex-suffragettes developed the discourse of proto-fascist militant feminism to fullest effect.

Elam constructed her own comparative history of the two movements and imagined much common ground, postulating Mosley to be the latter-day Mrs Pankhurst and fascist dictatorship the perfection of WSPU voluntary discipline and service:

> In this conception of practical citizenship, the women's struggle resembles closely the new philosophy of Fascism. Indeed, Fascism is the logical, if much grander, conception of the momentous issues raised by the militant women of a generation ago. Nor do the points of resemblance end here. The Women's Movement, like the Fascist Movement, was conducted under strict discipline, and cut across all party allegiances; its supporters were

drawn from every class and Party. It appealed to women to forget self-interest; to relinquish petty personal advantage, the privilege of the sheltered few for the benefit of the many; and to stand together against the wrongs and injustices which were inherent in a system so disastrous to the well-being of the race. Like the Fascist movement, too, it chose its Leader, and once having chosen gave that leader absolute authority to direct policy and destiny, displaying a loyalty and devotion never surpassed in the history of this country. Moreover, like the Fascist movement again, it faced the brutality of the streets; the jeers of opponents; the misapprehensions of the well-disposed; and the rancour of politicians.[48]

Reflecting upon the unfulfilled legacy of the pre-war women's struggle and the laxity of British women's commitment to national service by the 1930s, Allen became convinced that 'it is women, perhaps, who are in need of a dictator – but, I hasten to add that I am not qualifying for that unenviable post'.[49] The BUF's ex-suffragettes regarded feminine militancy and fascism as twin political impulses, and saw in their conglomeration the potential for the resurrection of the spirit of *their* earlier suffragette struggles.

Rather than having to discard their suffrage identities in order to wear the new black shirt, former suffragettes Elam, Allen and Richardson were encouraged to call upon the past to propagate the fascist future. In recompense for their noteworthy support, the BUF rewarded them by granting publicity to their personal histories and representing them as heroic agitators in a feminist revolution. Mary Richardson was advertised as 'a pioneer worker for the "rights of women" '[50], an 'ex-suffragette and a leading protagonist for women's emancipation. ... During the seven years prior to 1914, Miss Richardson took an active part in the suffrage movement, for which she was sentenced to terms of imprisonment totalling more than three years.'[51] Notably, however, while the BUF's newspapers publicized Richardson's souvenirs from the WSPU, such as the medal in her possession that had been given to Mrs Pankhurst by the 'Women of America' and the first suffrage petition carried to the House of Commons demanding the female franchise, conspicuously absent from the distinctions listed were her acts of arson and her slashing of the 'Rokeby Venus'.[52]

Norah Elam was described as 'one of the leaders of the Women's Suffrage Movement in pre-war days, [who] served three terms of imprisonment and endured several hunger strikes'.[53] Elam provided further favourable publicity for the BUF by being one of its prospective parliamentary candidates. In 1936 the BUF announced its first list of 100 candidates and took gleeful pride in the fact that ten of these first 100 were women, a higher percentage than for any other party in Britain.[54] When Mosley presented Elam to her prospective constituents at the Northampton town hall in November 1936, he stated that he was glad indeed to have the opportunity of introducing this first candidate, and it killed for all time the suggestion that National Socialism proposed putting British women back into the home. Mrs Elam, he went on, had fought in the past for women's suffrage ... and was a great example of the emancipation of women in Britain.[55]

With the emphasis placed on their pre-war activities, the ex-suffragettes served as mascots for the BUF's women's policy, and their membership was fully exploited to drive home before a sceptical public the distinctions between British and Continental variants of fascism.

In addition to applauding their suffragette past, the BUF provided a forum in which the women could record their memories of suffrage days and secure for posterity their top billing in the WSPU. When Mrs H. Carrington-Wood, a north-west London organizer for the BUF, resigned from the movement in 1935 – alleging that 'the promises made on Fascist platforms and in Fascist literature are inadequate to appease the anxiety of the womenfolk, who naturally do not want to risk going back to where they were before the days of the Suffragettes' – it was Norah Elam who took vehement exception to her claim, and derided her for 'exploiting the Suffragettes' for her own purposes. From Elam's perspective, only the women who had engaged in the earlier struggle had licence to evoke the memory:

> what really 'gets one's goat' is the exploitation of the fight made by women such as myself who suffered imprisonment and the horrors of the hunger and thirst strike, in order to vindicate our principles in the days of the Suffragette battle ... those of us who bore the heat and burden of that day have, at any rate, earned the right to challenge those who now want to make capital of the sacrifices of militant women.[56]

The suffragette inheritance was only to be partitioned by the former militant women themselves, and Elam passed on her own share of the bequest to the BUF.

For Elam, suffragette experiences had been formative and she was keen to share her own memories with younger fascist women, especially once her life had come full circle and she was again imprisoned in Holloway. For instance, in Holloway Prison in 1942, Officer Baxter recorded the following exchange between Diana Mosley and her mother, Lady Redesdale:

> Lady Riddesdale [sic] said she wanted to go see the lady in Logan Place (meaning Mrs Elam) and Lady Mosley said 'Oh do, she is such a sweet dear soul and you will probably find her in the midst of a large tea – she is very fond of her food, which makes her all the more marvellous as she was here in the Suff. time and went on hunger strike 3 times and Mrs Pankhurst gave her a medal with three bars and she is so proud of it; the officers in those days were so different to now, they absolutely tortured those poor women – do get her to tell you all about it, it's so interesting and six of the officers

couldn't bear it, and all resigned on the same day stating as their reason that they hadn't joined the service to torture women so they left' (I was one of the officers at that time, so I was rather amused).[57]

Lady Mosley's reaction exemplified how Elam's part in the history of British feminism was appreciated by her fascist peers. It also suggested the manner in which Elam had kept alive and recycled her memories of the WSPU through fascism.

The BUF went beyond applauding individual militant actions by granting the pre-war suffragette movement as a whole a prominent place in its own historical memory. It was not considered too far-fetched to suggest that

> just as before the war the anti-parliamentary movement of Ulster Loyalists had within it the germ of a Fascist revolution, aborted by the war, so the Women's Suffrage movement might, uninterrupted by the same cause, have been the direct inspiration and forerunner of the Fascist movement in Great Britain.[58]

BUF historiography had the greatest reverence for the so-called Golden Age of Tudor Government and it was claimed that this had also been 'the Golden Age of women's accomplishments.... The reaction of anti-feminism came after, coincident with Puritanism, and the rise of Parliamentary power.'[59] Through this process of conceptualization (or misconceptualization), the BUF not only professed to be the rightful inheritor of the suffragette legacy, but also asserted British fascism's claim to represent true feminism. Doreen Bell, a young recruit, gave voice to a *leitmotif* in the BUF's women's policy when she explained that 'many ardent feminists have been induced by anti-Fascist propagandists to oppose the Movement, little realizing that through the Corporate State in BUF many of the ideals [for which] they have fought so hard and sacrificed so much will be realized'.[60] The negotiation of a merger between fascism and 'true' feminism was facilitated by charges of decadence and ineffectuality against the inter-war women's movement. Within the BUF the most vociferous critics of contemporary feminist organizations were the ex-suffragettes themselves.

The ex-suffragettes attacked inter-war British women for every political sin imaginable. In the same breath Elam characterized other former suffragettes as 'empty volcanoes'; castigated younger women for not appreciating the monumental achievements made for their freedom by militant women a generation earlier; indicted individual feminists for colluding with the party system; at one and the same time scoffed at women for acting as accomplices to warmongers and for serving international pacifism; faulted feminist organizations for the narrowness of their efforts for a single sex; and portrayed the whole female population as obtuse for believing that 'a woman is free because she also votes, or that democracy can offer anything but the careful and organised exploitation of men and women who suffer it to exist'.[61] Days after the Munich crisis, the anti-Semitic ex-suffragette borrowed the Dreyfussard rhetoric to exclaim 'J'ACCUSE: failure of the women's movement', and wondered 'where is there to-day an organised body of women which is protesting against the intrigues of democracy?'[62] Similarly, Allen had exhibited signs of deep disenchantment with organized feminism before she joined the BUF and, from the vantage point of her position as policewoman, she shuddered at many of the immoral choices made by modern women.[63] With the coming of war, Allen articulated the essence of feminized fascism when she advised 'that women drop for good and all the tiresome reiteration of "Women's Rights" and substitute for it "Women's Responsibilities"'.[64] Perturbed by what they perceived as the retreat of British women from action into decadent individualism, Elam and Allen renewed their demand for 'deeds and not words', this time to light the flame of fascist revolution.

The triumph of deeds over words became the order of the day when women Blackshirts complemented their rhetorical attacks by disrupting the meetings of competing women's organizations. In March 1937 the British Union fought the London County Council elections and among those protesting against their campaign was none other than Flora Drummond, with her Women's Guild of Empire. Elam described Drummond's own operation to encourage East End women to vote against the BUF as an 'anti-fascist circus'. When women Blackshirts interrupted one of Drummond's meetings at the Bethnal Green Library, they made their exit with cries of 'Hail Mosley!'[65] As part of their own Women's Peace Campaign, BUF women organized the disruption of a peace meeting hosted by the Women's League Against War and Fascism at the Kingsway Hall on 31 January 1940.

The ex-suffragettes' offensive action against women's organizations and contemporary feminism was motivated by their disillusionment with the outcome of female enfranchisement. Their sense of lost promise and even betrayal culminated in an uncompromising rejection of parliamentary democracy. Discourses on women and the vote in the BUF were clearly predicated on this assault on the democratic system as such. The arguments were essentially tautological, as fascism would in effect dispense with parliamentary suffrage, both male and female. However, by polemicizing the significance and consequences of female enfranchisement, women in the BUF could distinctly isolate those aspects of interwar feminism which pointed to the necessity for the fascist revolution and national reconstruction by way of the corporate state.

The vote was variously described as an 'empty vessel', 'merely a symbol'[66] and 'a barren girl'.[67] Anne Brock Griggs subtitled her prescriptive pamphlet *Women and Fascism: 10 Important Points* with the defeatist statement 'You Have the Vote – Yet You Are Still Powerless'. Looking at developments abroad, Muriel Currey averred that 'the fact that women have not a parliamentary vote in Italy has blinded some ardent feminists to the importance and power of women in the Italian Corporate State'.[68] The notion was that there was a definite incongruity between sign and signifier, and the symbolism of the female franchise had been undermined by the conquest of 'financial democracy'. Rarely, however, was it acknowledged as ironic that the BUF intended to come to power constitutionally, by appealing to male and female voters, and to use democracy to defeat democracy.[69]

In light of the BUF's dismissal of any respect for the franchise, it was ironic that the suffragettes who turned to fascism embraced their title as 'suffragettes' at all. They retained their identification with a cause that they admitted was anathema to the political destiny they prescribed for Britain during the 1930s. They worked through issues of revisionary feminism in the BUF, divorced from the context of a democratic nomenclature, principles of representation, and liberal tolerance.[70] Over three decades of political activism, the former suffragettes in the BUF managed a monumental shift from an extra-parliamentary struggle for rights for inclusion in the democratic process to a willingness to employ democratic methods in order to overthrow parliamentary democracy. Ridden with paradox as this shift might seem, the fascist ex-suffragettes demonstrated that there was a certain logic in this progression.

Notes

1. O. Mosley, *The Greater Britain*, London, BUF Publications, 1932, p. 40. The emphasis is Mosley's.

2. A. K. Chesterton, 'Return to manhood: regiment of old women routed', *Action*, No. 21, 9 July 1936.

3. The estimate of 30 per cent is taken from R. Thurlow, *Fascism in Britain: A History, 1918–1985*, New York, Basil Blackwell, 1987, p. 126. For the percentage of women's participation at meetings, the figure is based on my own tabulation of estimates of the composition of BUF meetings as recorded by the Special Branch. See also The Regulation 18B British Union Detainees List, British Union Collection, 6/1, Sheffield University.

4. 'Women Blackshirts: helping to build a Great Britain', *Blackshirt*, No. 58, 1 June 1934.

5. Advisory Committee to Consider Appeals Against Orders of Internment, 3 July 1940, Home Office Papers (HO 283/14/2–117), Public Record Office, Kew, London (hereafter PRO).

6. K. Thomas, *Women in Nazi Germany*, London, Victor Gollancz, 1943, p. 28.

7. N. Elam, 'Fascism, women and democracy', *Fascist Quarterly*, Vol. 1, No. 3, July 1935, pp. 290–8. In 1918 she came second in the poll, winning 3615 votes (20.2 per cent) and losing to C. B. Edgar, a Conservative Coalition candidate.

8. Home Office Papers (HO45/24895/9-12), PRO.

9. Home Office Papers (HO283/48/27), PRO. It is presumed that the eight names, all men, were those who were entrusted to become leaders of the British Union when and if Mosley himself was put out of commission. MI5 presumed that Elam's Anti-Vivisection Society, with offices in Victoria Street, was simply a BUF front organization. This may have been the case, but confusion has arisen owing to the fact that the largest organization of this type was the British Union for the Abolition of Vivisection (BUAV), with offices at 47 Whitehall. The BUAV's organ vehemently denied any connection with Mosley's BUF. See 'The single aim of the BUAV', *The Abolitionist*, July 1940. For further discussion see also H. Kean, *Animal Rights: Political and Social Change in Britain since 1800*, London, Reaktion, 1998, pp. 192-3, 258.

10. Visited by Sir Walter Monckton on 26 April 1941, Diana Mosley brought forward the case of the older women internees, and spoke of Elam: 'She has an old husband who is not very strong, has been interned and had a very bad time at Stafford and some other prison – she is worried that she may have to go to the Isle of Man.' Home Office Papers (HO144/21995/99), PRO.

11. Letter from the Governor, H. M. Prison, Holloway, G.2 Division, to the Home Secretary, Herbert Morrison, 25 March 1943, Home Office Papers (HO45/24891/342), PRO.

12. 'Ex-suffragette joins the BUF: Mussolini's predictions', *Fascist Week*, No. 7, December 1933, pp. 22-8. I am grateful to Jeffrey Wallder for the information about Richardson's acquaintanceship with Mussolini in pre-war London.

13. *Ibid*.

14. Quoted in N. Mosley, *Beyond the Pale*, London, Secker and Warburg, 1983, pp. 91-2.

15. Documents in the Public Record Office would suggest that she left the BUF in 1935, while John Warburton, President of the 'Friends of O. M.', recalls that she was still in the movement in 1936. Letter from John Warburton to the author, 27 February 1997.

16. '"Commandant" Mary Allen who, at her headquarters, is addressed as "Sir", was wearing a long dark blue tight-fitting tunic, dark blue breeches, black top-boots and a peaked cap which sat on her close-cropped grey hair with just a shade of Beatty angle.' *Daily Herald*, 8 November 1933.

17. *Evening Standard*, 29 January 1934.

18. M. Allen, *Lady in Blue*, London, Stanley Paul, 1936, pp. 150-1.

19. Home Office Papers (HO144/21933/244), PRO.

20. Home Office Papers (HO144/21933/330-331), PRO. It was also alleged that Allen had attended meetings at the flat of Miss Margaret Bothamley (a pro-Nazi who would broadcast for German radio during the war) in July 1939, and that she was associated with Mrs Domvile (wife

of the founder of the Link) and Mrs Muriel Whinfield (a prominent member of the BUF).

21. Home Office Papers (HO144/21933/404-430), PRO.
22. *Ibid.*
23. N. Elam, 'Women and the vote', *Action*, No. 6, 26 March 1936.
24. C. Pankhurst, *Unshackled*, London, Hutchinson, 1959, p. 288.
25. A. Rosen, *'Rise up, Women!' The Militant Campaign of the Women's Social and Political Union 1903-1914*, London, Routledge and Kegan Paul, 1974, p. 250.
26. M. Richardson, *Laugh a Defiance*, London, Weidenfeld and Nicolson, 1953, p. 190.
27. Allen, *Lady in Blue*, p. 24.
28. *Ibid.*, p. 25.
29. 'Prospective BU parliamentary candidates: the first twelve with their prospective constituencies', *Action*, No. 40, 21 November 1936.
30. See M. Pugh, *Women and the Women's Movement in Britain, 1914-1959*, London, Macmillan, 1992, p. 45.
31. Allen, *Lady in Blue*, pp. 93-4.
32. B. Harrison, *Prudent Revolutionaries*, Oxford, Clarendon Press, 1987, p. 35.
33. Pankhurst, *Unshackled*, p. 297.
34. On 19 September 1907, precipitating the split which led to the formation of the Women's Freedom League, WSPU headquarters issued the following letter to all organizers: 'We are not playing experiments with representative government. We are not a school for teaching women how to use the vote. We are a militant movement and we have to get the vote next session. ... It is after all a voluntary militant movement; those who cannot follow the general must drop out of the ranks.' Quoted in A. Raeburn, *The Militant Suffragettes*, London, Michael Joseph, 1973, pp. 40-1.
35. See V. Coleman, *Adela Pankhurst: The Wayward Suffragette*, Melbourne, Melbourne University Press, 1996.
36. M. Durham, 'Suffrage and after', in M. Langan and B. Schwarz (eds), *Crises in the British State 1880-1930*, London, Hutchinson, 1985, pp. 179-91.
37. 2 February 1924, Home Office Records (PRO30/69/221), PRO.
38. 'The work of the women's units during the strike', *Fascist Bulletin*, Vol. 3, No. 41, 29 May 1926.
39. C. Hamilton, *Life Errant*, London, J. M. Dent, 1935, p. 68.
40. E. Pethick-Lawrence, *My Part in a Changing World*, London, Victor Gollancz, 1938, preface.
41. W. Holtby, 'Shall I order a black blouse?', *News Chronicle*, 4 May 1934. The ideal of near-religious conversion to the cause was shared by suffragettes and fascist women. Mary Richardson remembered how she reacted the first time she stewarded a meeting for the WSPU at the Albert

Hall in the following manner: 'I cannot remember a single word of what was said on that, for me, so memorable occasion. But at the time the words did not matter. In some strange way I was inspired by the atmosphere of the great gathering. "We will fight," I kept repeating to myself.' Richardson, *Laugh a Defiance*, p. 5. Similarly, Mary Allen was 'converted' by a speech she heard given by Annie Kenney and 'abandoned home, parents, friends and comfort to follow a vision'. Allen, *Lady in Blue*, p. 15.

42. N. Mitford, *Wigs on the Green*, London, Thornton Butterworth, 1935, p. 195.

43. H. Fye, 'Fascist meeting at Olympia', *The Times*, 13 June 1934.

44. 'Behind fascist brutality', *New Leader*, NS Vol. 26, No. 22, 15 June 1934.

45. 'Bluebird', 'Brutal Liberal assaults on women', *Action*, No. 80, 28 August 1937.

46. For feminist reaction to fascism see J. Alberti, 'British feminists and anti-fascism in the 1930s', in S. Oldfield (ed.), *This Working-Day World*, London, Taylor and Francis, 1994, pp. 111-22. An enduring theme in Elam's fascist journalism was the wrong turns taken by former suffragettes after the struggle was over. Of her former allies, she wrote, 'With few notable exceptions, we find these extinct volcanoes either wandering about in the backwoods of international pacifism and decadence, or prostrating themselves before the various political parties, which for years they denounced as cesspools of corruption and chicanery.' N. Elam, 'Suffragette in anti-fascist circus: Flora Drummond tries bluffing the women', *Blackshirt*, No. 230, 25 September 1937.

47. M. Richardson, 'My reply to Sylvia Pankhurst', *Blackshirt*, No. 62, 29 June 1934.

48. N. Elam, 'Fascism, women and democracy', *Fascist Quarterly*, Vol. 1, No. 3, July 1935, pp. 291-2.

49. M. Allen and J. H. Heyneman, *Woman at the Cross Roads*, London, Unicorn, 1934, pp. 136-7.

50. O. Hawks, 'Youth and womanhood turns to Fascism', *Blackshirt*, No. 70, 24 August 1934.

51. 'Ex-suffragette joins the BUF: Mussolini's predictions', *Fascist Week*, No. 7, 22-28 December 1933.

52. While the BUF did not draw attention to Richardson's more outrageous acts of law-breaking, the Special Branch – always voyeuristic about British fascists' transgressive behaviour – placed emphasis on her criminal pedigree. She was described as 'an ex-Suffragette, who has convictions for wilful damage, arson, assault on police etc. incurred in connection with her "votes for women" activities'. Home Office Papers (HO144/20140/102-120), PRO.

53. 'Prospective BU parliamentary candidates', *Action*, No. 40, 21 November 1936.

54. While 10 per cent of BUF prospective parliamentary candidates were women, for the general election of 1935 only 3.2 per cent of Conservative candidates, 6.3 per cent of Labour and 6.8 per cent of Liberal candidates were women, and throughout the inter-war period only 36 women sat in the House of Commons.

55. 'Northampton meets prospective BU candidate: Mosley's great meeting', *Action*, No. 41, 28 November 1936.

56. 'Fascism will mean real equality: by an old suffragette', *Blackshirt*, No. 96, 22 February 1935.

57. From the Governor of Holloway, 6 February 1942, Home Office Records (HO45/24891/444), PRO. The recollections of another former internee tells us something of how Elam, a woman in her sixties, endured prison life: 'I met Mrs Norah Elam when I was in F Wing in Holloway. I was a little in awe of her – she was of course a much older woman, and highly intelligent and erudite. Lady Mosley sometimes invited me to her cell with a few others for a small friendly get-together. All sorts of topics – art, music, literature etc. were discussed, and Mrs Elam was invariably there. ... I was never close enough to her to hear about her suffragette experiences, but she was certainly a staunch member of BUF.' Letter from Louise Irvine to the author, 6 May 1996.

58. 'Women as orators: the woman's part in British Union', *Action*, No. 151, 14 January 1939.

59. *Ibid.*

60. D. Bell, 'Women's world: by women for men and women', *Action*, No. 199, 6 January 1938.

61. N. Elam, 'Fascism, women and democracy', pp. 290–8.

62. N. Elam, 'J'ACCUSE: failure of the women's movement', *Action*, No. 138, 8 October 1938.

63. 'A convinced militant suffragette myself, I cannot help feeling that we started a fire that has consumed far more than we had envisioned.' Allen and Heyneman, *Woman at the Cross Roads*, p. 56.

64. M. S. Allen, 'Women's responsibilities', *Action*, No. 220, 23 May 1940.

65. See N. Elam, 'Suffragette in anti-fascist circus' and 'Women's anti-fascist circus', *Blackshirt*, No. 234, 23 October 1937.

66. Elam, 'Fascism, women and democracy', pp. 290–8.

67. P. Alderidge, 'Women demand results: valueless vote', *Action*, No. 121, 11 June 1938.

68. *Blackshirt*, No. 58, 1 June 1934.

69. When it came to the anti-war campaign, however, the woman's vote took on a renewed significance and was represented as having a positive role to play in the bid for peace: 'Rise Up! the remedy is in your hands. You have the vote for which an earlier band of brave women fought. Use your right, it is not too late. Demand peace.' A. K. Wood, 'Stop this war: to British women, wives, mothers, daughters and sisters', *Action*, No. 186, 23 September 1939.

70. To varying degrees, all three exhibited sympathy for the BUF's policy of racialism and anti-Semitism. Richardson wrote articles condemning the anti-Christian act of profiteering and usury, and saw the freedom of British workers threatened by 'the wage-slavery of the Orient'. M. Richardson, 'New and old Rome', *Blackshirt*, No. 75, 28 September 1934. In her list of charges against inter-war feminists, Elam observed how 'they once again wear the primrose in memory of the Jew Disraeli, the rosette in honour of Sir Herbert Samuel, the red emblem in commemoration of Karl Marx'. See Elam, 'Women and the vote'. When Allen's home in Nanquindo Valley, St Just, was searched by officers of the Special Branch in 1940, they found copies of many anti-Semitic pamphlets and books, including the works of Arnold Leese, leaving little doubt of her views on the 'alien menace'. Home Office Papers (HO144/21933/345-346), PRO.

7 'It Is Only Justice to Grant Women's Suffrage': Independent Labour Party Men and Women's Suffrage, 1893–1905

Laura Ugolini

Men in the Independent Labour Party (ILP) are usually associated with support for women's suffrage and some of them make their appearance in suffrage histories, particularly individuals such as Keir Hardie and Philip Snowden, the miner turned journalist and the crippled ex-civil servant, who were both prominent ILP members.[1]

However, a close look at the period from 1893 to 1905 reveals interesting variations in their attitudes as well as changes over time. While ILP support for women's suffrage was – at least on paper – well established by 1905, the prior arguments for and against it provide insights into a group of socialist men – men who shared common ideological baggage which affected their views not only on women's enfranchisement, but also on the roles of women and men in society generally.

As long ago as 1978 Brian Harrison provided a study of opponents of women's suffrage, many of whom were men,[2] but only recently have historians turned their attention to men who supported the movement.[3] And just as Karen Hunt has challenged the stereotypical image of the Social Democratic Federation (SDF) as being composed of at best anti-feminist and at worst misogynist men, so it is time to reassess the position of ILP men.[4] Their attitudes towards women's enfranchisement must be placed within the context of their identities as socialists and as men, and changes and developments reconsidered.[5]

This chapter, which covers the period from 1893, the year of the ILP's foundation, to 1905, the year which marked the onset of the Women's Social and Political Union's (WSPU) militancy, delves into male ILPers' attitudes to women's enfranchisement before 'suffrage' became headline news. The years prior to the beginning of the militant suffrage campaign can be divided into two periods, with the central break being the general election of 1895. Although the 44,000 votes received by 32 socialist parliamentary candidates (including four fielded by the SDF) have been described as 'not an unsatisfactory total',[6] the fact remains that none of the ILP's candidates was elected. Perhaps an even greater blow to members' morale was the fact that Keir Hardie (at the time the party's president) lost his seat in West Ham South. This setback led to a considerable shift in the ILP's ideology, and also in its attitude towards women's emancipation.

The ILP was founded in 1893 when around 120 delegates, mostly from the industrial north of England and Scotland, met in Bradford. Its antecedents can be found on the one hand in the context of long-standing demands for the representation of the labouring classes on governing bodies – demands which certain sections of the labour movement felt the main political parties had not satisfied. On the other, the impetus to form the ILP can be found in the 'revival' of socialism which had taken place in the 1880s and 1890s, and which had also led to the establishment of a number of other socialist societies – the SDF, Socialist League and Fabian Society – in 1884.[7] From its first conference, the ILP was committed not only to obtaining the election of Labour MPs, but also to achieving the collective ownership of the means of production, distribution and exchange.

As the title of the party suggests, the ILP's immediate aim was to ensure the representation of 'labour' on public bodies independently of both the main parties, as neither Liberals nor Tories were seen as capable of representing the interests of the 'workers'.[8] However, the ILP's ultimate aim was the achievement of the economic emancipation of the worker and the establishment of a socialist society. ILP electoral politics, both at a national and at a local level, were engaged with the aim of establishing a 'socialist commonwealth'.[9]

As a result, 'political' reforms were perceived as largely irrelevant to the needs of the working class and were constantly downplayed, with priority given instead to industrial, economic change.[10] This attitude led to a remarkable lack of interest in campaigns for political reforms, including those relating to the franchise. It was assumed that the workers whose independent representation in Parliament and local government was being sought already possessed political power. This was in spite of the fact that as late as 1911 only about 59 per cent of the adult male population was registered to vote in parliamentary elections.[11] Significantly, women's suffrage was *never* mentioned as a necessary precondition for the establishment of labour representation in Parliament. The outcome was the advocacy of a form of emancipation for 'workers' from which women (in addition to a good number of men) were in fact debarred.

Therefore, it is within this context of the ILP's rejection of what it saw as a liberal-radical emphasis on the primary importance of political reforms[12] that support among ILP men for women's suffrage must be placed. This rejection explains the decision taken at the Bradford conference of 1893 to shelve a motion which had included adult suffrage and payment of election expenses and replace it with a motion 'in favour of every proposal for extending electoral rights and democratising the system of government'. Shaw Maxwell, an ex-land reformer who became the ILP's first general secretary, considered that this made the party's position clear without laying it open to accusations of taking planks out of 'ordinary political parties'.[13]

There is no evidence of any substantial contact between male ILPers and suffrage organizations before the twentieth century. Individuals such as Richard Pankhurst, a lawyer active in radical causes in Manchester since the 1860s (including women's suffrage) and a leading member of the Women's Franchise League, who joined the ILP together with his wife, Emmeline Pankhurst, in 1894, were the exception rather than the rule.[14] Nevertheless, many within the ILP were clearly aware of the existence of a women's suffrage movement and looked favourably on its demands. At the ILP's 1895 annual conference an explicit commitment was made to women's suffrage which was partly a result of the pressure exerted by the Glasgow Women's Labour Party and its representative, Isabella Bream Pearce. At Keir Hardie's suggestion, the original National Administrative Council (NAC) proposal that 'the ILP is in favour of every proposal for extending electoral rights and democratising the system of government' was amended to include 'to both men and women'.[15]

The wording clearly left the door open for the possibility of supporting a measure of women's suffrage in advance of full adult suffrage, and on some occasions this opportunity was taken up. One instance was in June 1894 when ILPers, both male and female, were called upon in no uncertain terms to make their presence felt at a suffrage meeting organized by the North of England Society for Women's Suffrage at the Manchester Free Trade Hall: 'Verily, if any recreant stays away for any less cause than his own funeral, I will pronounce upon him, that new, improved malediction which I have hitherto strictly reserved for city councillors and compositors'.[16]

Nevertheless, the reasons why such support should be given were hardly ever spelled out. References to women's suffrage before the general election of 1895 tended to be incidental and brief. A contradiction in ILP policy existed between supporting a form of emancipation for 'workers' which used political power as a tool while scorning it as an end in itself, and supporting another for 'women' which centred on the empowerment brought by political enfranchisement.

It is possible, although never explicitly stated, that a democratic franchise was not really considered by male ILPers to be essential to the establishment of a 'socialist commonwealth'. It may have been assumed that a restricted number of (presumably male) working-class voters would have been able to achieve this commonwealth for the benefit of all the 'workers'. It is important to note that the definition of 'worker' deployed here included working-class women; it is certainly the case that, to a remarkable extent, both working-class men and women were portrayed by ILP men as waged workers who shared an experience of workplace exploitation. For both sexes waged work was portrayed as badly paid drudgery in poor and sometimes dangerous conditions: Manchester tramway men were compared with girl shop workers, male miners and engineers with sewing girls. Their very bodies marked both sexes off from the rest of the population: the man 'with his bowed and twisted body ... his legs bent with much standing and moving about under heavy burdens', while for the woman, 'the good colour fades, the teeth decay, the form becomes scraggy, the voice harsh and quarrelous [sic]'.[17] Both therefore would benefit from changes in the economic system which would result from the establishment of a socialist society.

At this stage ILP men placed very little emphasis on the identification of women as domestic beings, although by the same token there was little concern about their domestic problems. In 1895 Keir Hardie received a letter demanding that 'you should arrange that women like myself work eight hours in our families and no more'. However, he effectively managed to evade the issue of domestic drudgery by simply observing that socialists should be as pleasant at home as they were outside.[18] Excessive attachment to the domestic sphere on the part of women was actually condemned as detrimental to the development of a strong commitment to the labour movement. Nevertheless, it is significant that such attitudes were not mirrored in male socialists' own domestic practices: a domesticated wife was clearly deemed essential to their comfort and well-being. In his autobiography Robert Smillie, the ILPer and Scottish miners' leader, recalled that 'wherever my duties called me, however long they kept me away, the children and the home were cared for with uncomplaining devotion'.[19] Such recollections give no indication that male ILPers, even if they did publicly support women's emancipation, undertook household chores in order to enable their wives to pursue political interests.[20]

Although the identification of women within the broad category of 'worker' can explain why women's suffrage was not considered a necessary precondition to the establishment of independent labour representation, it does not really explain the continued presence among male party members of support for women's suffrage. On the contrary, given the emphasis placed on economic change, one would expect to find a condemnation of special attention being devoted to grievances relating to women outside their role as 'workers'. For example, in a letter published in the *Labour Leader*'s women's column,[21] 'X' recognized the injustice of women's lower wages in the workplace and unpaid drudgery in the home, but considered these to be simply side issues compared to the really important question of workers' industrial emancipation. He believed that women's oppression was one of the consequences of the timeless 'scramble for power and property', with its ideology of

130   Laura Ugolini

aggressive individualism. 'X' concluded, unsurprisingly, with the view that the only effective solution could be the establishment of a socialist society. After all, '*All* wage earners are in a state of "absolute dependence on the whims" not of men, but of an all-pervading spirit of mutual hostility named "competitive commercialism".' 'X' did not mention women's suffrage, but it is unlikely that he would have viewed this with a greater degree of approval than other issues relating to women's specific exploitation. It was only through socialism that workers, including women, were to achieve their real emancipation.[22] Such a position, however, was taken only very rarely.[23]

The reason for this lies in the ideology adopted and developed by male ILPers in the party's earliest years. Although the need for workplace changes was central to their thinking, there was at the same time a widespread belief that socialism involved also personal and cultural changes which were part of what has been termed the 'religion of socialism'. As Stephen Yeo has observed, all contemporary socialist organizations to some extent were influenced by a denial of the separation between personal and wider structural change, between politics, socialism and 'the rest of life'.[24] In consequence, disapproval of separating out women's issues on a par to that expressed by *Labour Leader* reader 'X' was rare. On the contrary, it was more common, particularly in the period up to 1895, to find a belief that socialist moral imperatives and desire for change should also be applied to the question of women's emancipation. Archibald Hunter, for example, pointed out that

> As a humble member of the Labour Party this question of women's social and economical [*sic*] freedom has often spurred me to greater effort on their behalf, because they are *my sisters*, because of the unnatural position the bulk of them occupy in our midst today, because we *must* have the women with us.[25]

Alongside such affirmations of cross-gender solidarity, the rejection by the ILP of any notion of class struggle also permitted the development of a positive attitude towards women's suffrage when in other circumstances it might have been rejected as a 'middle-class' measure. The existence of a conflict of interests between capital and labour was recognized, but the notion of the ILP as a class party was rejected, and instead claims were made about the representative nature of 'labour'. On this basis Fred Hammill argued in 1893 that 'The labouring community are more than a class, we are the nation. We constitute the overwhelming majority of the State, we produce the wealth of the country, and by this our cause is noble, sacred and dignified.'[26]

The dual emphasis in male ILPers' ideological positions on cultural as well as economic change allowed scope for some ILP men to be sympathetic to issues which affected women as a sex, such as their lack of the parliamentary franchise, and also their vulnerability in terms of their sexual and personal relations with men. Although male sexuality was not viewed entirely unproblematically, it was perceived that women would benefit most from changes in the nature of sexual relations. Most of the comments relating to such issues can be found in *Labour Leader* book reviews, especially of 'New Woman' fiction, for example Sarah Grand's *The Heavenly Twins*[27] or Iota's *A Yellow Aster*.[28] As Lucy Bland and other historians have pointed out, while the 'New Woman' was in some ways a journalistic invention, it nonetheless had its origin in social trends which had opened up new educational and employment opportunities for middle-class women. 'New Woman' fiction explored the problems encountered by women who took advantage of such opportunities, but also challenged conventional ideas about marriage and sexual relations.[29] Many ILP men were extremely sensitive to any action which might lead to accusations of sexual licence. When, for example, John Trevor, the founder of the Labour Church movement, remarried in 1895 only a few months after the death of his first wife, Keir Hardie wrote to him:

> You have given the movement such a blow as it will not recover from in a hurry, and if you really desire to serve it you can best do so by resigning all connections with the Labour Church. ... I value most, as you know, the moral side of our agitation, and it is there you have smitten us heavily.[30]

Despite the desire to maintain a 'respectable' image, 'New Woman' writers were mostly warmly welcomed and their arguments in favour of changes in the relations between the sexes accepted. Reviewers writing for the *Labour Leader* acknowledged the need for openness in discussing sexual matters and welcomed initiatives which aimed at educating young people and especially girls for 'the function they will by and by be called upon to fulfil in society'.[31] The importance of changing contemporary marital relations was recognized among others by one *Labour Leader* contributor going by the name 'the Octopus', who questioned whether

> anyone really believes that the mere form of legality can make the relation between man and woman pure and good? Does anyone see any real difference between the woman who sells herself to a man for a night and the woman who sells herself for a position, ease and luxury for life?[32]

The conclusion to be drawn from the ideas expressed by male ILPers in the period up to 1895 is that their support for women's suffrage cannot be traced to any one simple motive. Such support originated within two different, but coexisting, ideological frameworks, which also reflected both the ILP's building of a common 'workers'' identity and its emphasis on the importance of personal, cultural changes, rather than on class struggle. Women were identified as 'workers', and as such were considered to be part of, and represented by, the socialist movement.

They were also perceived to suffer from distinctive problems, in particular centring on their sexuality, which were treated with considerable sympathy: male ILPers were called upon to bring their commitment to end all forms of oppression to bear on their attitudes towards women's emancipation.

The general election of 1895, though, marked a considerable shift in ILP ideology with important consequences in terms of attitudes towards women's suffrage. Only for a brief period just after the election does there seem to have been any awareness of the possible negative effect the limited parliamentary franchise had on the party's electoral showing.[33] Even so, women's lack of the franchise was still rarely singled out for mention, and very soon, renewed optimism about the power of the workers at the ballot-box silenced any residual doubts. During a lecture in Glasgow, Keir Hardie, now no longer an MP, told his audience that in 'Glasgow, in West-Ham, all over the country the people are beginning to use their vote to assert their manhood'.[34] Keir Hardie's allusion to male workers *only* was a telling indication of the changes to come.

The ILP's commitment to parliamentary politics and its rejection of political reform as an end in itself remained unchanged. Instead it was believed that the solution to the party's electoral weakness would be found in the development of closer links with trade unions. This shift in policy eventually led to the establishment of the Labour Representation Committee in 1900, which in 1906 took the name of Labour Party, and this in turn was to have significant repercussions for ILP ideology.

Workers remained central to the ILP's ideology, and waged work under present conditions was still portrayed as exploitative. But now the 'worker' on whom attention was focused had become almost invariably male. Women workers did not entirely disappear from male ILPers' discourses after 1895, but a strand of thought developed which emphasized that waged work in general was 'unsuitable' for women. The Liverpool socialist John Edwards, for example, believed that in a socialist society women would not 'enter the arena of labour. ... The Socialists would leave the women to constitute the home, and let the lighter work now performed by them be given to men beyond forty.'[35] During the same period, images of women as wives and mothers multiplied. In this sense the *Labour Leader*'s fiction is particularly interesting. Whether it used 'fallen' women, or innocent girls in search of a marriage partner, as central characters, the attractiveness of marriage and domesticity were particularly emphasized.[36]

It is possible that this shift in the representation of women from workers to wives and mothers can be traced to the ILP's desire to form a closer partnership with trade unions, particularly given the latter's notoriously ambivalent attitude towards women's presence in the workplace. As Eleanor Gordon has shown in relation to Scotland, although by the turn of the century trade unionists were rejecting 'old' sectionalist policies, they still gave wholehearted 'support to the exclusive policies pursued by most of the skilled unions which sought to eliminate women from their trades'.[37] Furthermore, in his study of Preston, Michael Savage observes that it was the unions most threatened by female competition, such as the printers, which showed themselves most enthusiastic about the labour alliance.[38]

A strand of thought which emphasized the primacy of men's over women's work, and advocated the establishment of a family wage, became the dominant one among male ILPers. For most this was probably by no means a traumatic shift. R.J. Morris, for example, suggests that the Glasgow ILP was 'imbued with the ideology of Glasgow's "labour aristocracy"', whose ethos was based on the need to 'keep women out of the labour force, and then earn a family wage to maintain the domestic ideal'.[39] Even in the West Riding, where Isabella Ford's work among women textile workers, and Leeds tailoresses in particular, had received the support of sympathetic trade unionists and ILPers such as Ben Turner and Allen Gee throughout the 1890s, there were limits beyond which men were not prepared to go. As June Hannam has observed, 'It was one thing to support a general improvement in women's wages and work conditions, but quite another to challenge their secondary status within industry.'[40]

Other ideological shifts took place in the post-1895 period. First of all, the terms 'worker' and 'trade unionist' came increasingly to be used as if identical, being seen as forming the 'labour' whose independent representation was being sought. The class nature of this alliance was clear, although notions of 'class war' were still rejected and middle-class people continued to be welcomed into the party.[41] However, the gendered nature of this alliance was also clear: Labour was increasingly portrayed as a masculine entity. In a flight of rhetoric, a contributor to the *Labour Leader* (possibly Keir Hardie) asked:

> Are not the great Trade Union and Cooperative movements, children of the same great mother as ourselves? Were not they too born of the oppression of the worker? Were not they suckled at the same teats? They are our Elder Brothers, and as such must fight with us.[42]

The 'spiritual' side of socialism apparent before 1895 was not entirely forgotten. Keir Hardie, among others, continued to state his belief that socialism was more than a new economic system, but was rather an ethical and idealistic movement: 'a philosophy altogether beautiful'.[43] Nevertheless, the importance of economic, material change gained much greater prominence. By 1896 a strand of thought had developed among male ILPers which condemned as 'fads' any issues unconnected with economics. This did not necessarily imply a lack of sympathy for 'advanced' positions on issues such as marriage, but nevertheless considered them irrelevant to the socialist debate. As Gordon Holbeck pointed out, issues such as the relations between the sexes, antivivisection or Malthusianism were not unimportant, but were quite simply not socialism. Not surprisingly, perhaps, it was the economic question that was seen to unite and set apart socialists from other pressure groups. 'Are we divided as to the iniquitous workings of the private ownership of land and capital? Do we haggle and dispute over the unemployment problem?'[44]

This does not mean that issues considered to be of special interest to women were suddenly forgotten. Particular attention continued to be paid to the issues of marriage and of relations between the sexes, out of which women were still perceived to be the losers.[45] Once again, though, this did not lead to socialists questioning their own domestic practices or challenging the idea of the monogamous family unit. Solutions to perceived problems were also thin on the ground. The observation made in a *Labour Leader* editorial following a discussion of marriage, that 'It is time surely that women had a share in the making of laws which can so unjustly oppress them',[46] was very much an exception. The closest that male ILPers generally came to a solution was a vague implication that once established, socialism would right all wrongs. How it would do so was not discussed.[47]

Significantly, interest in exploring issues centring on the relations between the sexes did not remain constant throughout the period, but rather seems to have decreased. In the *Labour Leader*, for example, as attention to these issues diminished there was a significant increase in the number of short pieces, usually without comment, describing the often successful efforts of women in different parts of the world to enter professions, achieve educational qualifications or election to office, (especially in local government) and so on. Since these achievements would have involved almost exclusively middle-class women, this development appears rather inconsistent, especially if one considers the effort male ILPers were putting into presenting the ILP as a workers' and working-class party in this period. It is possible that this development made good sense, as the issues of opening up the professions and public office to women could be perceived as straightforward, and as not requiring a reworking of socialist priorities or personal politics. Furthermore, by 1900 any serious discussion in the *Labour Leader* about relations between the sexes had been largely substituted by jokey pieces, usually at the expense of wives, and usually relegated to the paper's last page.

On the whole, male ILPers' attitudes towards women's suffrage between 1895 and 1905 developed against a backdrop of an overwhelming emphasis on a working-class, masculine, trade unionist 'Labour' and a concentration on workplace, economic changes. As women lost their identity as members of 'Labour', a commitment to women's specific interests could also be dismissed as a 'fad'. Even so, there were still plenty of cases in which the justice of women's claim to the vote was accepted without discussion. The progress of women's suffrage all over the world was recorded with approval on the pages of the *Labour Leader*. In the spring of 1901, for example, the paper reported the vicissitudes of suffrage within the Norwegian Storthing, culminating with the granting of the communal franchise.[48]

Nevertheless, rather more critical attitudes towards separating out women's specific interests, including women's suffrage, were increasingly being expressed by some male ILPers. Views on this issue varied considerably, and yet they can all be traced back to shifts in wider ILP ideology as it emphasized its working-class status and at the same time the economic basis of its socialism. First, suffrage measures such as the suffrage bill before Parliament in the spring of 1897 were dismissed by some male ILPers as 'middle-class', and fears were expressed that women would use their votes to impede the establishment of socialism. In a letter to Lily Bell, published in the *Labour Leader*, 'C.H.' asked rhetorically whether women were not naturally more conservative than men. He also claimed that giving women the vote would retard the establishment of socialism.[49] Other male ILPers emphasized that 'a sixpence advance in wages' would improve women's position much more dramatically than the vote, although, as we have seen, these arguments were not accompanied by any renewed interest in the conditions of women workers.[50] On the other hand, a Robert M. stated in the *Labour Leader* that for women 'domestic' emancipation was more important than the political; what he meant exactly by 'domestic' is unclear, but his belief that women did not need the vote was on the other hand made perfectly clear.[51]

The argument put forward by Robert M. could easily be turned around, and suffrage justified in terms of women's domestic role and separate interests. An anonymous male ILPer, for example, wrote to Lily Bell,

> expressing his surprise that the mother who had given birth to him and to whom he owed his education in all that was good ... should be regarded by any as other than the equal of man ... it is only justice to grant women's suffrage all round.[52]

By the beginning of the new century, while support for women's suffrage was still widespread among male ILPers, it lay on shaky ideological foundations. Consequently, the articulation of an anti-suffrage position by some male ILPers was all too easy. It was in this rather uncertain context that things began to change noticeably between 1901 and 1902.

It was from 1901 that the party started to take notice of the activities among women workers of a group of Lancashire suffragists. Other historians have already chronicled the activities of those whom Jill Liddington and Jill Norris have termed 'radical suffragists': a group of activists which included the Manchester graduate Esther Roper and the Irish poet Eva Gore-Booth, and for a brief period Christabel Pankhurst, as well as a number of working-class women, such as Selina Cooper, Sarah Dickenson and Sarah Reddish, whose political background lay in socialism, trade unionism and the Women's Cooperative Guild.[53] Their activities, first noticed when Lancashire mill-workers took a petition to Parliament in March 1901, were obviously followed with approval by the party press.[54] They certainly galvanized a number of male ILPers into a more active stance towards suffrage. The Halifax town councillor James Parker, an early member of the Halifax ILP, pledged himself, if elected to Parliament, 'to put the vote for women first on his programme'.[55] The following year a deputation of radical suffragists found Philip Snowden's attitude towards women's enfranchisement 'exceedingly satisfactory'.[56] At a national level, in September 1902 it was decided that the chairman and the secretary of the party should sign a petition in favour of women's suffrage on behalf of the NAC.[57]

In the context of the discussion here, the significance of the radical suffragists lies in the fact that they were themselves active within the labour movement, and furthermore in the fact that they adopted and adapted the ILP's own rhetoric and ideology in order to advocate the extension of the franchise to working-class women. Just as the ILP advocated independent representation on governing bodies for 'workers' in order to improve their industrial position, so these activists advocated women's suffrage so that women waged workers could obtain their own 'independent representation' and improve their own economic and industrial position. In 1902 David Shackleton, the secretary of the Darwen weavers, had won a by-election victory as Labour candidate for the Clitheroe division. In response, ILP member Emmeline Pankhurst wrote to the *Labour Leader* that the women textile workers and trade unionists of the constituency, without whose financial support Shackleton could not have been elected, 'understand quite as clearly as does any Labour leader in the country how necessary it is to the workers to have direct representation in Parliament'.[58] The emphasis on both sides was – once again – on the identification of both men and women with waged workers.

The challenge this new strand of thought presented to male ILPers is obvious. If they were to endorse it, the result would have been a subversion of accepted gender identities within ILP ideology; the association of 'Labour' with masculine workers could no longer have been taken for granted, nor the identification of women as domestic beings. The question is, how many male ILPers were prepared to take this step? 'Gavroche' (William Stewart, until 1904 a *Labour Leader* staff member) was one man who was prepared to endorse changes in the perception of gender relations. He pointed out that political equality is an essential corollary to economic equality. Labour is one and indivisible ... the claim for women's suffrage is, at bottom, the claim for the wage-earning woman for the opportunity to work out her economic emancipation on a footing of equality with wage-earning man.[59]

In Stewart's eyes, 'Labour' was composed of both male and female wage-earners, although he recognized that the latter suffered also from traditional assumptions of inferiority.

Unsurprisingly, attitudes among the majority of male ILPers were generally more ambivalent. After 1904 support for women's suffrage was expressed much more often in terms of the special role women could play in society. According to F. J. Sheur in a letter to the *Labour Leader*, they could put across 'the feminine point of view',[60] as well as becoming fit mothers of the socialist citizens of the future. After all, 'the woman who is a drudge only, will produce sons unworthy of the fathers who have gone before them'.[61] Even more revealing is the extent to which ILP men rationalized women's claim to the vote by drawing on an older, radical tradition, which emphasized the importance of political reform as an end in itself and which they had seemingly rejected when they chose to place greater prominence on the importance of economic, rather than political, reforms.

However, identification with this radical tradition of political reform was developed in the first decade of the twentieth century under new circumstances, in particular in the context of the debate then gathering steam over the relative value and expedience of adult versus equal suffrage. In spite of male ILPers' differing views, both equal and adult suffragists shared a rejection, sometimes explicit, of the radical suffragists' rhetoric, and both used similar language to justify why women should be enfranchised. Adult suffragists chose to emphasize that equal suffrage would enfranchise only propertied women. As William Anderson[62] put it in a letter to the *Labour Leader*,

> It is inconsistent for a Socialist party to favour a limited bill, which would extend the vote to middle-class and rich women, while the vast majority of working-women would not qualify even as lodgers. ... It is inconsistent for a socialist to bolster up a class disability under the guise of removing a sex one.[63]

At times adult suffragist men did betray a certain impatience with a measure which they hardly considered vital anyway. As Albert Mitchell, the Stockton representative at the 1905 ILP conference, put it, 'there were other measures of much greater importance than ... the Enfranchisement Bill'.[64] But more telling still was the reluctance to place what were termed 'sex' issues at the forefront of the ILP agenda:

> Every industrial evil which afflicts women afflicts men to a greater or lesser degree. The evils we want to remove are not confined to one sex. ... The

conviction of the unity of the sexes in the Human Family so completely possesses the Socialist that he cannot separate the family into two classes.[65]

Male ILPers who favoured the introduction of an equal suffrage measure responded to the challenge of the adult suffragists in their party in two ways. First of all, they pointed out that equal suffrage had nothing to do with property, but was a measure to eliminate a 'sex disability'. As such, it was a necessary preliminary step towards adult suffrage.[66] In response to adult suffragists' dislike for the emphasis on 'sex' issues, they pointed out that sex disabilities *did* exist: 'The great historical subjection of women is a wrong that must be righted.'[67] Furthermore, the emancipation of women was in the party's own interest. At present, the party was divided between enfranchised male workers and unenfranchised female ones, and 'the effect of this inequality between men and women is … to engender conflicting interests, and to produce dissension instead of unity'.[68] Second, equal suffragists rejected the notion that only a tiny minority of working-class women would have been enfranchised by an equal suffrage measure.[69] The 1904 ILP conference had (unanimously) resolved to introduce an equal suffrage measure in Parliament. But 'some opposition having been raised against the Bill on the allegation that it will chiefly enfranchise middle and upper class women',[70] at an NAC meeting in January 1905 it was decided to send a questionnaire to branches in order to assess the proportion of working women (defined as 'those who work for wages, who are domestically employed, or who are supported by the earnings of wage-earning children'[71]) on municipal registers.[72] Although less than 50 out of 300 branches completed the questionnaire, the results were used as evidence that working-class women numbered 80 per cent of a female electorate of 1,250,000.[73]

Nevertheless, what these male equal and adult suffragists had in common was, in a way, as significant as their differences. In discourses about women's suffrage, the term 'citizen' replaced the term 'worker' as men's and women's equal rights and responsibilities within civil society were emphasized. This is not to suggest that when the emancipation of working men was being advocated, notions of 'citizenship' were not made use of. Despite Keir Hardie's and Ramsay MacDonald's[74] claims that words dear to Liberals such as 'right' and 'liberty' 'give no guidance in solving present-day problems',[75] ILPers had by no means entirely abandoned this rhetoric. John Bruce Glasier,[76] for example, reminded ILPers of what 'could be done in a year or two, by availing ourselves of our rights and performing our public duties as citizens'.[77] Nevertheless, there was no substitution of the economic identification of 'worker' with the political identification of the 'citizen'. Citizenship, founded on the possession of the vote, was rather an added dimension to working men's identity, and an additional weapon in their fight for economic emancipation.

Unlike for men, waged work was not a component of women's 'citizenship'; their role as 'citizens' took the place of that as waged workers. Adult suffragists believed that both men and women should be entitled to vote on the basis of their 'citizenship', not their property, or, as they called it, 'bricks and mortar'.[78] Equal suffragists agreed, but believed that at present women were in fact excluded by law from citizenship. As Keir Hardie never tired of pointing out,

> the law ... presumes the man to be a potential citizen upon whom the vote may be conferred. With him, the franchise is but the concession of a right already possessed but hitherto withheld. In the case of women, no such right exists, and must be created.[79]

According to male ILPers, women's claims to an equal franchise were based on their intellectual equality, as well as on notions of abstract 'justice'.[80] Old slogans such as 'taxation without representation is tyranny',[81] and all those 'who have to submit to the laws of the country should have a voice in shaping those laws',[82] were once more put to use. Harry Snell, the son of agricultural labourers, who had become a socialist in the late 1880s, asserted that he had never been 'a believer in the chivalrous fiction that women were the special guardians of moral treasure for mankind ... I ... approached the question of votes for women solely from the standpoint of citizenship'.[83]

To ILP men, masculinity was not a subject of discussion in the same way that class issues were. This was particularly true of the period after 1895, as the gendered nature of the party's ideology became more entrenched, and 'labour' came to be seen as composed of male trade unionists. It was femininity and 'the woman question' which were the subject of discussion. Out of the recognition that women suffered from special disabilities, and at the same time possessed distinctive qualities, there developed positive attitudes towards women's suffrage. Nevertheless, support for women's suffrage was made to fit within the background of a strongly masculine socialism, rather than to challenge it. Male ILPers for the most part rejected radical suffragists' advocacy of votes for women in their guise as waged workers. Instead, both equal and adult suffragists elaborated an older, 'radical' language in order to emphasize women's claim to citizenship. But even if the radical suffragists were unable ultimately to subvert the gendered nature of male ILPers' socialism, they were nevertheless successful in raising enormously the profile of suffrage within the party, and were central in ensuring its support for the extension of the franchise to women on the same basis as men.

The cautious and variable attitudes towards women's suffrage adopted by male ILPers were soon to be overwhelmed by a rapid, and for some unexpected, upsurge in suffrage agitation by women within their own party ranks, including after 1903 socialist women in the WSPU. As Russell

Smart put it, although significantly choosing to ignore the suffrage agitation of the past forty years,

> The ILP has hitherto deliberately ignored constitutional tinkering and political reform in order to concentrate popular attention upon economic questions. Political fruit has, however, a habit of ripening suddenly.... Women's enfranchisement, for example, has been sprung upon us, with alarming suddenness.[84]

The actions of a renewed and vigorous women's suffrage movement forced even the most reluctant among male ILPers to recognize that an easy dismissal of 'constitutional tinkering' was no longer acceptable.

Notes

1. See, for example, E. S. Pankhurst, *The Suffragette Movement: An Intimate Account of Persons and Ideals*, London, Virago, 1977 (first published 1931); J. Liddington and J. Norris, *One Hand Tied Behind Us: The Rise of the Women's Suffrage Movement*, London, Virago, 1994 (first published 1978).

2. B. Harrison, *Separate Spheres: The Opposition to Women's Suffrage in Britain*, London, Croom Helm, 1978.

3. A. V. John and C. Eustance (eds), *The Men's Share? Masculinities, Male Support and Women's Suffrage in Britain, 1890–1920*, London, Routledge, 1997.

4. K. Hunt, *Equivocal Feminists: The Social Democratic Federation and the Woman Question 1884–1911*, Cambridge, Cambridge University Press, 1996.

5. Such an analysis must be placed alongside studies which have focused on ILP women. See, for example, J. Hannam, *Isabella Ford*, Oxford, Basil Blackwell, 1989; J. Liddington, *The Life and Times of a Respectable Rebel: Selina Cooper 1864–1946*, London, Virago, 1984.

6. H. Pelling, *Origins of the Labour Party 1880–1906*, Oxford, Oxford University Press, 1965 (first published 1954), p. 167.

7. Pelling, *Origins*; D. Howell, *British Workers and the Independent Labour Party 1888–1906*, Cambridge, Cambridge University Press, 1983.

8. *Labour Leader* (hereafter *LL*), 9 March 1895; R. H. Smart, *The Independent Labour Party: Its Programme and Policy*, Manchester, Labour Press, 1893, pp. 14–15.

9. *LL*, 27 April 1895.

10. *LL*, 8 May 1891. See also 31 December 1892.

11. N. Blewett, 'The franchise in the United Kingdom 1885–1918', *Past and Present*, No. 32, December 1965, pp. 27–56.

12. Anon., *To the Workers of Great Britain and Ireland: Greetings*, ILP Circular No. 1, April 1894, ILP 5, 1894/14, ILP Archive, British Library of Political and Economic Science, London School of Economics. See also

L. Barrow and I. Bullock, *Democratic Ideas and the British Labour Movement, 1880-1914*, Cambridge, Cambridge University Press, 1996, pp. 75-87.

13. ILP Conference Report, 1893, p. 12. But see also P. Thane, 'Labour and local politics: radicalism, organised labour and party politics in Britain, 1850-1914', in E. Biagini and A. Reid (eds), *Currents of Radicalism: Popular Radicalism, Organised Labour and Party Politics in Britain, 1850-1914*, Cambridge, Cambridge University Press, 1991, pp. 261-70.

14. For the earlier period of suffrage activity see S. S. Holton, *Suffrage Days: Stories from the Women's Suffrage Movement*, London, Routledge, 1996, pp. 7-90.

15. ILP Conference Report, 1895, p. 10.

16. *LL*, 23 June 1894; 30 June 1894. See also 19 May 1894.

17. J. Leatham, *Was Jesus a Socialist?*, London, ILP Publication Department, n.d. (*c.* 1890), pp. 10-11. But see also the different features highlighted for each sex.

18. *LL*, 27 April 1895.

19. R. Smillie, *My Life for Labour*, London, Mills and Boon, 1924, pp. 28-9.

20. B. Turner, *About Myself, 1863-1930*, London, Humphrey Toulmin, 1930, pp. 73-4; G. Lansbury, *My Life*, London, Constable, 1928, pp. 76-9.

21. Until 1904, when it was bought by the party, the *Labour Leader* was owned and edited by Keir Hardie. Although it emphasized its role as the ILP's 'unofficial' newspaper, it reflected to a large extent Keir Hardie's own views. The women's column was written by the Glasgow feminist and socialist Isabella Bream Pearce, under the pseudonym of 'Lily Bell'. See H. Lintell, 'Lily Bell: socialist and feminist, 1894-1898', unpublished MA thesis, Bristol Polytechnic, 1990.

22. *LL*, 10 November 1894.

23. *LL*, 2 February 1895; 4 May 1895.

24. S. Yeo, 'A new life: the religion of socialism in Britain, 1883-1896', *History Workshop Journal*, Issue 4, Autumn 1977, pp. 5-56.

25. *LL*, 4 August 1894. See also C. W. Pearce to J. K. Hardie, 9 March 1894, Francis Johnson Correspondence, ILP 4, 94/42, ILP Archive.

26. F. Hammill, *The Necessity of an Independent Labour Party*, Newcastle, J. Dowling, 1893, p. 11.

27. *LL*, 5 May 1894.

28. *LL*, 23 June 1894.

29. L. Bland, *Banishing the Beast: English Feminism and Sexual Morality 1885-1914*, London, Penguin Books, 1995, pp. 143-9; E. Showalter, *Sexual Anarchy: Gender and Culture at the Fin de Siècle*, London, Virago, 1992, pp. 38-58.

30. J. K. Hardie to J. Trevor, 23 April 1895, Francis Johnson Correspondence, ILP 4, 95/78, ILP Archive.

31. *LL*, 16 June 1894. See also 11 May 1894.
32. *LL*, 2 June 1894. See also 2 March 1895.
33. *LL*, 3 August 1895.
34. *LL*, 19 November 1898. See also 2 April 1898; 7 May 1898.
35. J. Edwards, *What Is Socialism?*, ILP Platform Leaflet No. 25, 21 December 1901, ILP 6, uncatalogued, 'box 56', ILP Archive. See also Anon., *Labour Laws for Women: Their Reasons and Their Results*, London, City of London ILP, 1900.
36. *LL*, 23 May 1896; 21 November 1896; 5 August 1899. Notable for its absence, once more, despite the belief in the appropriateness of the domestic environment for women, was any concern for women's specific needs, for example in relation to housing. See, for example, H. R. Smart, *Municipal Socialism*, Manchester, Labour Press, n.d. (*c.* 1895).
37. E. Gordon, *Women and the Labour Movement in Scotland 1850-1914*, Oxford, Clarendon Press, 1991, p. 89. Gordon makes the interesting suggestion that in Scotland's socialist circles it was women (although certainly not all women) who defended women's right to work.
38. M. Savage, *The Dynamics of Working-Class Politics: The Labour Movement in Preston, 1880-1940*, Cambridge, Cambridge University Press, 1987, pp. 152-6.
39. R. J. Morris, 'The ILP, 1893-1932: introduction', in A. McKinlay and R. J. Morris, *The ILP on Clydeside, 1893-1932: From Foundation to Disintegration*, Manchester, Manchester University Press, 1991, p. 13.
40. J. Hannam, '"In the comradeship of the sexes lies the hope of progress and social regeneration": Women in the West Riding ILP, *c.* 1890-1914', in J. Rendall (ed.), *Equal or Different: Women's Politics 1800-1914*, Oxford, Basil Blackwell, 1987, especially pp. 223-5. See also L. Ugolini, '"By all means let the ladies have a chance": *The Workman's Times*, independent labour representation and women's suffrage, 1891-4', in John and Eustance (eds), *The Men's Share?*, pp. 62-87.
41. J. B. Glasier, *Labour: Its Politics and Ideals*, London, Independent Labour Party, 1903.
42. *LL*, 6 April 1901.
43. J. K. Hardie, *Young Men in a Hurry*, London, Labour Leader, n.d. (*c.* 1898), p. 5. See also *LL*, 9 October 1897; 12 August 1899.
44. *LL*, 14 March 1896. See also *ILP News*, June 1898.
45. *LL*, 10 October 1896; 12 December 1896; 22 July 1899.
46. *LL*, 2 July 1898.
47. *LL*, 10 October 1896; 3 April 1897; 22 July 1899.
48. *LL*, 30 March 1901; 18 May 1901; 25 May 1901; 8 June 1901.
49. *LL*, 5 December 1896. See also 27 February 1897; 5 June 1897.
50. *LL*, 27 February 1897. See also 5 December 1896.
51. *LL*, 27 February 1897.
52. *LL*, 2 October 1897.
53. Liddington and Norris, *One Hand Tied Behind Us*. See also

G. Lewis, *Eva Gore-Booth and Esther Roper: A Biography*, London, Pandora Press, 1988.
54. *LL*, 23 March 1901. See also 28 November 1903; 12 March 1903.
55. *LL*, 28 November 1903.
56. *LL*, 29 July 1904. In April 1904 Snowden still adopted an adultist position, but by the beginning of 1905 he was supporting equal suffrage. His view had changed, probably through the combined pressure of Leeds socialist Isabella Ford and of his future wife, Ethel Annakin, both active ILPers. Hannam, *Isabella Ford*, pp. 91, 110-11.
57. NAC minutes, 29/30 September 1902, ILP 1, 1/4, ILP Archive.
58. *LL*, 2 August 1902. The arguments in favour of women's suffrage expressed by Emmeline and Christabel Pankhurst in this period were similar to those of the radical suffragists. I have found no evidence, though, that Emmeline was directly involved in their campaigns.
59. *LL*, 9 January 1904.
60. *LL*, 30 April 1904.
61. J. K. Hardie, 'Speech by Mr. Keir Hardie, M. P., at Chelsea, February, 1902', in *What Labour Leaders Think of Women's Suffrage*, London, National Union of Women's Suffrage Societies, 1909, p. 3. See also *LL*, 21 April 1905.
62. A prominent member of the Shop Assistants' Union, before leaving it in 1907, Anderson in 1908 had joined the NAC. In 1911 he married Mary Macarthur, the women's trade union organizer. J. M. Bellamy and J. Saville, *Dictionary of Labour Biography*, London, Macmillan, Vol. 2, 1974, pp. 11-16.
63. *LL*, 18 November 1904. See also 16 April 1904; 25 November 1904; 27 January 1905; 28 April 1905. For a discussion of the adult versus equal suffrage debate, which, though, underestimates the extent of support for adult suffrage within the ILP, see S. S. Holton, *Feminism and Democracy: Women's Suffrage and Reform Politics in Britain 1900-1918*, Cambridge, Cambridge University Press, 1986, pp. 53-66. See also Hunt, *Equivocal Feminists*, pp. 152-84.
64. *LL*, 28 April 1905.
65. *LL*, 16 April 1904. See also 18 November 1904.
66. *LL*, 7 October 1904; 25 November 1904; 9 December 1904; 3 February 1905; 17 February 1905; 28 April 1905.
67. *LL*, 3 February 1905.
68. *LL*, 7 October 1904.
69. *LL*, 9 December 1904; 3 February 1905.
70. P. Snowden and F. Johnson, 'Census of women municipal voters', 4 March 1905, ILP 3, cards 47-48, item 52, ILP Archive.
71. Snowden and Johnson, 'Census'.
72. NAC minutes, 28 January 1905, ILP 1, 1/5, ILP Archive.
73. *LL*, 7 April 1905; 5 May 1905. J. K. Hardie, *The Citizenship of Women: A Plea for Women's Suffrage*, London, Independent Labour Party, 1906 (first published 1905), pp. 12-13. The questionnaire's

methodology was the subject of contemporary controversy. See, for example, *LL*, 7 April 1905.

74. A Scot of modest background, who had moved to London in search of a career, MacDonald was then a member of the ILP's NAC, and was soon to become the LRC's first secretary. D. Marquand, *Ramsay MacDonald*, London, Jonathan Cape, 1972.

75. J. K. Hardie and J. R. MacDonald, 'The Independent Labour Party's programme', *Nineteenth Century*, No. 263, January 1899, p. 21.

76. An architectural draughtsman by trade, in 1897 Bruce Glasier was elected to the NAC, by which time both he and his wife, Katharine Bruce Glasier, were well known as tireless speakers and propagandists. L. Thompson, *The Enthusiasts: A Biography of John and Katharine Bruce Glasier*, London, Victor Gollancz, 1971.

77. J. B. Glasier, *On Strikes*, Glasgow, Labour Literature Society, n.d. (*c.* 1897).

78. *LL*, 28 April 1905. See also 16 April 1904.

79. *LL*, 9 December 1904. See also Hardie, *The Citizenship of Women*, p. 10; *LL*, 9 December 1904; 3 February 1905; 19 May 1905.

80. *LL*, 26 March 1904; 16 April 1904.

81. *LL*, 20 May 1904.

82. *LL*, 18 November 1904; 17 February 1905.

83. H. Snell, *Men, Movements and Myself*, London, J. M. Dent, 1936, p. 182.

84. *LL*, 9 August 1907.

8 Between the Cause and the Courts: The Curious Case of Cecil Chapman

Angela V. John

The image of the suffragette in prison, denied her freedom as well as the vote, is a familiar one. Yet there were also other ways in which the cause of women's suffrage could come into dramatic collision or even collusion with the law. The marked presence of lawyers active in male support groups advocating women's suffrage is an under-researched area and this chapter focuses on such a lawyer.

Cecil Maurice Chapman is a particularly intriguing individual since he was also simultaneously a Metropolitan Police magistrate, a law enforcer as well as a potential law breaker. An active member of several women's suffrage societies, he sat on the executive committee of the largest of the men's support groups, the Men's League for Women's Suffrage (MLWS).[1] In 1911 he was elected chairman of this society, although rapid intervention from the Home Office ensured that he soon stood down.

Investigating the story behind this lawyer's enforced resignation raises questions about the significance of women's suffrage for a liberal-minded professional man radicalized by the politics of gender. It puts under the spotlight the sort of person who tended not to make headline news but could cause some consternation among the authorities behind the scenes. Indeed, it is surely no coincidence that suffragettes were never brought before him. Chapman's tale therefore reveals something of government fears about maintaining law and order at a time of heightened tension,[2] showing how easy it was to jump to erroneous conclusions about the MLWS. And it suggests that in the last resort, sympathetic men like Chapman still stood to lose much less than the women needed to gain. It thus demonstrates how women's suffrage always needs to be set against the wider context of gender relations, particularly expectations about the behaviour of men and women in the public domain.

At first sight Cecil Chapman (1852–1938) of Roehampton seems an unlikely rebel.[3] An Oxford graduate, he had been called to the Bar in 1878. He joined the south-eastern circuit and Surrey sessions. Between 1896 and 1898 he was the Conservative member for Chelsea on the

London County Council. A member of the Athenaeum Club, in 1899 after twenty years at the Bar this respectable establishment figure opted for what he dubbed 'the Courts of the Poor', becoming a Metropolitan Police magistrate.[4] During the years of suffrage militancy he was at Tower Bridge Court. A firm believer in explaining the workings of the law to the lay person, he became a frequent speaker at social and educational gatherings where he would advocate developments such as children's courts and the probation acts.

Neither did Chapman's membership of the MLWS denote revolutionary leanings. Founded on 2 March 1907 in the chambers of Herbert Jacobs, a middle-aged London barrister specializing in banking law, this all-male society sought to promote women's enfranchisement, arguing for the vote for women on the same terms as men.[5] It was constitutionalist in its methods, working through speeches and propaganda as a pressure group and publicist. It prided itself on being non-party and non-political, pre-dated anti-suffrage organizations and was overwhelmingly supported by men who already had the vote. Indeed, members argued that precisely because they were voters they commanded attention. Unlike the women – and indeed a sizeable proportion of working-class men – they were not requesting something for themselves. This gave them a useful rationale, providing a justification for their existence which marked them out from every other women's or mixed suffrage society. They argued that their rational demands must be heeded. It was their task, their duty, to get the voter to put pressure on the men in Parliament.[6] As civilized men of the new century, they presented themselves as progressive and caring. At times their apparent magnanimity could make them appear somewhat smug.

Suffrage men and women drew upon the past as well as the present to demonstrate that they were fighting a just cause. This involved a teleological argument for the completion of the evolution of democracy for both genders but they could also invoke historical examples to demonstrate how the present should learn from more enlightened eras. In a pamphlet called *Custodia Honesta*, Professor George Sigerson, who had been a member of the Royal Commission on Prisons in the 1880s, examined cases in Chartist and other earlier popular protests to demonstrate the retrogressive nature of the present government in relation to the treatment of political prisoners.[7] Even Magna Carta was invoked by pro-suffrage men in their argument that women were being denied justice.[8] In 'The argument from history', one of a series of articles commissioned by the MLWS for its handbook, the barrister J. Arthur Price stated the women's case by citing instances of medieval women exerting authority.[9]

Cecil Chapman would have found a number of other barrister members of the MLWS. The members so far identified (over 950)[10] include a significant percentage of academics, writers, clergy, solicitors and barristers. Ten per cent of the first 300 members were lawyers, perhaps reflecting the influence of their founder and chairman, Herbert Jacobs. On the whole they were established professionals. One of them described their contingent at a suffrage demonstration in London in June 1910 as 'a sober, grey-coated and somewhat grey-haired company in the middle of the army of triumphing women'.[11] The Liverpool barrister W. Lyon Blease, one of their younger members, published a book entitled *The Emancipation of English Women* (1910) as well as a pamphlet on the status of political prisoners, condemning forcible feeding in no uncertain terms.

Clearly the expertise of such men was valuable in giving validity and status to arguments about the questionable legality of the actions of police and government, as were the opinions of those doctors and surgeons who were prepared to speak out against the wishes of so many in the medical profession. Radical lawyers were hardly new to the cause. The first women's suffrage bill, introduced in Parliament in 1870 by Jacob Bright, had been drafted by the barrister Richard Pankhurst. The MLWS chairman, Herbert Jacobs (who was also a vice-president of the Jewish League for Women's Suffrage and a director of the International Women's Franchise Club), had long been active in suffrage circles.[12] He had been influenced as a young Liberal lawyer by John Stuart Mill's seminal work *The Subjection of Women* and knew Jacob Bright. Jacobs had even sat on the committee of the Central Society in the 1880s.[13]

Some suffragist lawyers became MPs. Despite the opposition of Mrs Pankhurst and other members of the Women's Social and Political Union (WSPU), who travelled to Pembrokeshire to obstruct the Liberal candidate in the by-election of 1908, the young Cardigan solicitor Walter Roch was successful. He was the first MLWS member to become an MP. A committed supporter of women's suffrage, he played a useful role on the cross-party Conciliation Committee, which worked hard to produce a compromise measure of suffrage.

A small number of pro-suffrage lawyers linked their profession to their political practice by defending suffragists and even themselves in court. The Irishman Tim Healy MP and Frederick Pethick-Lawrence, financial backer of the WSPU, provide two eminent examples of such commitment. For someone like Cecil Chapman, however, the situation was more complicated since he was not in private practice.

The iconography of suffrage was littered with references to justice. For example, Mary Lowndes's banner 'Justice – at the door', published by the National Union of Women's Suffrage Societies (NUWSS) in 1912, portrayed justice as a woman, thereby suggesting that by excluding women from the proposed reform bill they were also denying justice, which was traditionally represented symbolically in the form of a woman.[14] Such associations could also serve to distance male suffragists from militancy. Thus, Councillor H.M. Lloyd, chairing an NUWSS meeting at Merthyr Tydfil in 1912, stressed that 'The great women's cause was going to be won not by violence but by justice.'[15] One of the men's societies working for women's suffrage was actually called the Men's Committee for Justice to Women.

In a speech to the MLWS, Herbert Jacobs declared that men as well as women were slaves until suffrage freed them since men were at present 'bound to give support to this reform'.[16] Abstract concepts of natural justice and rights deserved and denied formed an important part of their arguments about women's need for the vote. At their Queen's Hall rally in 1909 the Reverend Silvester Horne declared that the first condition of social amelioration was that every class of the community should be able to stand before the state to demand justice.[17] For Chapman, legal and social justice for women became paramount in his speeches and writing although, unlike many pro-suffrage men, he was demanding reforms extending beyond simply granting the vote to women.

In 1911 Chapman published his *Marriage and Divorce* as the first book in the Woman Citizen series. This was a topical subject, given the publication of the majority and minority reports of the Royal Commission on Divorce. Chapman had personally given evidence to the Commission. He suggested in his book that marriage should be regarded as a civil contract and advocated a civil ceremony as the only valid legal marriage ceremony. In his view, religious services should be reserved for committed believers. He sought a higher legal age of marriage for both men and women, the compulsory maintenance of a wife and children, and a reform of the bastardy laws so that men and women shared equally responsibility for their children. Indeed, 'All distinction of sex should be abolished before the law, and everything should be done to create or maintain the freedom and equality of women in marriage.'[18] While carefully stressing that rather than undermining marriage he was actually seeking to increase respect for it, he nevertheless strongly urged, both here and in his speeches, the need to extend the grounds for legal separation and increase facilities for divorce. Gender equality in law must be paramount.

The MLWS printed Chapman's views in its monthly newspaper. In an article entitled 'Obedience in marriage' he ridiculed the notion that Saint Paul's injunctions were relevant to present law-making:

> It was to the women of Ephesus and Colossae in the first century of the Christian era that he was writing and it would be nothing short of a miracle if his injunctions were adapted to our present stage of civilisation upon anything except moral and spiritual ideas.[19]

He urged the evolution of a higher morality 'by substituting freedom and equality in the state of marriage for obedience and domination'. He attacked the restrictive and humiliating conditions facing many women within marriage, maintaining that obedience to any dictate but that of conscience and reason was as unbecoming to a woman as to a man. His conclusion was that it was time the people, and the Church in particular, expressed faith in the competence of women to take charge of their own lives.

Some MLWS members were enlightened enough to appreciate such thinking. Indeed, some who were men of the cloth were already challenging the Church's gendered strictures. For example, Chapman's brother, the Reverend Hugh B. Chapman MA, chaplain of the Chapel Royal, Savoy, conceived of women's suffrage as involving 'the whole reconstruction of the attitude of the sexes towards one another' and got into trouble with the Archbishop of Canterbury for his opposition to women's having to use the word 'obey' in the marriage ceremony.[20] When he officiated at the wedding of prominent suffragists Una Dugdale and Victor Duval, the Archbishop sent along two priests to insist on the bride obeying![21]

Both Chapmans appear to have understood that 'the fundamental question was the future of a particular idealisation of womanhood'.[22] Yet the majority of men viewed votes for women essentially as a central plank in a just and necessary move towards the democratization of society, a case of putting the matter straight. A more radical analysis which appreciated that the vote was only part of the need for a more fundamental readjustment of gender relations could appear quite threatening. Certainly Cecil Chapman's pronouncements on marriage and divorce offended some within his own suffrage society. The Reverend T. E. Lacey, for example, wrote a passionate letter to the MLWS paper repudiating Chapman's conception of marriage as a contractual relation.[23]

Chapman not only argued for legal change (and joined the Divorce Reform Union), but also implied that men as well as women needed to investigate their own practices. And even though it might be argued that he nevertheless subscribed to a predictable gendered notion of what constituted masculine and feminine characteristics, he at least believed that they were not immutable. In a speech for the MLWS given at the Queen's Hall, London, he stressed that

> the common interests of men and women could never be humanly dealt with till both sexes were represented. The spirit of dominance in man and the spirit of subservience in woman both must be removed: civilization demanded from men something of the gentleness associated with women, but also from women something of the fearlessness and independence which true manliness implied.[24]

It is highly debatable as to how far male suffragists were prepared to rethink their own sense of manhood even if they believed that women's lives should change. Carolyn Spring's examination of pro-suffrage men's speeches from within and beyond Parliament suggests that their perceptions of gender did not necessarily differ fundamentally from those of the 'antis'.[25] They tended to be predicated upon stereotypical, deeply entrenched wider assumptions about the nature of both women and men. Women's suffrage might appeal, and even appear as an early twentieth-century version of being 'politically correct', but it was not incompatible with these same men feeling challenged and worried by feminism and any questioning of accepted notions of masculinity. It was one thing to demand women's recognition as citizens. It was quite another to disturb personal politics, and a sense of manly worth. This partly explains why the concept of chivalry resonates through the language of pro-suffrage men. It is no coincidence that the point at which relations became most strained between men and women suffrage supporters was at the very time when women appeared to be repudiating their femininity through their assumption of militancy and at the same time denying men their customary role of being in charge.

It seems clear from Chapman's talks and books that his commitment to women's suffrage developed from his experience in the police courts, where he witnessed daily the injustices facing poor working-class women in particular. Although a supporter of women's suffrage since his student days, Chapman admitted that it was his dealings in the police courts which had brought home to him the realities of gender inequalities.[26] Jennifer Davis's research into the mid- and late nineteenth-century London police courts shows that they occupied a special role in the criminal justice system of the time, being used by the London populace to press for changes, resolve disputes and even as advice centres. She argues that the magistrates sometimes acted on behalf of their working-class clientele in ways which could bring them into conflict with the police. Apparently working-class women in particular used legal sanctions to give them protection. Although by the Edwardian period there had been some erosion of the advisory and non-punitive aspects of these police courts, it would seem that Chapman combined his progressive attitudes towards gender issues with subscribing to an older, humane tradition of administering law which recognized popular notions of seeking and utilizing social justice.[27] In July 1912, when the suffragette Elizabeth Robins was gathering material for a novel, it was to Chapman that she turned. Another suffragette, Evelyn Sharp, had first told her that Chapman 'is on our side'.[28] Robins therefore discussed his work with him, then attended his court. She was shocked by what she saw and heard – 'a strange and terrible lot of people' – yet also impressed by Chapman 'most humanly' resisting the imposition of unrealistically high fines.[29] A fellow member of the MLWS described him as 'just and tender on the bench to the poor and them that have no helper'.[30]

It does, however, also seem likely that Chapman's views on women's rights, especially in matrimonial law, were informed by events quite literally closer to home. His wife, Adeline Mary Chapman, who was also his cousin, had suffered an unhappy first marriage to the wealthy railway director Arthur Guest. When Guest, a former Tory MP for Poole, had unsuccessfully contested Southampton in 1888, his mother, the translator, businesswoman and collector Lady Charlotte Schreiber (formerly Guest), had commented in her journal that her son's cause had not been helped by the circulation of 'the old wicked lying story' that he was unkind to his wife.[31] The couple separated and Guest died in 1898, Adeline remarrying in 1900.

June Balshaw's research[32] is demonstrating the importance of political partnerships in advocating women's suffrage, and the Chapmans seem to provide yet another example of a husband and wife both committed to the cause. Adeline Chapman had been converted to women's suffrage at a meeting of anti-suffragists! She became president of the New Constitutional Society for Women's Suffrage and her niece and Cecil Chapman also actively supported the society (he sat on its committee in 1911).[33] Founded in 1910, it sought to unite all suffragists who believed in anti-government electoral policy and it urged, despite its own constitutionalist slant, abstention from public criticism of all those who adopted different methods for winning the vote. Adeline also participated in tax resistance and attended the 'Cat and Mouse' Committee. Mildred Mansel, Adeline Chapman's married daughter from her first marriage, became Honorary Secretary of the Bath WSPU and was imprisoned in Holloway in 1911 for breaking windows in the War Office.[34]

Cecil Chapman's own brushes with authority were not so dramatic, though considered no less serious since the Home Office clearly believed that suffrage activities were both inconsistent and incompatible with the position of police magistrate. A careful watch was kept on his activities, even when he appeared in highly respectable company. On 18 February 1909 the Conservative and Unionist Women's Franchise Association held a meeting at the Westminster Palace Hotel, London.[35] Its president, Lady Knightley, was in the chair and there was a marked presence of titled ladies. Chapman was one of the three speakers. He emphasized the primacy of women's suffrage, adding that when he viewed 'the glaring grievance and great injustice' facing women, he was 'not inclined to preach the gospel of patience'.

The meeting had been announced a week earlier in *The Times* with Chapman's name printed as a speaker. This had prompted Sir Albert De Rutzen, the Chief Magistrate, to consult the Home Office, then warn Chapman that it was undesirable for him, given his position, to participate in a suffrage gathering. Chapman conveyed the impression that he would withdraw. De Rutzen was therefore incensed when he read in the press that he not only had spoken but also appeared to be 'inciting woman suffragists to greater activity'.

Chapman's account of his behaviour is revealing. He was only too well aware that magistrates were not supposed to participate in public meetings of a contentious or political character or become connected with matters which might compromise their judicial role. With the increasingly frequent appearance of suffrage activists before the London courts, his situation was especially sensitive. In his defence he therefore sought to dissociate his remarks from any taint of militancy, stressing that the reference to 'patience' was simply an allusion to the words of the speaker who preceded him. This had been L. S. Amery, Unionist candidate for Wolverhampton, who had actually advocated 'patience with constant endeavour and constant persuasion' and implied that Unionism was a more urgent priority than suffrage. Chapman (who was to become a member of the Suffrage First Committee, which argued that women's suffrage was the most urgently needed of contemporary reforms and should take precedence over all others) explained that he had merely been responding to Amery's remarks. He stressed that his audience had *not* misunderstood him and that he had been quoted out of context by the press. He claimed that his speech had not been written in advance. After all, he had only expected to say a few words and, being abroad at the time when the meeting was announced, he had been surprised on his return to learn that he had been billed as a speaker. He had expected a small, private affair but when so many turned up and an overflow meeting had become necessary, he had merely obliged the needs of the moment by giving an impromptu speech. And like a wily lawyer summing up his client's activities and seeking to establish him as a responsible person, he made sure that he stressed how he always adhered to the rule that those in official positions should not take part in public political meetings. He expressed regret that a chapter of accidents had resulted in an unintentional contravention of the rules.

In the House of Commons the pro-suffrage MP MacNeill seized the opportunity to link Chapman's words to a plea for giving suffrage prisoners first-division status.[36] When the Home Secretary was then asked whether magistrates preaching politics should not be removed from their posts, Herbert Gladstone rehearsed Chapman's excuses but added that he personally felt it undesirable for magistrates to make speeches.

In fact Chapman continued to embarrass the magistracy and Home Office. And far from withdrawing from politics, he continued and even extended his public speaking. In 1910 he was described in *The Vote* as 'one of the most important and convincing speakers to be had on any suffrage platform'[37] and he helped defray the expenses of the MLWS when it moved from Bloomsbury to more strategically placed headquarters in the heart of Westminster. He marched with the MLWS in the vast suffrage demonstration of June 1910.

He used various means to exculpate himself from accusations of improper behaviour. He maintained a narrow definition of politics as synonymous with party politics and claimed that he was really simply describing his work experiences in his speeches even though he actually used these experiences to demonstrate how justice was continually denied to women. His audiences were still mainly composed of men and women committed to suffrage, some of whom were now personally familiar with both court and prison. He continued to address the essentially law-abiding societies such as the Conservative and Unionist Women's Franchise Association, the Hove Women's Suffrage Society, his own MLWS and special-interest groups such as the Actresses' Franchise League. He also spoke to militant groups such as the North Islington and Chelsea branches of the WSPU. He took part in a suffrage debate for the New Constitutional Society and in March 1911 moved the vote of thanks at a large MLWS rally at the Queen's Hall.[38]

Soon after this last public appearance he came close to losing his job. There were two incidents which alarmed the Home Office. The first was a meeting of the Chorley Wood branch of the WSPU at a local hotel on 25 May 1911.[39] Here, in familiar tones, Chapman stressed how the law disadvantaged women. He illustrated how they were not treated as responsible beings by citing the case of a man charged with deserting his wife and five children. She died in the workhouse but because the children were born out of wedlock he was not held responsible. Chapman referred to the 'nonsense' of the marriage vows and the degradation for women in saying they would obey: 'The law made the man a tyrant and the woman a "doormat".' He spoke of the advantage that women's equality before the law would bring to the entire community, suggesting that their contribution to the home should be remunerated financially, and at the same time he made some pointed remarks about the conditions of sweated workers. Here he was indirectly alluding to the statement made in Parliament in mid-March where it had been revealed that in future women's wages for making service dress trousers in the Army Clothing Factory in Pimlico were to be reduced. He was equally topical in his remarks about the Poor Law. A fortnight before his speech, Margaret Wynne Nevinson's play *In the Workhouse* had been performed in London by the Pioneer Players. Based on her stories about workhouse 'characters' in the *Westminster Gazette* which in turn emanated from her own considerable experience as a Poor Law Guardian, they had provided a damning indictment of women's vulnerability in relation to marriage and the Poor Law by an active member of the Women's Freedom League.[40]

The MP for Chorley Wood was the committed 'anti', Arnold Ward. One of the suffrage speakers, the Honourable Mrs Haverfield, had pointed to the irony of Mrs Humphrey Ward having to withdraw from an anti-suffrage meeting in Manchester because she was helping to get her son into Parliament. No doubt incensed by this reference to his mother, Arnold Ward drew Parliament's attention once more to Chapman's utterances.[41]

Once again the magistrate found himself having to account for his actions and their publicity. Chapman tried to exculpate himself by using some of the same excuses as before, a tactic which served to question both his sincerity and his opinion of his employers. He claimed, somewhat disingenuously, that the Chorley Wood meeting had been described in advance as 'a small social gathering intended to be of a purely educational character' – hardly a description most people would associate with the WSPU! He argued that the material for his talk was in the public domain, though he chose not to dwell on his construction and interpretation of that material and denied that he had actually accused the government of sweating women. Once again he pleaded that a reporter had misrepresented his words, an excuse that had to be taken seriously since so many newspaper articles *did* embellish the truth when it came to describing what were disparagingly called the 'antics' of the suffragettes.

Chapman also wrote a personal letter to the Under-Secretary of State, Sir Edward Troup. Here he explained that women's suffrage was for him 'a purely social and moral question entirely removed from party politics'. Troup, a Balliol man like Chapman, put in a good word for him. The Liberal Home Secretary Winston Churchill decided not to take action, largely because by now Chapman was facing a more serious charge and one potentially embarrassing to the Home Office since it raised questions about loyalty, law and order involving a stipendiary *Justice* of the *Peace*. On 16 May 1911 after a stormy MLWS meeting, Chapman (already on the executive committee) had beaten Jacobs by one vote and been elected their chairman. At the same meeting the committee had passed unanimously the resolution that:

> With a view to preventing the recurrence of the abuses which have occurred on previous occasions, the League, in the event of a renewal of public demonstrations by the Women's Suffrage Societies, shall organize a corps of witnesses who will be willing to serve at short notice.[42]

This had been sent one week later (on MLWS notepaper and signed by Chapman and the society's secretary) to the Chief Commissioner of Police. It had also been published in the MLWS newspaper.

Churchill was outraged by Chapman's endorsement of such a position, with its implied acknowledgement of police abuses and threats.[43] He deputized an embarrassed Chief Magistrate – who described Chapman's latest behaviour as 'monstrous' – to remonstrate with him, spelling out the gravity of the situation and requesting Chapman to withdraw from active participation in the work of the MLWS and any similar society. He stipulated that if he did not immediately provide a satisfactory response he must be dismissed forthwith: 'Such conduct in a Stipendiary Magistrate is quite intolerable.'

Chapman confirmed that the offending letter and signature were genuine but instead of expressing remorse, initially defended himself by stressing his responsibilities as the society's chairman. He was adamant that nothing contrary to the law had been contemplated and that no reflection was intended upon police behaviour. Indeed, he explained that he had agreed to become chairman only on the understanding that he would not have to take part in public occasions. How this lawyer chose to define such terms was not made clear.

The Home Office papers reveal that there was in fact considerable confusion about what exactly Chapman was chairing. Their reference to 'a society whose past activities have been closely associated with acts of illegality and disorder and in some cases violence' was hardly an accurate description of the MLWS. In fact, as Chapman soon realized, it was actually a reference to the rival, smaller men's support group, the Men's Political Union for Women's Enfranchisement (MPU), which the Home Office had confused with the MLWS. Founded in 1910, the MPU tended to represent a younger, less patient set of men than the MLWS and seems to have perceived itself as the male equivalent of the WSPU, sporting the latter's colours of purple, white and green (whereas the MLWS had its own colours of black and gold). It deliberately sought attention in ways which worried the MLWS and caused concern among suffragettes.

The MLWS, in contrast, was characterized by words rather than deeds, highly appropriate since it included so many writers and academics.[44] It prided itself on encompassing the spectrum of party politics and taking an incrementalist stance, though admittedly positions did change somewhat over time. As various suffrage bills faltered and as government positions and those of other political groupings shifted, so the MLWS was forced to come off the proverbial fence. Asquith's evident intention to prevent further discussion of the Conciliation Bill prompted it to hold, in September 1910, a special meeting where, by a majority of 136, it adopted a policy of distinct opposition to the government. The league had now, as they put it, 'crossed the Rubicon'.[45] Not surprisingly the veteran suffragist Walter McLaren and H. G. Chancellor, both Liberal MPs, had felt obliged to vote against such a move. Chancellor resigned from the committee, though he remained a paid-up member and was soon made a vice-president. In the December election the MLWS opposed all government candidates except those sitting Liberal members who had already proved themselves effective on the Conciliation Committee. It published lists (as did other suffrage societies) so that members were clear as to who should or should not be supported.

This anti-government stance lasted until July 1911. When, four months later, the future of the Conciliation Bill hung in the balance with Asquith's dangling of a Manhood Suffrage Bill, the MLWS found itself divided once more over tactics. It now agreed to oppose every parliamentary candidate who did not pledge himself to vote against the government on the third reading of the Reform Bill.

Yet none of this politicking amounted to conspiracy or activities of the sort now being encouraged by the WSPU. Many of the MLWS pronouncements were inevitably reactive, seeking to repair damage after the prevarications and betrayals of Asquith and Lloyd George. Compared with the MPU activists and in contrast to the militant women, MLWS meetings generally involved protracted debates and resolutions over policy and acceptable positions. Indeed, the war correspondent and journalist H.W. Nevinson was bored by the procedural tendencies of the MLWS and particularly critical of 'lawyer Jacobs', whom he found to be 'a great nuisance with points that could not win'.[46] Jacobs was an international chess champion and not a man who made hasty moves.

The Home Office's confusion about the league and MPU does, however, become more comprehensible when it is appreciated that the MPU was founded by MLWS supporters impatient with their society's caution. Moreover, there remained some overlap in personnel. Nevinson, one of the original 40 men who founded the MLWS, sat on the MLWS executive and edited its paper for a time but also chaired the MPU. He soon found the rank and file of the latter hard to restrain and acknowledged in his diary that many of the MPU members seemed to be spoiling for a fight. By the time of its second annual report (in 1911) the MPU was proudly asserting that it was now recognized 'in all quarters as the chief centre for militant men'.[47]

To compound matters Churchill had personal reasons to be wary of the MPU, which, as a matter of course, was consistently anti-government. He had already been physically attacked by Hugh Franklin, Honorary Assistant Organizer of the MPU (Franklin had resigned from the MLWS in 1911, preferring the more interventionist society, which gave him a much more prominent role).[48] Franklin saw himself as a soldier fighting for a cause and had held Churchill responsible for the police assaults on suffragettes on 'Black Friday' in November 1910. He had then interrupted several of Churchill's meetings and after a meeting in Bradford had attempted to strike him with a dog whip during his train journey home, for which offence he was imprisoned. In March 1911 Franklin threw a stone at Churchill's house and received a further prison sentence, during which he was forcibly fed.

Chapman had never been a member of the MPU. Most of his fellow MLWS members deplored the actions of individuals such as Franklin, whom they saw as attention-seeking young mavericks. Fully aware, however, that his job really was now on the line, Chapman visited the Home Office 'in a very humble state of mind'.[49] He withdrew the letter which had caused so much trouble, promising that he would 'take no further part in any proceedings of the Men's League or any other similar association'. He thereby managed to avoid a double resignation, probably aided by the fact that the Home Office had so palpably got its facts wrong. Indeed, he remained in his post until 1924 and in retirement wrote books about the magistrate's role in administering justice, taking care to stress the value of the new women JPs and to reiterate his passionate belief in the individual's right to divorce, regardless of class or gender.

So, just three weeks after being chosen to head the MLWS, Chapman announced that he would be resigning his chairmanship. Nevinson wrote in his diary that this represented 'a great loss'.[50] Ironically, it seems that Chapman's leadership could have galvanized the society into more effective action, though he could only have stayed on had he been prepared to sacrifice his job. Eleven days later Jacobs resumed office. The society's monthly paper announced that it was with great regret that Mr Chapman had 'felt compelled to resign', though he remained 'one of the truest friends of the League, and one of the most effectual supporters of the movement'.[51] The annual report simply included a terse, euphemistic statement that 'in view of his judicial duties' Chapman had found that he was unable to continue serving.[52]

Chapman had not been prepared to give up his job, yet despite his promises to the Home Office he did not turn his back on women's suffrage. Unrepentant, he had continued to speak at suffrage gatherings and addressed the International Suffrage Club in October 1911. Perhaps by announcing his subject in advance as being that of penal reform he thought he might forestall possible criticism. He chaired meetings of his wife's New Constitutional Society, spoke to Conservative suffragists in Liverpool on 'The Doctrine of Coverture and the Moral Side of Women's Suffrage' and even addressed the occasional WSPU gathering[53] – this body was by now unequivocally committed to militancy – as well as attending MLWS meetings.[54] He had remained a member of the MLWS and by April 1914 was back on its committee. He attended what proved to be its final AGM (in the same month a new edition of *Marriage and Divorce* was published). In 1913 at a reception for his society's new secretary he reiterated his 'unalterable conviction that the cause for which the League stands is one which belongs to the highest aspirations of mankind'.[55] He continued to urge the importance of the vote as a protection against oppression, stressing that where misery was at its greatest and education at its lowest ebb, 'there is more necessity for women to have the vote than elsewhere'.[56] And in his recollections of 1925 he stressed that women's suffrage had been a matter of justice and law, therefore important for a magistrate to understand and explain.

In October 1920 Chapman was an expert witness before the Joint Standing Committee on the Criminal Law Amendment Bill. As a result of a note he passed to its chairman about including women in the bill, there took place the first recorded parliamentary discussion of criminal sexual relations between women. Studying Chapman's evidence, Laura Doan has argued that his intervention seems to have had more to do with feminism than with homophobia.[57] His concern appeared to be for sexual equality, for an equal treatment of men and women before the law in order to protect against the possible exploitation of girls by adults of both sexes. Yet whereas Chapman had been involved in discussions of 'sexual inversion' with his fellow members of the radical

British Society for the Study of Sex Psychology (whose chairman was his old fellow MLWS committee member Laurence Housman), the wider climate of ignorance and prejudice[58] simplified and elided such concern with fears about all lesbians.

During the suffrage years it had been Chapman's paradoxical roles as dispenser of justice and advocate of legal justice for voteless women which had made him seem a threat to the establishment. Not surprisingly, the idea of collusion with the suffrage cause from someone charged with promulgating law and order worried his employers. In the end, faced with arson attacks and greater threats to security, and not just from women's suffrage, the authorities let this partisan metropolitan magistrate escape.

Cecil Chapman never had to face anything approaching the sort of punishment meted out frequently to suffragettes by his fellow justices. Admittedly, most of these women did not have prestigious jobs to lose and sought to be, if not martyrs to the cause, then at least brave enough to sacrifice some of their freedom for it. Chapman's gender and his friends and connections in high places no doubt assisted him in holding on to his job, as did his skills of negotiation and prevarication when confronted with his 'misdemeanours'. And it might be argued that, although in some respects a progressive thinker who effectively critiqued the current laws, Chapman nevertheless ultimately subscribed to a somewhat optimistic belief in the efficacy of legislation which time would show to be questionable.

Yet the case of Cecil Chapman JP, frustrated leader of the Men's League for Women's Suffrage, is an illuminating one. It amounts to more than an individual case history since it questions what may or may not constitute 'radical' behaviour. It reminds us that all activists have to negotiate – in differing ways depending on the individual and their circumstances – a complex set of needs and public demands. Chapman's experiences underscore the centrality of gender in determining the outcome of such negotiations. They also illustrate the extent to which individuals crucial to the maintenance of the state and to 'good order' were signalling that earlier certainties and broader consensus seemed to be breaking down.

Moreover, through Chapman we can discover something about the way in which respectable and respected male supporters had to learn rapidly from their novel experiences challenging the current laws. Chapman found himself, like many women of the time (though in a very different manner), caught between the court and the cause. Yet his defence and treatment were unlike theirs. But although he did not sacrifice his job, neither did he turn his back on women's suffrage and it might be argued that by remaining in his influential position he was able to be of more use to women than had he quit. Henry Nevinson wrote that he could not 'imagine a magistrate more open to reason, more careful in his judgment, and at the same time more humane, more compassionate towards the poor'.[59] Moreover, unlike many of his fellow supporters, he *did* make links between his daily work and his beliefs about gender transformation, while he clearly saw the vote as only part, albeit an essential part, of a wider struggle for legal and social justice.

Notes

I am grateful to this book's editors and to History Workshop, London, and Oxford Brookes University, where I tried out a version of this chapter.

1. For information about the various men's groups see A. V. John and C. Eustance (eds), *The Men's Share? Masculinities, Male Support and Women's Suffrage in Britain, 1890–1920*, London, Routledge, 1997.

2. See I. Fletcher, '"A star chamber of the twentieth century": suffragettes, Liberals and the 1910 "Rush the Commons" case', *Journal of British Studies*, Vol. 35, No. 4, 1996, pp. 504–30, for an analysis of suffrage which is also concerned with state responses.

3. For Chapman see *Who's Who*, London, 1938.

4. He was at Clerkenwell Police Court (1899–1901), Southwark (1901–8), Lambeth (1908–10), then Tower Bridge, the new name for the old Southwark Court (1910–16). C. Chapman, *The Poor Man's Court of Justice: Twenty-five Years as a Metropolitan Magistrate*, London, Hodder and Stoughton, 1925.

5. Men's League for Women's Suffrage (MLWS), first annual report (1907–8), Suffragette Fellowship, Museum of London.

6. See, for example, comments made at a Welsh meeting reported in the *Glamorgan Free Press*, 14 May 1909.

7. G. Sigerson, *Custodia Honesta*, London, Woman's Press, 1913.

8. *Manchester Guardian*, 25 August 1912.

9. *The Men's League Handbook for Women's Suffrage*, London, MLWS, 1912. See too S. Strauss, *'Traitors to the Masculine Cause': The Men's Campaigns for Women's Rights*, Westport, CT, Greenwood Press, 1982, p. 227.

10. In John's and Eustance's research.

11. *MLWS Monthly*, July 1910.

12. *The Vote*, 6 August 1910.

13. In 1888 the National Society for Women's Suffrage split, resulting in the creation of the Central National Society for Women's Suffrage and the Central Committee of the National Society for Women's Suffrage. See S. S. Holton, *Suffrage Days: Stories from the Women's Suffrage Movement*, London, Routledge, 1996, p. 75, for an explanation. Jacobs does not make it clear to which group he belonged.

14. L. Tickner, *The Spectacle of Women: Imagery of the Suffrage Campaign, 1907–1914*, London, Chatto and Windus, 1987, poster V. See too p. 40 ('Justice demands the vote').

15. *Merthyr Express*, 1 June 1912.
16. *The Vote*, 14 May 1910.
17. MLWS pamphlet (Queen's Hall, 26 January 1909), Museum of London Pamphlets 5-7. 116/2.
18. C. Chapman, *Marriage and Divorce: Some Needed Reforms in Church and State*, London, David Nutt, 1911, p. 44.
19. *MLWS Monthly*, April 1913.
20. H. Carter, *Women's Suffrage and Militancy*, London, Frank Palmer, n.d. (c. 1911), p. 8. I am grateful to June Balshaw for drawing my attention to this booklet.
21. Diaries of H. W. Nevinson, 12 January 1912, Bodleian Library, Oxford (hereafter Nevinson Diaries), MS Eng. Misc. e 617/1.
22. A. Young, '"Wild Women": the censure of the suffragette movement', *International Journal of the Sociology of Law*, Vol. 16, 1988, p. 292.
23. *MLWS Monthly*, May 1913.
24. *Ibid.*, March 1911.
25. C. Spring, 'The political platform and the language of support for women's suffrage, 1890-1920', in John and Eustance (eds), *The Men's Share?*, pp. 158-81.
26. Chapman, *The Poor Man's Court*, p. 58.
27. J. Davis, 'A poor man's system of justice: the London police courts in the second half of the nineteenth century', *Historical Journal*, Vol. 27, No. 2, 1984, pp. 309-35. See too Evelyn Sharp's fictional representation of the old and understanding London magistrate in the children's court, which was 'more like a Council school-room than a police-court'. E. Sharp, *Who Was Jane?* London, Macmillan, 1922, pp. 104-19.
28. Evelyn Sharp to Elizabeth Robins, 10 August 1907, Harry Ransom Humanities Research Center, University of Texas at Austin.
29. Diary, 25 July 1912, also memorandum within 1912 diary. Elizabeth Robins Papers, the Fales Library, New York University Library.
30. *MLWS Monthly*, July 1910.
31. Lady Charlotte Schreiber's journal, 22 May 1888, National Library of Wales, Aberystwyth.
32. See, for example, J. Balshaw, 'Sharing the burden: the Pethick Lawrences and women's suffrage', in John and Eustance (eds), *The Men's Share?*, pp. 135-57.
33. See A. J. R., *The Suffrage Annual and Women's Who's Who*, London, Stanley Paul, 1913, pp. 98, 203.
34. *Ibid.*, p. 300.
35. For this incident see *The Times*, 19 February 1909, and correspondence in the Home Office Papers (HO144, 1033/175. 878, fo. 15, Public Record Office, Kew (hereafter PRO).
36. Hansard Parliamentary Debates. Commons, n.s. Vol. I, 4 March 1909, c. 1590.
37. *The Vote*, 8 October 1910.

38. For his speaking commitments see the columns outlining forthcoming meetings in the *MLWS Monthly*.

39. *West Herts and Watford Observer*, 27 May 1911. See also Home Office Papers (HO45/11057/234294), PRO.

40. M. W. Nevinson, *In the Workhouse*, London, International Suffrage Shop, 1911.

41. Hansard Parliamentary Debates, Commons, ms. Vol. 26, 1 June 1911, c. 1210, 1213.

42. *MLWS Monthly*, June 1911.

43. For the correspondence and details of this incident see Home Office Papers (HO144/1148/209446), PRO.

44. See A. V. John, 'Men, manners and militancy: literary men and women's suffrage', in John and Eustance (eds), *The Men's Share?*, pp. 88-109.

45. *MLWS Monthly*, October 1910.

46. Nevinson Diaries, 31 January 1911, e 616/3.

47. MPU second annual report (1911), UDC 396.11 (06) B, Fawcett Library, London Guildhall University, London.

48. For Franklin see Franklin Papers 226, Fawcett Library, and S. S. Holton, 'Manliness and militancy: the political protests of male suffragists and the gendering of the "suffragette" identity', in John and Eustance (eds), *The Men's Share?*, pp. 110-34.

49. HO144/1148/209446, PRO.

50. Nevinson Diaries, 6 June 1911, e 616/3.

51. *MLWS Monthly*, March 1911.

52. MLWS fifth annual report (1911-12).

53. Nevinson commented that he spoke 'admirably' from the chair at a London WSPU meeting held in Warwick House. Nevinson Diaries, February 1911, e 616/3, 1. I am grateful to Krista Cowman for the Liverpool reference.

54. See, for example, *Votes for Women*, 9 January 1914.

55. *MLWS Monthly*, January 1913.

56. *North Wales Chronicle*, 13 December 1911.

57. I am very grateful to Laura Doan for letting me read a draft of her article '"Gross indecency between women": policing lesbians or policing lesbian police?', *Social and Legal Studies*, Vol. 6, No. 4, 1977, pp. 533-51.

58. When the Metropolitan Police issued a lawsuit against the Women's Police Service for wearing uniform resembling that of its own personnel, Chapman presided over the hearing. Adeline and Cecil Chapman were in fact Patrons of the Women's Police Service. Thanks to Laura Doan for letting me read part of the manuscript of *Fashioning Sapphism: The Origins of a Modern English Lesbian Culture*, New York, Columbia University Press, forthcoming.

59. *New Leader*, 8 January 1926.

9 Journeying Through Suffrage: The Politics of Dora Montefiore

Karen Hunt

The whole point seems to me to lie in this – shall we, as Liberal women, believing as we do in Liberalism being a progressive cause, and a cause which carries on a grand tradition as regards the extension of the franchise, continue to work for so-called Liberal candidates, who virtually go back on their Liberal principles by refusing to extend that franchise to properly qualified women?[1]

I, as a Socialist and an Adult Suffragist, oppose the policy of Manhood Suffrage as being undemocratic and likely to put back the just claims of women. And other comrades are opposing the granting of the franchise to women on the same terms as it is or may be granted to men, because by some process of reasoning, unknown to my less logical mind, they consider such a measure opposed to the principles of equality and democracy for which we all stand. We can surely both hold and work for our opinions, aye, and criticise each other's attitude in a friendly way.[2]

These two public statements were made by the same woman, Dora Montefiore; the first in 1898, the second in 1905. At first it might seem that the two statements are contradictory – people can, after all, change their minds. At minimum the political affiliations claimed have changed markedly – from liberalism to socialism. What is clear is that on both occasions a suffragist is speaking, but a suffragist whose strategy is changing. In this chapter I want to raise some issues for a 're-visioned' suffrage history by examining the evolution of the suffrage politics of one particular woman.

Dora Montefiore[3] (1851–1933) had an expansive and evolving politics which included the suffrage alongside her eventual commitment to a socialism and a feminism informed by a clear internationalist perspective. The suffrage organizations she was part of, and often held office within, included the Womanhood Suffrage League of New South Wales, the Union of Practical Suffragists, the National Union of Women's Suffrage Societies (NUWSS), the Women's Social and Political Union (WSPU), the Adult Suffrage Society (ASS) and the British Dominions Woman Suffrage Union. Was such a range of apparently contradictory organizational affiliations idiosyncratic? Part of feminist historians' revision of the history of women's politics in the late nineteenth and early twentieth centuries[4] suggests the permeability of apparently discrete and often competing organizations and the multiple affiliations of individuals. So what does Dora Montefiore's journey through the various overlapping campaigns for women's enfranchisement tell us about British suffrage history more generally? If we consider an individual's suffragism as a process rather than a static position, what questions does this raise for suffrage historiography?

Women's suffrage was crucial to Dora Montefiore's politicization as well as to her later political practice. Born in 1851 into a large middle-class family, she not only received an education but debated social and political questions with her Conservative father, whose amanuensis she became on leaving school. In the years before her marriage she travelled widely with him, acting as his interpreter (she was a skilled linguist) and helping in the preparation of papers for the British Association and Social Science Congresses.[5] How did a relatively privileged young Victorian woman become an imprisoned suffragette and later still a founder member of the Communist Party of Great Britain?[6] Although she later recalled that hers was a happy childhood she also remembered herself as the dark-haired tomboy who felt different from other people. This, combined with what was an exceptionally wide-ranging education for a mid-Victorian girl, provided fertile soil from which her later political activities would spring.

In 1874 Dora went to Australia to keep house for her eldest brother and his family and there met George Barrow Montefiore, a merchant. After their marriage in 1881 they lived prosperously in Sydney, where their two children were born. In 1889 her husband died at sea and Dora subsequently discovered that she had no rights of guardianship towards her own children unless her husband had willed them to her. His will did not contain such a declaration; nevertheless, it was agreed that in this case she would be allowed to keep the children. This experience of so-called 'sex disability' led her to meet other women in the same position and to make the connection with the most obvious sex disability of all, the lack of a vote.[7] As a result, the first meeting of the Womanhood Suffrage League of New South Wales was held at her home in March 1891. In its earliest days she acted as the group's Honorary Secretary and then became its first Recording Secretary,[8] but by 1892 she had returned to Europe. She settled for a time in Paris so that her children could learn French and finally returned to England so that her son could attend prep school.

Plotting out the exact genesis of Dora Montefiore's political involvement in the 1890s is not easy. She had returned from Australia as a relatively inexperienced suffrage activist. She had done some organizing, as secretary of the Womanhood Suffrage League, and had spoken once at a public meeting.[9] It seems that the limitations of being a single parent, albeit a middle-class one, and her lack of experience of British politics – she had been living outside the country for nearly two decades – did not deter her. In her not entirely reliable memoir, *From a Victorian to a Modern*, she talks of working with the 'old Suffrage Society under the Presidency of Mrs Fawcett, at Victoria Street, Westminster'.[10] This sounds like the Central Committee of the National Society for Women's Suffrage, although *The Woman's Signal* lists Dora Montefiore as a speaker for the rival Central National Society for Women's Suffrage.[11] She recollected that she was on the Executive Committee but that she found it

> depressing work as the Press would give us no publicity.... Many of us felt rebellious and realised that as long as we continued to help men into Parliament who did nothing to help us, we were simply wasting our time and our political energies.[12]

Early in 1896 she published an article in *Shafts*, the feminist monthly, whose subtitle was unequivocal: 'Why we need Woman Suffrage, and why we need it NOW'.[13] Clearly her interest in the franchise had not waned since her return from Australia. But she now found herself in a different political context. As Rose Scott, the pioneer Australian suffragist, pointed out,

> It must be remembered that the English effort to secure the franchise for women is confined to women with certain qualifications, thus it is so far on a conservative basis, whereas the battle in the Australian colonies has always been on the basis of one woman one vote. In England the question of women's suffrage has unfortunately been rather too much involved in mere party politics.[14]

Dora Montefiore's assessment of this new and dynamic political context, particularly of a property-based franchise, but also of the peculiarities of British political parties' attitudes to women's suffrage, was to guide her journey through the suffrage campaigning of the 1890s and the early decades of the twentieth century. In Australia suffragists were, in effect, adult suffragists. In terms of property qualification and the exclusion of married women, the context for Australian suffragists was much more inclusive than that of Britain. Where it was not inclusive was over the issue of race. Scott had argued when campaigning for women's suffrage that women should be given the rights 'which had long since been accorded to the very blackfellows of New South Wales'.[15] When Australian women were enfranchised in 1902, Aboriginal voters were simultaneously disqualified.[16] Australian women's suffrage may have appeared to have been adult suffrage but it was clearly only *white* adult suffrage. The context and the debate were very different in Britain and Dora had to come to terms with these differences and develop her own position. This journey took her through various political organizations.

She seems to have become involved in a local Women's Liberal Association in Sussex (Cuckfield, Hayward's Heath and Lindfield), speaking on women's suffrage at a public meeting organized by the Association in November 1896.[17] She continued to be mentioned in reports of local Women's Liberal Associations until the turn of the century.[18] Her principal interest was clearly women's suffrage, although she also made interventions on other topics. She was part of the Union of Practical Suffragists,[19] formed in 1896 within the Women's Liberal Federation (WLF), which sought to make women's suffrage a 'test question' – that is that women Liberals should only work at elections for the return of pro-suffrage candidates. Practical suffragists pressed their case within the Federation so that, for example, the suffrage debate at the 1898 annual meeting of the Federation's council was taken up entirely by a heated and protracted discussion on the test question.[20] It was during this debate that Dora spoke, including in her speech the quotation that begins this chapter. Here she made a case for prioritizing women's suffrage within the Liberal political agenda but it soon became clear, as her speech proceeded, that she felt that women's suffrage should be a test question for all political parties.[21] The Practical Suffragists failed to persuade the meeting and although Dora spoke at the WLF annual meeting the following year[22] there is other evidence to suggest that she had not found her political home in the Liberal Party. In 1899 the Union of Practical Suffragists published Dora Montefiore's pamphlet *Women Uitlanders*,[23] which pointed out the double standard of a British government willing to fight a war in South Africa over the Uitlanders' disenfranchisement while refusing to act on a similar case much nearer to home, that of voteless British women. Once again she made a strong case for making women's suffrage a test question. At the same time as Dora worked with the Union of Practical Suffragists within the WLF, she was also working with the Women's Local Government Society to promote women candidates for the Boards of Guardians and School Boards and to ensure that women voted where they could.[24] By the end of the 1890s Dora Montefiore had become a more assured public speaker, was becoming more successful at publishing her views as a journalist and as a correspondent to various journals, and was a sometime committee woman – all in the suffrage cause.

Meanwhile Dora Montefiore was stretching out beyond liberalism and what she saw as the 'male policy' of the Liberal Party, and was seeking an organization which reflected her evolving politics. Although she had admiration and respect for individual Liberal women, she was critical of organized women Liberals – 'There was too much of the village pump politics' – and she remembered, 'I found it difficult after a time to put my best energies into the Liberal pint-pot, which was not as "liberal" in its dimensions as I would have wished'.[25] Reading labour history, corresponding with Julia Dawson (a columnist of the socialist newspaper *Clarion*) from 1897, two weeks as an itinerant propagandist with the *Clarion* van in 1898 and attendance at the Independent Labour Party Annual Conference in 1899 were all part of her journey to socialism.[26] It is not clear when she joined the marxist Social Democratic Federation (SDF) but by 1901 she was writing for its papers and by 1903 she was on the party executive.

However this political journey is 'read', it should not be seen as one which was in any way separate from, or a substitute for, Dora's commitment to women's suffrage. The first letter she wrote to the *Clarion* was on the subject of women's suffrage. Just as when she was working among suffragists her concern was with tactics, so in writing to a socialist newspaper she argued that the current Women's Enfranchisement Bill was not 'anti-democratic' but was 'the thin end of the wedge, the first crack in the great wall of "privilege" which has to come down before either the workers or women are freed'. She suggested that half a loaf was better than no bread.[27] Her concern was always with ensuring that women's suffrage was democratic, for as more progressives became persuaded by the arguments for women's enfranchisement so, she argued, it became increasingly important to emphasize that adult suffrage was the ultimate goal. She always stressed that the suffrage she was fighting for was for working women. This was a position she had arrived at before she called herself a socialist. In the 1890s she was more than willing to be part of a limited suffrage campaign but the way in which she expressed that support indicates that the potential already existed for the later fracturing of the suffrage campaign over the issue of adult suffrage. At this stage Dora did not feel that she had to choose and she was not alone in expressing her support for one demand (women's suffrage on the same terms as men's) as a means to achieve the full demand (adult suffrage). Indeed, as late as 1905 Christabel Pankhurst spoke of 'We, who seek Adult Suffrage'.[28] It was important to Dora, even in the 1890s, to consider the implications of any women's suffrage bill for *all* women; thus in 1897 she wrote to the editor of the *Daily Chronicle* to correct the perception of the women's suffrage bill before Parliament:

> Under the Bill ... no woman of property, *as owner only*, will have a vote; she must be also an occupier in order to become a qualified voter. In other words, this Bill will enfranchise a large number of working women who are tenants of small houses, and it is therefore in no sense of the word a 'property measure', increasing the strength of the property vote, but, as far as it goes, an impartial and democratic enlarging of the bounds of the parliamentary franchise.[29]

Despite her own position as a woman of property, Dora was clear that she wanted the most democratic measure possible and that if that had to be based on a property franchise then it should clearly be understood as a means and not as an end in itself.

It was the emphasis on working-class women in the early propaganda of the WSPU, founded in 1903, which attracted her and on which she reported favourably in her 'Women's Interests' column in the radical weekly *New Age*, which she wrote from 1902 to 1906. Her journalism in this period is saturated with her concern for women's suffrage, reporting on international developments as well as making links between suffrage and other issues such as education. It is clear that apart from reading widely in the British and foreign radical press, she gained material for her column from the correspondence network centred on Elizabeth Wolstenholme Elmy.[30] She had been part of this group for most of the period discussed here, first appearing in Mrs Elmy's letters in 1897.[31] This friendship network sustained Dora Montefiore's suffrage activism over a crucial period in her life.

In January 1904 Dora reported to her readers in *New Age* that she had joined the WSPU and called on others to do likewise.[32] As with earlier political affiliations, this was to be no paper membership: she was to be an organizer, public speaker and militant for the cause. Yet at the same time, it seems, she continued her membership of one of the local committees of the London Society of the NUWSS, for this committee was suspended from the national body in 1905 because of Dora's association with militancy.[33] Dora was an active WSPU organizer in London in the years when the Pankhursts were still based in Manchester. It was also in 1904 that Dora first used a tactic which she did not invent but to which she brought considerable publicity: tax resistance. There had been earlier suffragist tax-resisters, such as the Priestman sisters in 1870 and Henrietta Muller in 1884,[34] although it is not clear that Dora Montefiore knew of her predecessors when she responded to a piece in *The Woman's Signal* in 1897.[35] In her letter Dora said that some time previously she had suggested this form of action to other suffragists, drawing on the successful example of the Society of Friends and its protest against paying church tithes. She called for a league to be formed of suffragist tax-resisters. She thought it would probably take at least a year to have its desired effect if five to ten thousand women organized and all refused to pay their taxes. The public auction of the goods of quiet law-abiding citizens 'for conscience' sake' would convince the most sceptical, she thought, that the time had come to grant suffrage to women.[36] As became plain to Dora, the key was to move from individual to collective action and to maximize publicity. In response the *Yorkshire Herald* warned 'women who contemplate joining the suggested league that such an extreme course is likely to alienate, rather than to attract, sympathy'.[37] Although the Women's Tax Resistance League did not form until 1909, individuals, including Dora Montefiore herself, were not deterred from taking action on their own initiative.

In 1904, Dora began what she called the 'only logical passive resistance' by refusing to pay her taxes. Her stand of 'no taxation without representation' resulted in the seizure and sale of her dining room sideboard and chairs, dressing table and washstand and bicycle to cover a debt of £9 15s 6d.[38] Her suffragist friends noted that her action was against the injustice that 'in New South Wales she was a voter, here she is a political non-entity' but also recognized that 'unless the case is made public and other women follow her example, her protest will be in vain'.[39] The following year, when Dora again refused to pay her taxes, she was determined to make the resulting auction of her goods a clearer propaganda statement. The sale was attended by friends and sympathizers, among whom were several of Dora's fellow members of the newly formed Hammersmith Society for Women's Suffrage. After the sale, the auctioneer allowed Dora to speak and she explained her reasons for passive resistance. A resolution was then passed by those present demanding voting rights for women on the same terms as men.[40] Yet as a tactic in the fight for women's enfranchisement, tax resistance could be further refined. In 1906 much more publicity was gained for the cause when Dora was besieged in her home, christened 'Fort Montefiore' by the press, for six weeks by bailiffs attempting to distrain her goods. Nailed high on a summerhouse in full view of passers-by was a huge banner, 'WOMEN SHOULD VOTE FOR THE LAWS THEY OBEY AND THE TAXES THEY PAY'. Suffragists, including Annie Kenney and Teresa Billington, held solidarity meetings outside the house on Upper Mall in Hammersmith while Dora addressed the crowds from an upper window.[41] Later, when taunted for no longer supporting the WSPU, Dora wrote of the personal cost that this aspect of militancy had brought for her, stressing that she not only lost the value of the furniture sold, but also

> endured the annoyance and indignity of having the bailiff in my house, [and] ... I suffered also the loss of friends, for many of my relations were extremely annoyed with me, and refused to speak to me after this action on my part.[42]

She also described the effect that tax resistance had on her personal finances, dependent as she was on a trust set up by her late husband. She seems to have had to move from the Hammersmith house to a much smaller flat.[43] Nevertheless, she continued, more quietly, to refuse to pay income tax for some time after the 'Fort Montefiore' incident. But, as she underscored for her critics in 1911,

> All this involved me in much extra work and inconvenience, which I cheerfully bore in the cause of the enfranchisement of women. But I certainly would not have borne it to enfranchise women of property. Those who are working for the property qualification, far from suffering financially, are making a very good living out of it.[44]

This was to become her quarrel with the WSPU but for a time she thought that it was an organization through which she could campaign for a more democratic franchise. Dora was clear that she was only interested in working towards adult suffrage although her views on how best this might be achieved did change over time.

Dora Montefiore's particular path through suffrage politics seems to have led to her marginalization from the central narrative of women's suffrage and from the particular stories of organizations in which she played an active part. This may be because Dora Montefiore's relationship to other suffragists was not without its problems. Although Dora had represented the WSPU internationally, for example at the International Council of Women's congress in Berlin in 1904 and the International Woman Suffrage Alliance (IWSA) congress in Copenhagen in 1906, when the Pankhursts moved to London their proximity seemed to result in considerable tension. And yet in her autobiography, written long after the height of the suffrage campaign, Dora quoted from personal letters from both Christabel and Emmeline Pankhurst which suggest that theirs had not always been a strained relationship. There are also positive comments about the Pankhursts in Dora's column in *New Age*.[45] Indeed, in her unpublished writings Sylvia Pankhurst remembered her mother and Dora in May 1905 in a way which suggests that they had once been close: 'My mother and Mrs Montefiori [sic] discuss tripping up Mr Labouchere, who is expected to talk out the Bill, with a piece of string.'[46] Yet you could be forgiven for thinking that Dora Montefiore had never been part of the WSPU if you relied on the published accounts of any of the Pankhursts or Annie Kenney (with whom Dora had worked closely in London's East End when Kenney first came to London).[47] On the contrary, the minutes of the Canning Town branch of the WSPU show that Dora was viewed with respect and affection – feelings which she reciprocated by presenting them with the banner which had hung outside 'Fort Montefiore' throughout the siege.[48] Elizabeth Wolstenholme Elmy had become worried in early 1906 about Dora's relationship with the WSPU. She reported of one of her stays in London with Dora that 'she did nothing but find fault all the way with everybody and everything connected with the WSPU ... they undertook to do things but "left" all the doing to her'.[49] It seemed that Dora felt that no notice was being taken of all the hard work she was doing. Yet Elmy's concerns soon melted away, only to return a year later when in early 1907, after further extensive suffrage work including arrest and imprisonment in Holloway, Dora and the WSPU parted company.

It is not entirely clear what happened. Sandra Holton argues that Dora was the first of the original WSPU leadership to be expelled. She says this was possibly because of unsubstantiated suggestions of financial dishonesty but that it is more likely that the reason was the personal following Dora was building up within the London WSPU.[50] In her autobiography Dora said somewhat enigmatically, 'I broke off my working relations with the WSPU', implying that she took the matter into her own hands.[51] Moreover there was considerable disquiet in the Canning Town branch at 'the treatment which Mrs Montefiore had received from the Central branch of the WSPU'.[52] By way of explanation Dora recounted her disagreements with Mrs Pankhurst: unease at the increasing physical violence at demonstrations; concern at the secrecy over the source of WSPU funds; and the autocratic rulings of Mrs Pankhurst herself, particularly over the Westminster branch of the WSPU which Dora had helped to form. There were rumours within the WSPU that Dora's offence had been to write to a great friend of hers who was a Liberal, thereby breaking the rules of the Union.[53] Ironically, the letter which disbanded the Westminster branch, and which may have ended Dora's WSPU membership, was in the name of Charlotte Despard, who, as Dora pointed out, 'was the next to find herself "not wanted"'.[54]

With hindsight Dora's understanding of the WSPU during 1906 seems out of step with what the organization was to become. By this time Dora was describing herself as one of 'we women agitators' and talked of 'revolutionary methods'.[55] She described the WSPU to the IWSA congress that year as 'a movement of working women led by Socialist women of intellect and culture, bringing to downtrodden women the gospel of their rights as human beings'.[56] Summarizing suffrage politics for 1906, she concluded:

> Judging from recent 'inspired' utterances, the present Government is in a 'coming-on attitude' towards manhood suffrage; could not the working women of England make use of the stream they have already set running in that direction, and uniting with it the great tide of democratic demand for equality of opportunity, force universal adult suffrage in the place of manhood suffrage ... ?[57]

This analysis of the nature of the suffrage movement and the strategies needed to achieve women's enfranchisement could no longer be sustained within the WSPU. For, at least at the leadership level, the antipathy towards a socialist analysis of suffrage had become more explicit from the summer of 1906 when Christabel Pankhurst unilaterally introduced a policy of attacking Labour as well as Liberal candidates at by-elections.[58] For Dora the price of her estrangement from the WSPU was the loss of her cherished friendship with the pioneer suffragist Elizabeth Wolstenholme Elmy.[59] Nevertheless, Dora Montefiore continued to campaign for the suffrage, now explicitly as an adult suffragist. She was a member of the Hammersmith Suffrage Society and joined the Adult Suffrage Society (ASS) in 1907 and was elected its Honorary Secretary in 1909. She continued to write and speak for adult suffrage, for example in set-piece debates with limited woman suffragists. In one such debate in 1910, she argued:

> the way to success lay rather in asking for all that was wanted at once, especially as women's suffrage was in any case considered a revolutionary

measure. Also, as the right to vote at present involved in general either the paying or the receiving of rent, few working men's wives would be enfranchised, which would place them in an unfair position.[60]

Her focus on a democratic and inclusive measure remained from her earlier years as a suffragist but she now felt that a strategy based on limited women's suffrage as a stepping-stone to full adult suffrage was no longer tenable. She continued to make her case wherever she could. In Australia in 1911 Dora argued that 'Beneath the suffragette skirt peeps the cloven hoof of extension of political power to property and privilege.'[61] Increasingly she saw suffrage as a class issue, even claiming against limited women's suffrage that 'This movement is a desperate and spasmodic effort of entrenched capitalism to keep back the rising waves of democracy.'[62] Back in Britain, she was not idle. She argued for a new Womanhood Suffrage League to take the place of the old ASS and founded a journal, *Adult Suffragist*.[63] She used whatever forum was available to make the case for the enfranchisement of all women, whether it was in *The Times* or the new organization, the British Dominions Women's Suffrage Union (BDWSU), which had been formed in 1914 to bring together suffragists from Australia, New Zealand, Canada and South Africa.[64] During the war she continued her suffrage work through the BDWSU, the Women's Suffrage National Aid Corps (formed by the Women's Freedom League to work with women and children during the war) and the Workers' Suffrage Federation (formerly Sylvia Pankhurst's East London Federation of Suffragettes).[65] When it became clear that there was to be a new Representation of the People Act, Dora argued forcibly that woman suffragists should be pushing for full womanhood suffrage: 'It is no longer, in the twentieth century, property that must be enfranchised, but the individual human being.'[66] Although the resulting Bill was less than she had hoped, she nevertheless chaired a 'Victory Dinner' at her club, the Lyceum, to celebrate the enfranchisement of 6 million British women and acknowledged in her speech stalwarts of the women's cause such as Mrs Fawcett, Mrs Pankhurst, Mrs Despard and the Pethick-Lawrences.[67] This was hardly the action of a bitter opponent of women's suffrage, as adult suffragists are so often represented, but that of a committed suffragist whose journey through suffrage politics was a principled and energetic one which reveals much about the complexity of those politics.

If these are some of the traces of Dora Montefiore's journey through suffrage, it is important to contextualize that journey by noting that at the same time as she attempted to find a suitable setting for her energy and commitment within suffragism, Dora was also working within the SDF, developing her own woman-focused socialism.[68] She often came into conflict with the party leadership over suffrage, but also over the gap between socialist rhetoric and practice on the woman question. She was one of the SDF women who began the party's Women's Socialist Circles in 1904 and was one of the few women to be elected to the SDF executive – in 1903, 1904, 1908 and 1909. She remained an energetic although often dissident worker for the SDF until the end of 1912. She resigned from what was now the British Socialist Party in protest against militarism and returned to the party only in 1916 when the Hyndmanite 'old guard' left. Her political activity continued: she spoke at the Leeds Soviet in 1917 and became an early executive member of the Communist Party of Great Britain. Having become politically active in her forties, she sustained her passion and principle into her seventies, only taking a less active part once her health, and particularly her sight, deteriorated.

It seems her family regarded her as a 'crank', and there were those who found her difficult. It was observed in 1905 that she 'is not everywhere well received, there having been heterodox passages in her private life which people resent'.[69] Her detractors seized on rumours of the abuse of cocaine lozenges[70] and suggestions that she had had an inappropriate relationship with an ILP organizer who was both married and working-class. The gossip surrounding the latter events led to a libel case between George Belt, the man concerned, and Margaret MacDonald in 1900.[71] Olive Banks has called Dora Montefiore a 'courageous and unconventional woman'[72] and she certainly straddled campaigns and organizations which have often been thought to have been incompatible, always giving not only financial support but also her time and her skills in organizing, public speaking, networking and journalism.

When Dora Montefiore died nearly twenty years after the suspension of the militant campaign and five years after adult suffrage had finally been achieved, *The Times* still remembered her for her militant suffragism, including her association with Mrs Pankhurst and her daughters, as well as for her socialism.[73] She presented herself, through her autobiography, as principally a non-violent suffragist who was also a militant and always an adult suffragist.

What does her story, or that part I have tried to tell, have to say for us now as we seek to reassess the suffrage campaigns and their histories? First, stories like Dora's do not fit easily, or even at all, into the traditional historiography of organizations and leaders. Even when Dora achieves a walk-on part in these other dramas, this fails to capture the complexities of, on the one hand, the interrelationship between suffragism and other politics (such as liberalism and, in this case particularly, socialism) and, on the other hand, the changing debates about strategy and tactics within the broader political context. Although Dora's particular journey may have been idiosyncratic, Stanley and Morley have alerted us to others who sprawled across organizations and campaigns and did not fit neatly into the stereotypes of militant versus constitutionalist or socialist versus suffragette.[74] Dora's experience also alerts us to the need for a suffrage history which can incorporate an understanding of an individual's suffragism as a process rather than a static position. She was hardly alone in her sincere belief in adult suffrage: yet this position remains marginal to the suffrage story, too often stereotyped and dismissed.[75] As we ask more questions about what the struggle for women's enfranchisement meant for women and men in the years before 1918, so we need to find a way to incorporate the insights of biography into the broader histories. This seems to be more difficult than it sounds. We need to find a way to write of the complexity and process that is the politics of women's suffrage, and part of the way towards this is to understand more about individual journeys through suffrage.

Notes

I am grateful for an Australian Bicentennial Fellowship and British Academy support which enabled me to explore the Australian sources for the life and politics of Dora Montefiore.

1. Women's Liberal Federation (WLF), Annual Meeting of Council, 1898, p. 45.
2. *Clarion*, 26 May 1905.
3. For varying accounts of Dora Montefiore's life see her autobiography, *From a Victorian to a Modern*, London, E. Archer, 1927, and the following biographical dictionary entries: O. Banks, *Biographical Dictionary of British Feminists, 1800-1930*, Brighton, Wheatsheaf, 1985, pp. 133-4; *Australian Dictionary of Biography*, Vol. 10, Melbourne, Melbourne University Press, 1986; *New Dictionary of National Biography*, forthcoming.
4. For example: J. Rendall (ed.), *Equal or Different: Women's Politics 1800-1914*, Oxford, Basil Blackwell, 1987; S. S. Holton, *Feminism and Democracy: Women's Suffrage and Reform Politics in Britain, 1900-18*, Cambridge, Cambridge University Press, 1986; J. Hannam, 'Women and politics' in J. Purvis (ed.), *Women's History: Britain, 1850-1945*, London, UCL Press, 1995, pp. 217-45.
5. Montefiore, *From a Victorian to a Modern*, pp. 26-8.
6. For a broader discussion of the politicization of socialist women see K. Hunt, 'Making socialist woman: politicisation, gender and the Social Democratic Federation, 1884-1911', paper to Ninth Berkshire Conference on the History of Women, Vassar College, 1993.
7. Montefiore, *From a Victorian to a Modern*, pp. 30-1. It was only in 1912 that the state of Victoria gave the mother automatic guardianship of the children on the death of her husband. These rights did not apply to all of Australia until 1934. See A. Oldfield, *Woman Suffrage in Australia: A Gift or a Struggle?*, Melbourne, Cambridge University Press, 1992, p. 206.
8. Minute Book of Womanhood Suffrage League, in Rose Scott Papers, Mitchell Library, Sydney, ML MSS 38/33/1/, pp. 2, 8.

9. See *Woman's Suffrage Journal* (Sydney), 15 March 1892, for a copy of a speech given by Mrs George Montefiore on 6 May 1891.

10. Montefiore, *From a Victorian to a Modern*, p. 40.

11. *Woman's Signal*, 1 October 1896. For a useful overview of the various suffrage organizations, see S. S. Holton, 'Women and the vote', in Purvis (ed.), *Women's History*.

12. Montefiore, *From a Victorian to a Modern*, p. 40.

13. *Shafts*, January 1896.

14. Newspaper cutting of letter from Rose Scott, n.d. but between 1894 and 1902, in Rose Scott Papers, ML MSS 38/35/4/290.

15. Womanhood Suffrage League address to New South Wales legislators signed by Rose Scott, n.d. (c. 1897-8), Womanhood Suffrage Correspondence 1887-99, Rose Scott Papers, ML A2271/416.

16. M. Lake, 'Between old worlds and new: feminist citizenship, nation and race, the destabilisation of identity', in C. Daley and M. Nolan (eds), *Suffrage and Beyond: International Feminist Perspectives*, Auckland, Auckland University Press, 1994, p. 279.

17. *Woman's Signal*, 3 December 1896.

18. See *Summary of Federation News*, 1897-9.

19. For the formation of the Union of Practical Suffragists see the *Woman's Signal*, 19 November 1896. For a very brief history see H. Leeds, *Origin and Growth of the Union*, Union of Practical Suffragists Leaflet No. 13, 1898. See also L. Walker, 'Party political women: a comparative study of Liberal women and the Primrose League, 1890-1914', in Rendall (ed.), *Equal or Different*, esp. pp. 188-9. For Liberal women and the suffrage see R. Billington, 'Women, politics and local Liberalism: from "female suffrage" to "votes for women"', *Journal of Regional and Local Studies*, Vol. 5, No. 1, 1985, pp. 1-14; C. Hirshfield, 'Fractured faith: Liberal Party women and the suffrage issue in Britain, 1892-1914', *Gender and History*, Vol. 2, No. 2, 1990, pp. 173-97.

20. WLF Annual Meeting of Council, 1898, pp. 34-56.

21. *Ibid.*, pp. 45-7.

22. *Ibid.*, 1899, pp. 56, 78.

23. D.B. Montefiore, *Women Uitlanders*, Union of Practical Suffragists Leaflet No. 14, 1899.

24. Mrs E. C. Wolstenholme Elmy to Mrs McIlquham, 14 November 1897, Correspondence of Mrs E. C. Wolstenholme Elmy, British Library Manuscripts (BLM), Add Ms 47,451.

25. Montefiore, *From a Victorian to a Modern*, p. 60.

26. *Ibid.*, pp. 61-3. See also *Clarion*, 20 February 1897; 23 October 1897; 4 June 1898; 25 June 1898; 9 July 1898; 8 October 1898.

27. *Clarion*, 20 February 1897.

28. *Clarion*, 6 January 1905.

29. *Daily Chronicle*, 4 February 1897, a cutting in Rose Scott Papers, ML MSS 38/35/4/228.

30. For example, *New Age*, 6 November 1902.
31. See Mrs E. C. Wolstenholme Elmy to Mrs McIlquham, 4 July 1897, Correspondence of Mrs E. C. Wolstenholme Elmy, BLM, Add Ms 47,451.
32. *New Age*, 7 January 1904.
33. Holton, *Feminism and Democracy*, p. 36. See also Mrs Frances Rowe to Mrs Harriet McIlquham, 29 August 1905 and 26 September 1905, Harriet McIlquham Papers, Fawcett Library Autograph Collection.
34. M. K. Parkes, *The Tax Resistance Movement in Great Britain*, Women's Tax Resistance League, n.d., pp. 1-2.
35. *Woman's Signal*, 8 June 1897.
36. *Woman's Signal*, 17 June 1897.
37. Quoted in *Woman's Signal*, 6 August 1897.
38. *New Age*, 26 May 1904.
39. Mrs E. C. Wolstenholme Elmy to Mrs McIlquham, 19 May 1904, Correspondence of Mrs E. C. Wolstenholme Elmy, BLM, Add Ms 47,453.
40. *New Age*, 21 December 1905.
41. A. Raeburn, *The Militant Suffragettes*, London, Michael Joseph, 1973, pp. 19-20.
42. *Maoriland Worker* (Wellington), 29 September 1911.
43. Mrs E. C. Wolstenholme Elmy to Mrs McIlquham, 3 November 1906, Correspondence of Mrs E. C. Wolstenholme Elmy, BLM, Add Ms 47,455.
44. *Maoriland Worker*, 29 September 1911.
45. Montefiore, *From a Victorian to a Modern*, pp. 116-18; for example, *New Age*, 20 August 1903.
46. S. Pankhurst, 'The inheritance: a life of struggle', p. 10 in 'Women, suffrage and politics: the papers of Sylvia Pankhurst', microfilm reel 5/55, Marlborough, Adam Matthew, 1994. Originals are held at the Internationaal Instituut voor Sociale Geschiedenis, Amsterdam.
47. For example, S. Pankhurst, *The Suffragette Movement*, London, Virago, 1977 (first published 1931); C. Pankhurst, *Unshackled*, London, Hutchinson, 1959; A. Kenney, *Memoirs of a Militant*, London, Edward Arnold, 1924.
48. Minutes of Canning Town branch of WSPU, 25 October 1906, the Suffragette Fellowship Collection, Museum of London, 50.82/1133.
49. Mrs E. C. Wolstenholme Elmy to Mrs McIlquham, 6 January 1906, Correspondence of Mrs E. C. Wolstenholme Elmy, BLM, Add Ms 47,454.
50. Holton, 'Women and the vote', p. 291.
51. Montefiore, *From a Victorian to a Modern*, p. 108.
52. Minutes of Canning Town branch of WSPU, 1 January 1907.
53. *Ibid*.
54. Montefiore, *From a Victorian to a Modern*, pp. 108-13.
55. *New Age*, 5 April 1906; 10 May 1906.
56. *New Age*, 16 August 1906.
57. *New Age*, 3 January 1907.

58. Holton, 'Women and the vote', p. 291.

59. See, for example, Mrs E. C. Wolstenholme Elmy to Mrs McIlquham, 29 January 1907, 12 February 1907, 10 May 1907, Correspondence of Mrs E. C. Wolstenholme Elmy, BLM, Add Ms 47,455. Others also broke with Dora Montefiore; see Aletta Jacobs to Rosika Schwimmer, 16 December 1907 in M. Bosch with A. Kloosterman, *Politics and Friendship: Letters from the International Woman Suffrage Alliance, 1902-42*, Columbus, Ohio State University Press, 1985, p. 74.

60. *The Vote*, 12 March 1910.

61. *The Socialist* (Melbourne), 10 March 1911.

62. *Maoriland Worker*, 11 August 1911.

63. *Daily Herald*, 6 November 1912. For *Adult Suffragist* see advertisement in *Labour Leader*, 30 July 1913. I have been unable to locate copies of this: can anyone help?

64. *The Times*, 10 June 1914; *The Vote*, 17 July 1914.

65. See, for example, *The Vote*, 28 August 1914, 15 October 1915; *Jus Suffragii*, 1 October 1917.

66. *The Vote*, 19 November 1915.

67. *The Vote*, 1 February 1918.

68. See K. Hunt, *Equivocal Feminists: The Social Democratic Federation and the Woman Question, 1884-1911*, Cambridge, Cambridge University Press, 1996.

69. Mrs Rowe to Mrs McIlquham, 26 September 1905, Harriet McIlquham Papers.

70. Mrs E. C. Wolstenholme Elmy to Mrs McIlquham, 6 January 1906, Correspondence of Mrs E. C. Wolstenholme Elmy; Mrs Rowe to Mrs McIlquham, 9 June 1907, Harriet McIlquham Papers.

71. For the Belt case see Francis Johnson Correspondence, British Library of Political and Economic Science; C. Collette, 'Socialism and scandal: the sexual politics of the early Labour movement', *History Workshop Journal*, Vol. 23, 1987, pp. 102-11.

72. Banks, *Biographical Dictionary*, p. 134.

73. *The Times*, 1 January 1934.

74. L. Stanley and A. Morley, *The Life and Death of Emily Wilding Davison*, London, Woman's Press, 1988.

75. For adult suffrage see Hunt, *Equivocal Feminists*, chapter 6.

10 Suffrage Autobiography: A Study of Mary Richardson – Suffragette, Socialist and Fascist

Hilda Kean

Suffrage feminists, who had so publicly and visually promoted a positive political identity for women, adopted the genre of autobiography to emphasize the sense of a united self and of collective strength found in the feminist movement. *The Suffrage Annual and Women's Who's Who*, published in 1913, contained a plethora of potted autobiographies of suffrage activists; once the vote was partially won for women in 1918, full-length autobiography followed.[1]

Histories of the suffrage movement written by participants were rare: rather, autobiography was the favoured genre for their narrative.[2] Indeed, both the form and the motifs employed within the texts were distinctive. The autobiographies of former Women's Social and Political Union (WSPU) activists such as the journalist Evelyn Sharp, the publisher Viscountess Rhondda or the writer Cicely Hamilton highlighted the action of the individual feminist, her lone acts of defiance, possible estrangement from family and her commitment to the cause.[3] Although this writing emphasized individual feats and hardships, it was within a context of what Susan Stanford Friedman has described as 'an interdependent existence that asserts its rhythm everywhere in the community'.[4]

Suffrage autobiography can be read almost as the collective expression of a political movement. This sense of collective identity was developed through the use of mythological and metaphorical devices not dissimilar to those identified by Luisa Passerini and Alessandro Portelli in their work on the development of popular memory among the left in Italy.[5] Frequently found in suffrage autobiography are stories of 'conversion', of a women explaining how a small vivid incident – usually a personal encounter with a member of the Pankhurst family – led to a rejection of an earlier life and an embracing of the suffrage cause. Such autobiographical writing became almost a collective invention of the past, often written at a time in which there was a disjuncture between the political reality of the times and the imagined new world for women. Autobiographical writing in such politically bleak times for feminism helped to maintain women's dreams and their hopes.

Mary Richardson published her autobiography *Laugh a Defiance* in 1953 towards the end of her life (she died in 1961 aged 70).[6] Taking the title from the suffragettes' anthem *March of Women*, Richardson's book is full of dashing deeds. She had been a member of the WSPU, a hunger striker, and had gained widespread publicity for slashing the 'Rokeby Venus' painting in the National Gallery. In common with many other suffrage accounts, her autobiography does not mention her life after suffrage and there is scant reference to a life outside the public political domain. Certainly there was no mention of her adopted son Roger, nor of her poetry published in the 1920s.[7] More significantly, there was nothing of her *public* life after suffrage although by 1931 she had stood for Parliament four times – on socialist platforms – and by 1934 was the women's organizer of the British Union of Fascists. In some respects these autobiographical omissions are similar to those found in other suffrage autobiographical writing; the impression given is that there is no life before or after suffrage.[8] And yet in Richardson's case a public life of a very different political character continued. It was not that Mary Richardson had left behind political, public life after the 1914–18 war, but that it had no part in the creation of her chosen identity as a militant suffragette.

Suffrage autobiography was a specific genre which aimed to create a collective identity. It arose directly out of the nature of the suffrage movement itself, which epitomized dislocation from family, job and a former way of life, while offering feminists a new idea of what it meant to be a woman.[9] It was because of the perception of the movement as one which gave such profound life-changing experiences that the 'conversion motif' was used so frequently in suffrage autobiographical writing.[10] In Mary Richardson's *Laugh a Defiance* there was a standard conversion story. In this case Mary rescued Mrs Pankhurst's son, then 'met' Emmeline herself and 'saw the light' in religious fashion. She declared that 'I had enlisted in a holy crusade'.[11] Richardson also employed the religious motif of 'laying on of hands' in her accounts of meeting or having contact with important suffragettes.[12] According to her autobiography, she met Emily Wilding Davison at Epsom on Derby Day before Davison's fateful demonstration involving the king's horse.[13] She told a story about Lady Constance Lytton, the popular aristocratic WSPU member,[14] and recalled how she 'converted' the Bishop of London to speak for suffrage in the House of Lords.[15] Life as a suffragette was presented by Richardson as very exciting. She described her pseudonym (Polly Dick), mentioned unsigned messages which came from Christabel Pankhurst and re-counted how she slashed the 'Rokeby Venus' with a small axe. She told of hunger strikes and force-feeding and of an escape from a dastardly 'double agent' (Mrs Penn). Mary Richardson's story was of a women at the centre of important events. And yet, although she appeared to reveal much of her life in the sense of describing illegal activities, in reality she disclosed very little, other than a penchant for creating exciting yarns.

Revealingly, *Laugh a Defiance* was by no means Richardson's first attempt at autobiography. Throughout her life she wrote and rewrote her life in a number of ways to give meaning and a sense of unity to her range of political, public activities and possibly to create a personal sense of unity and identity. Mary Richardson used the suffrage story to make sense of a life and to provide a framework of coherence to her fragmented existence. She used suffrage stories not to reflect a life of political continuity, but to construct a continuity to a life that was distinctly splintered and characterized by sharp breaks.[16]

Richardson used different suffrage narratives to 'explain' her contemporary preoccupations. It was as if suffrage words rather than suffrage deeds became important in defining and creating a place for her within the developing popular memory of suffrage. From the 1920s Mary Richardson created an identity for herself as a woman who continued to embody the ideals of the suffrage movement while in her political practice she was active in a number of organizations and campaigns which had no direct relationship at all with suffrage feminism. Coherence in her life came from the way she situated her motivations and past life rather than her current preoccupations.

In 1916, according to her account in the Women's Freedom League (WFL) paper *The Vote*, Mary joined Labour.[17] In 1922 and 1924 she stood as a Labour and then Independent Labour – that is left-wing socialist supported by the Communist Party – candidate in Acton, west London; on both occasions she lost to the Tory candidate. In 1924 Mary stood against the official Labour candidate, H. A. Baldwin.[18] Later, in 1931, she was the Labour candidate in the military town of Aldershot in Hampshire, having been selected at the last minute after the previous candidate had defected to support the National Government.[19] Thus during the 1920s and early 1930s her political activity was undertaken within the parameters of socialism. That the nature of her politics was left-wing can be seen both in the circumstances of her standing against an official Labour Party candidate and in the ideas she then espoused.

During this time Mary Richardson used stories from her suffrage past to explain her current politics without apparently espousing contemporary feminist ideas. The motif she developed in the 1920s was that of suffrage martyr; of the individual undertaking individual protests rather than collective action. Her public name had been earned by the slashing of the 'Rokeby Venus' – and one can understand her reluctance to raise this repeatedly, given the hostility her actions had aroused at the time. Nevertheless, it was personal suffering rather than collective sentiment that she deemed most important.[20] This theme was developed primarily because she constructed her life in the present through a sense of who she was and had been, rather than providing a political analysis of suffrage.

In 1922, as the Labour parliamentary candidate in Acton, Mary

Richardson expressed an interest in prison reform, ascribing this to her personal experience of periods of imprisonment and force-feeding during the pre-war suffrage campaign. She also described herself as a great friend of Mrs Despard. Charlotte Despard had been not only the president of the militant suffrage society the Women's Freedom League, but (conveniently) a former member of the left-wing Social Democratic Federation (SDF). Mary Richardson's own links to political history prior to her involvement in the suffrage movement were made tangible through reference to where she lived: North Street, Westminster, in 'an interesting historic house, once the property of Lord North with a secret passage to the House of Commons – which shall be very convenient when I am ultimately elected'.[21] However, in 1926, when Richardson wrote in the WFL paper *The Vote*, there was no mention of Mrs Despard, despite the links that still existed between the WFL and its former president. Instead Christabel Pankhurst, combined with Oliver Cromwell and Demeter, the Greek goddess of corn, were invoked to summarize the source of her political inspiration.[22] At the time Richardson was publicizing her adoption as prospective Labour candidate for Bury St Edmunds (although she never actually contested the election). Her politics, she declared to *Vote* readers, were derived not from the suffrage movement – as she had formerly implied in 1922 – but from her grandparents, who had brought her up. They were 'severe Puritanical. ... They instilled into me a dire respect for our greatest "Bolshie" Oliver Cromwell.'[23]

In the account in *The Vote* in 1926 she described her conversion to suffrage using the mythological convention of conversion found in many suffrage tales, but she used a story different from one she later employed in *Laugh a Defiance*. Here Richardson described meeting Christabel Pankhurst and exclaimed, 'I was x-rayed by those grey eyes of destiny – Christabel's.' Richardson also conveniently placed herself at the centre of suffrage events in Parliament Square on Black Friday in 1910.[24] As a result 'This decided me!' She 'revert[ed] to my childhood's hero, the great Oliver, I became a militant! I need not say more.' In terms of her political programme Richardson no longer mentioned prison reform; agriculture now took precedence – understandably, in a rural constituency like Bury St Edmunds. This interest was explained by references to history and art: her early love of the Greek statue of Demeter, the mother of corn, in the British Museum.[25]

Richardson analysed Labour's policies as advocating new and efficient public services, better houses, cheaper food, higher wages, shorter working hours, fewer idle rich and more healthy lives for all. Economic change was needed, and the exposure of middlemen, food rings and trusts so as to ensure purer food and milk. Her concerns were neither those of 'old feminists' in the WFL nor those of 'new feminists' in the National Union of Societies for Equal Citizenship (NUSEC).[26] It was a framework of labour, rather than feminist, politics that Richardson adopted, while maintaining the motifs of the suffrage narrative. Further, although she was a prospective Labour candidate in 1926 in Bury St Edmunds, albeit in an unwinnable seat, her political emphasis had shifted away from the concerns she had expressed a few years before when she stood in Acton. Economic change rather than prison reform was foregrounded.

When Mary Richardson again stood as a parliamentary candidate in Aldershot in 1931, Oliver Cromwell and Demeter had been forgotten. But the suffrage movement was remembered as having given her an excellent schooling in politics. Her political legitimacy now came direct from Emmeline Pankhurst and at her adoption meeting she exclaimed:

> I carry in my hand tonight what is to be my *talisman*. It is a piece of paper which Mrs Pankhurst carried in her hand when she went to the House of Commons to demand votes for women. On the piece of paper were the words: 'Thrice armed is she who knows her cause is just.'[27]

Richardson used her connections with the suffrage movement to legitimize a hopeless campaign in a reactionary military area. Unsurprisingly, the sitting MP, Lord Wolmer, a Conservative and a supporter of the National Government, was returned. It is possible that the suffrage motif used by Richardson in Aldershot was an attempt to inspire Labour voters with analogies of past political successes in equally difficult circumstances. It also suggests that Richardson interpreted her uphill fight in Aldershot as analogous to her difficult personal battles for the suffrage. Clearly the politics of the campaigns were very different; what was similar was the presence of Mary as a leading protagonist trying to explain to herself – as much as to her audience – why a former suffragette was standing in the constituency.

Her personal explanations of her understanding of socialism also changed for the Aldershot election. Mary now attributed it to her recognition of the horrors of poverty which she witnessed when she had visited Italy. 'Although an artist by profession she believes that it is a greater thing to bring joy and relief to the majority than to give pleasure to a few by painting pictures to hang on a wall.'[28] This statement may have been an attempt to explain retrospectively her attack on Velázquez's *The Toilet of Venus* (the 'Rokeby Venus') as a progressive protest. Other suffragettes had also attacked paintings in art galleries during the militant suffrage campaign and focused upon the financial implications of their actions. However, at the time of her protest Mary Richardson had made much of the content of the specific painting she had slashed. For Mary the most beautiful woman in art had little value compared to the life of Mrs Pankhurst, the most beautiful character in modern history.[29]

For the first time in her autobiographical election accounts in 1931, Mary Richardson mentioned her suffrage work in London's East End, where she had had contact with members of the East London Federation of Suffragettes, the organization aimed at working-class women which Sylvia Pankhurst had established.[30] The Federation, Richardson declared, had persuaded her that socialism was the only living, evolving policy that the country had. Such an awareness led, she suggested, to an emphasis on economic questions. Women had lost their rightful place under capitalism – Ramsay MacDonald was doing the work of the bankers – and society faced a struggle between capitalism and socialism.[31] Images of the suffrage movement were used to create a distinctive mood for her election campaign, a mood of defiance and commitment to a cause. Suffrage became a story of personal suffering, isolation, martyrdom and survival rather than a particular feminist politics.

In April 1934 Mary Richardson joined the British Union of Fascists (BUF) as the organizing secretary of the Women's Section. This was just four months after Rothermere's enthusiastic endorsement of the fascists in the *Daily Mail*: 'Hurrah for the Blackshirts.'[32] Obviously Mary Richardson was not unique in turning from left-wing socialism to fascism.[33] Other converts, apart from Mosley of course, included John Beckett, former Labour MP for Gateshead; ILP whip George Sutton, Mosley's secretary and former chair of North St Pancras Labour Party; and Wilfred Risdon, the former divisional organizer of the ILP in the Midlands, who became a director of propaganda in the BUF.[34]

Mary Richardson described her reasons for becoming a fascist in the weekly fascist paper *Blackshirt*. She made no mention of her considerable time in the Labour Party or of her perceptions of its failures. She again looked back to her earlier experiences of the suffrage movement both to inspire the fascist readership and to offer an explanation of her behaviour. She suggested a continuity in her own politics by telling (new) suffrage stories while overlooking the intervening two decades. Such stories were not just written accounts for *Blackshirt*, they were personally important to her. Recent interviews undertaken by Stephen Cullen have suggested that Mary Richardson's depiction of herself within the fascist movement as a suffragette was something she also spoke about informally.[35] Her stories were apparently so striking that they were recalled by a former BUF member some sixty years later:

> The moving spirit of this [women's HQ] was an ex-suffragette of great character. She was a fiery speaker particularly at street corner meetings and used to plaster her hair down with Grip-fix so that it would not blow about on these occasions. She had been with Emily Davidson [*sic*], the suffragette who threw herself under the King's horse at the Derby and was killed. This one escaped to Epsom Station where a sympathetic station master hid her in the ladies' loo until the hue and cry were over.[36]

In her written narratives in *Blackshirt*[37] Mary Richardson described working in the suffrage movement not with Christabel Pankhurst, whose eyes she had remembered so clearly in her earlier piece in *The Vote*, but with the socialist, and now anti-fascist, Sylvia Pankhurst, in Bow. She recalled being imprisoned with Sylvia in Holloway Prison.[38] Richardson also referred to the first petition Emmeline Pankhurst presented to Parliament – the talisman which she mentioned at Aldershot. However, there was also an important iconographic addition; Mary owned, she said, the medal presented to Mrs Pankhurst by the women of America in 1913, which she received on Emmeline Pankhurst's death. This narrative became more than another suffrage story of the encounter with a famous leader; the relationship was now portrayed as extending beyond death. In this story the mantle of the suffrage movement passed to Mary Richardson, fascist organizer, rather than to the anti-fascist daughter, Sylvia.

Although she was a relative newcomer to the BUF, it was Mary Richardson rather than other prominent fascist women such as the novelist Olive Hawks, Mrs Gueroult, Elizabeth Gill or Jenny Linton – all of whom wrote in *Blackshirt* and spoke at public meetings – who replied to Sylvia Pankhurst's attack on the fascists' violence at the Olympia rally in June 1934. Sylvia had also spoken at an anti-fascist rally in Trafalgar Square in 1934 demanding the arrest and detention of fascist sympathizers, including her erstwhile colleague Mary Richardson.[39] In her article responding to Sylvia Pankhurst, Richardson depicted the recent events as almost a contest for the soul of the suffrage movement, praising the Blackshirts as the current embodiment of the former militant suffrage movement:

> I was first attracted to the Blackshirts because I saw in them the courage, the action, the loyalty, the gift of service, and the ability to serve which I had known in the suffrage movement. When later I discovered the Blackshirts were attacked for no visible cause or reason, I admired them the more when they hit back, and hit hard.[40]

Mary compared the violence at the Olympia rally to that of Black Friday on 18 November 1910 when suffrage feminists demonstrating against the shelving of the Conciliation bill were physically attacked and sexually abused.[41] However, the analogy she drew was between the suffragettes and fascists as common *victims* of hooligan violence. Moreover, resistance to violent attack, which is how the actions of the anti-fascists were portrayed, was compared in favourable terms to the violent resistance to force-feeding which both Mary and Sylvia undertook. The appeal in her writing was not to disillusioned socialists but ostensibly to women formerly active in the suffrage movement over twenty years earlier and who, like Mary herself, were apparently seeking some sort of continuity with that time.

Although there were former suffrage feminists like Mary Richardson who joined the ranks of the BUF, those who repudiated fascism and campaigned against it as a betrayal of feminist ideas were far more numerous. As former WSPU member Cicely Hamilton explained, 'As a feminist, its doctrines did not attract me, most of my acquaintances were strongly opposed to them and the danger of Fascism spreading in England had often been impressed on me.'[42] When she witnessed the numbers of women on a fascist march in the 1930s, her reaction was that 'as a feminist, I noted the fact with regret'.[43] Certainly there were debates within the BUF on the position of women, and the 'anti-suffrage spinster' line became more prominent once Mary Richardson left, apparently in November 1934.[44] When Mrs Carrington Wood, the North West London organizer of the BUF, resigned and publicized this fact in *The Star* on 11 February 1935, she too drew on suffrage stories but used them to argue that women would be infinitely worse off under fascism and that they did not want to go back to where they had been before the days of the suffragettes.[45] It was an anonymous BUF member who called herself 'an old suffragette' and who had apparently suffered hunger and thirst strikes who was called upon to rebuff the public attack in the fascist press.[46]

When Mary Richardson wrote in February 1936 to the executive committee of the feminist Six Point Group (SPG) about the fascist attitude to women, the committee seemed singularly unimpressed and merely noted the correspondence.[47] They had, after all, been organizing against fascism both at home and abroad, quite effectively, without Mary Richardson's help. Richardson did not appear in the 1920s – or after – as an ex-fascist who had recanted; there were many activities organized by former suffragettes against fascism in which she seems to have taken no part. Nor did she apparently support any of the SPG's petitions and campaigns.[48] However, by November 1936, when she attended a suffrage reunion dinner, her attendance was reported without hostile comment in *Women Today*, the anti-fascist paper of the British Section of the Woman's World Committee Against War and Fascism, supported by none other than Sylvia Pankhurst. Appropriating the suffrage myth for its own purposes, the paper remarked that more of the suffragette spirit would be welcome in the 1930s.[49]

From 1936 to her death in Hastings in November 1961 there is little to suggest that Mary took either an active part in public life generally or remained in touch with former colleagues in the suffrage movement at Suffragette Fellowship gatherings. (The Suffragette Fellowship was an organization dedicated to commemorating the suffrage campaign.[50]) A reading of the Suffragette Fellowship newsletter, *Calling All Women*, or of the obituaries in the WFL *Bulletin*, reveals little information on her life after the mid-1920s and colludes, unwittingly, with the story Richardson presented in *Laugh a Defiance* – of no political life after suffrage.[51] Although she had many papers relating to the suffrage movement she chose not to leave them with the Suffragette Fellowship collection (deposited in the Museum of London); she claimed to *Calling All Women* that she had placed them in the Smith College for Women in Massachusetts in the United States.[52]

In the decades after the 1920s, feminists who had been active in the suffrage campaign continued to meet to commemorate dead suffrage colleagues or to keep alive the memory of those times in dwindling groups like the WFL or the National Union of Women Teachers.[53] Mary Richardson was not among them and yet her absence is in sharp contrast to the image she projected in *Laugh a Defiance* of a woman who had led a life structured by the suffrage movement. Words here did not reflect her deeds; they replaced them. When she died in 1961 the obituary in the WFL's *Bulletin* made no mention of her post-1918 activities and was distinctly dismissive of her contribution to the campaign for women's suffrage: 'She was one of the very militant members of the WSPU ... though only in the Union during the last two years of its life.'[54]

Mary Richardson's autobiography appeared later than those of many of her militant contemporaries who continued to be active in feminist politics between the wars and who used their writing to contest the political legacy of the suffrage movement.[55] Suffrage autobiography was indeed almost a collective creation of the suffrage movement; but Richardson's work also indicates the personal motivations involved. Mary did not write just one story of her life, she wrote and *rewrote* her own suffrage story: Acton 1922, Bury St Edmunds 1926, Aldershot 1931, London 1934, Cambridgeshire 1953. In doing so she helped to explain her disrupted life to herself and also helped to create an image of the suffrage movement in popular memory.

Notes

Thanks to the contributors to discussion at the Seeing Through Suffrage Conference, University of Greenwich, 1996, at which an earlier paper on this topic was read, and to my post-graduate Public History students at Ruskin College for their stimulating comments.

1. A. J. R., *The Suffrage Annual and Women's Who's Who*, London, Stanley Paul, 1913.
2. H. Kean, 'Searching for the past in present defeat', *Women's History Review*, Vol. 3, No. 1, 1994, pp. 57–80; L. E. M. Mayhall, 'Creating the "suffragette spirit": British feminism and the historical imagination', *Women's History Review*, Vol. 4, No. 3, 1995, pp. 319–44; R. Gagnier, *Subjectivities: A History of Self Representation in Britain 1832–1920*, Oxford, Oxford University Press, 1991; G. Norquay, *Voices and Votes*, Manchester, Manchester University Press, 1995; M. Joannou, 'She who would be free herself must strike the first blow: suffragette

autobiography and suffragette militancy', in J. Swindells (ed.), *The Uses of Autobiography*, London, Taylor and Francis, 1995.

3. E. Sharp, *Unfinished Adventure*, London, John Lane, 1933; C. Hamilton, *Life Errant*, London, J. M. Dent, 1932; Viscountess Rhondda, *This Was My World*, London, Macmillan, 1933.

4. S. S. Friedman, 'Women's autobiographical selves', in S. Benstock (ed.), *The Private Self*, London, Routledge, 1988, p. 38.

5. L. Passerini, *Fascism in Popular Memory: The Cultural Experience of the Turin Working Class*, Cambridge, Cambridge University Press, 1987; A. Portelli, 'Uchronic dreams: working-class memory and possible worlds', in R. Samuel and P. Thompson (eds), *The Myths We Live By*, London, Routledge, 1990.

6. M. Richardson, *Laugh a Defiance*, London, Weidenfeld and Nicolson, 1953.

7. M. R. Richardson, *Cornish Headlands and Other Lyrics*, Cambridge, Heffer, 1920.

8. L. Stanley with A. Morley, *The Life and Death of Emily Wilding Davison*, London, Women's Press, 1988, p. 74; Kean, 'Searching for the past'; unfortunately Weidenfeld have no records of the circumstances surrounding the publication of her book. Whether the focus of the writing was determined by the publisher or by Mary herself is not possible to determine.

9. See in particular L. Tickner, *The Spectacle of Women: Imagery of the Suffrage Campaign 1907-1914*, London, Chatto and Windus, 1987.

10. Kean, 'Searching for the past', p. 68; Norquay, *Voices and Votes*, p. 14.

11. Richardson, *Laugh a Defiance*, p. 6.

12. See similar events in Cicely Hale and Mary Conway's accounts: C. Hale, *A Good Long Time: The Autobiography of an Octogenarian*, London, Regency Press, 1973, p. 47; M. Conway, *Woman Teacher*, 5 October 1928, p. 4.

13. Richardson, *Laugh a Defiance*, p. 20.

14. *Ibid.*, pp. 25-6.

15. *Ibid.*, pp. 46-8.

16. H. Kean, 'Continuity and change: the identity of the political reader', *Changing English*, Vol. 3, No. 2, 1996, pp. 209-18; S. Frosh, *Identity Crisis: Modernity, Psychoanalysis and the Self*, London, Routledge, 1991; A. Giddens, *Modernity and Self-Identity*, Cambridge, Polity Press, 1991.

17. M. Durham, 'Gender and the BUF', *Journal of Contemporary History*, Vol. 27, No. 3, 1992, pp. 513-29.

18. In 1926 she had been adopted as prospective parliamentary candidate for Bury St Edmunds against Colonel Guinness although she never actually stood against him. She did not contest the 1929 election. In 1920 Richardson lived in Cambridge, in the Red House, Haslingfield, from where she published a book of terrible poetry called *Cornish Headlands and Other Lyrics*, with a foreword by Edith Picton Turberville.

19. *Aldershot Gazette*, 15 October 1931, p. 8.

20. At the time of the slashing Christabel Pankhurst declared 'the Rokeby Venus has, because of Miss Richardson's act, acquired a new human and historic interest. For ever more this picture will be a sign and a memorial of women's determination to be free.' *The Suffragette*, 20 March 1914, quoted in R. Fowler, 'Why did suffragettes attack works of art?', *Journal of Women's History*, Vol. 2, No. 3, Winter 1991, p. 122. Some eighty-odd years later no mention of the slashing is recorded in the information panel accompanying the picture in the National Gallery. However, in the new CD-ROM of the gallery's works there are illustrations of the slashing and the statement that it was undertaken by a (nameless) suffragette. It is in this most modern creation of the past that Christabel's hyperbole has become a reality.

21. *Middlesex County Times*, 4 November 1922, p. 7; 18 November 1922, p. 5.

22. *The Vote*, 24 September 1926.

23. *Ibid*.

24. *Ibid*. On Black Friday, 18 November 1910, a deputation of 500 suffrage activists protesting against the shelving of the Conciliation Bill were the subject of police brutality. C. Morrell, *Black Friday: Violence Against Women in the Suffrage Movement*, London, Women's Research and Resources Centre, 1981.

25. *The Vote*, 24 September 1926.

26. The terms 'old' and 'new feminists' were developed in the 1920s to distinguish those campaigners who wished to continue campaigning for equality with men, the 'old' or 'equality' feminists, and those 'new feminists' who emphasized women's role as wives and mothers.

27. *Aldershot Gazette*, 15 October 1931, p. 8.

28. *Ibid*., p. 9.

29. Fowler, 'Why did suffragettes attack works of art?', pp. 112 ff.

30. *Woman's Dreadnought*, 8 March 1914, as published in K. Dodd, *A Sylvia Pankhurst Reader*, Manchester, Manchester University Press, 1993, pp. 53-5.

31. *Aldershot Gazette*, 15 October 1931, pp. 8-9.

32. 'Hurrah for the Blackshirts', *Daily Mail*, January 1934, as reprinted in *Blackshirt*, 19-25 January 1934. The membership of the BUF reached c. 50,000, probably its highest figure, in July 1934, but by October 1935 had declined to c. 5000, with much of this decline attributed to middle-class disapproval after the violence towards opponents shown at the Olympia rally in June 1934. R. Thurlow, *Fascism in Britain*, Oxford, Basil Blackwell, 1987, p. 122.

33. Like several other BUF members, Mary Richardson had also been a member of the New Party. M. Durham, 'Women and the BUF 1932-1940', *Immigrants and Minorities*, Vol. 8, Nos. 1 and 2, 1989, p. 11.

34. R. Benewick, *The Fascist Movement in Britain*, London, Allen Lane,

1972, pp. 113-14; Thurlow, *Fascism*, p. 101. Risdon went on to become the national secretary of the National Anti-Vivisection Society in the 1940s and 1950s; see H. Kean, *Animal Rights: Political and Social Change in Britain since 1800*, London, Reaktion, 1998, pp. 192-3.

35. S. Cullen, 'Four women for Mosley: women in the British Union of Fascists, 1931-40', *Oral History*, Vol. 24, No. 1, Spring 1996, pp. 49-59.

36. 'Pauline', as quoted *ibid.*, p. 57.

37. M. Richardson, 'My reply to Sylvia Pankhurst', *Blackshirt*, 29 June 1934, p. 3.

38. As the East London Federation of Suffragettes (ELFS) paper *Woman's Dreadnought* of 8 March 1914 explained, Sylvia Pankhurst, Mary Richardson and four others were arrested after a rally in Bromley public hall in Bow Road in July 1913. The article of the time expressed the horror of the ELFS when they learned that Mary Richardson and Rachel Peace were being forcibly fed in prison.

39. B. Winslow, *Sylvia Pankhurst*, London, UCL Press, 1996, p. 188.

40. *Blackshirt*, 29 June 1934, p. 3.

41. Morrell, *'Black Friday'*. The Conciliation Bill was an ultimately unsuccessful all-party measure to legislate on the vote for women on a limited scale.

42. Hamilton, *Life Errant*, p. 226.

43. C. Hamilton, *Modern England*, London, J. M. Dent, 1938, p. 72.

44. *Blackshirt* reports in 5 October 1934 that she suffered a motoring accident on the way back from speaking at a meeting in Bedford and would be out of action for two weeks. After November 1934, when she is reported to have spoken at a Liberal Women's Association meeting in Hampstead Garden Suburb, there is no further mention of her involvement. *Ibid.*, 11 November 1934, p. 9. See also N. Mosley, *Beyond the Pale: Sir Oswald Mosley and Family 1933-1980*, London, Secker and Warburg, 1983, p. 92, for an account of the acrimony between Mary Richardson and Lady Mosley, Oswald's mother. For a discussion of the fascist position on women see T. Kushner, 'Politics and race, gender and class; refugees, fascists and domestic services in Britain 1933-1940', *Immigrants and Minorities*, Vol. 8, Nos. 1 and 2, March 1989, pp. 49-58; Durham, 'Gender and the BUF'; N. Elam, 'Fascism, women and democracy', *Fascist Quarterly*, Vol. 3, July 1935, pp. 290 ff.; A. Brock Griggs, 'Women and fascism', BUF, n.d.; O. Hawks, 'On the ideal of womanhood', *Blackshirt*, 5 October 1934, p. 8; J. Linton, 'Fascist women do not want equal rights with men: they desire only the true woman's place in the community', *Blackshirt*, 2 November 1934, p. 9.

45. 'Fascist organiser quits in disgust', *The Star*, 11 February 1935, p. 9.

46. *Blackshirt*, 7 February 1935.

47. Minutes of the Executive Committee of the Six Point Group, 11 February 1936, p. 1, Fawcett Library, London. Unfortunately Mary's letter is not included in the file.

48. By December 1935 the Six Point Group was already organizing on anti-fascist issues. For example, the pamphlet 'Women behind Nazi bars' had been issued; an exhibition against fascism was organized; it had protested to the German Embassy, held meetings about the plight of Abyssinia and participated in a demonstration against fascism in May 1936. See Minutes of Executive Committee of Six Point Group, Fawcett Library, London. When it organized subsequent petitions and telegrams to Hitler – for example in October 1937, concerning Lisalotte Herman and a boy of three sentenced to death – Mary Richardson's signature does not appear, neither does her name appear as a contributor to their financial international appeal.

49. *Woman Today*, November 1936, p. 3.

50. See the absence of material in the Suffragette Fellowship collection at the Museum of London. See too Mayhall, 'Creating the "suffragette spirit"', for an account of the activities of the Suffragette Fellowship.

51. Richardson did live abroad at some stage. See Richardson, *Laugh a Defiance*, p. ix. She was not present at major suffrage celebrations such as the unveiling of a plaque in the Manchester Free Trade Hall in July 1960.

52. *Calling All Women*, July 1960. Unfortunately Smith College has no information on Mary Richardson depositing papers, nor apparently any of her papers. Correspondence with Hilda Kean, 8 February 1996.

53. H. Kean, *Challenging the State? The Socialist and Feminist Educational Experience 1900–1930*, London, Falmer, 1990, pp. 149–50; H. Kean, *Deeds Not Words: The Lives of Suffragette Teachers*, London, Pluto, 1990, pp. 127–36.

54. Women's Freedom League, *Bulletin*, 17 November 1961.

55. Sharp, *Unfinished Adventure*; E. Pethick-Lawrence, *My Part in a Changing World*, London, Victor Gollancz, 1938; Rhondda, *This Was My World*; Hamilton, *Life Errant*. I am suggesting not that other autobiographies were not published after this date but that the examples cited here were part of a collective suffrage genre written by women still active in the feminist movement. See Kean, 'Searching for the past'.

11 'What a Lot There Is Still to Do': Stella Browne (1880–1955) – Carrying the Struggle Ever Onward

Lesley A. Hall

Frances Worsley Stella Browne (she always used the name Stella) crops up as a character of some interest in several manifestations of the 'first wave' of British feminism. She participated in early twentieth-century feminist debates on sexuality, the British birth control movement in the inter-war years, women's struggles within the Labour Party during the same period, and the abortion law reform movement. She was one of the founders of the Abortion Law Reform Association in 1936, the culmination of two decades of activism in which she had, almost alone, spoken out for safe and legal abortion as a necessary element in contraceptive provision. She has been depicted as representative of the 'new feminism' of the post-First World War era, defined as less concerned with political and civic rights and more with women's special biological needs, in particular those to do with reproduction.[1]

In fact Stella was nearly 40 and eligible for the limited suffrage when it was granted following the First World War, and had had at least a decade of activism in women's causes behind her. In 1916 she wrote that she had 'observed the Suffrage movement in England, from within and without, for some years':[2] assuming that the Miss S. Browne, Mrs Stella Browne, Miss Stella Browne and Miss Browne who thus variously appear in the Annual Reports of the Women's Social and Political Union[3] were all the same woman and that this was the same Stella Browne who was a vociferous participant in debates in the correspondence columns of *The Freewoman* in 1912, she was a veteran of the suffrage campaign.

Stella appears to have spent some time in Germany before the First World War and to have had contact with the more radical elements of the German feminist movement, for example the group around Dr Helene Stöcker, although it has not yet proved possible to ascertain the exact details of this period of her life. Certainly the issues with which she was associated were those to which German feminists were devoting their energies, focusing far more explicitly on issues of marriage, motherhood and sexuality than on questions of political rights. Stella, however, did not see commitment to causes such as divorce law reform, birth control and the reform of the legitimacy laws as excluding participation in the campaign for women to be recognized as fully equal citizens; rather she saw these as facets of a struggle taking place over many fronts. Reviewing Havelock Ellis's *The Task of Social Hygiene* in 1912 for the *English Review*, she suggested that he underestimated 'the moral value of this active and articulate revolt against *tradition as well as present conditions*' embodied in the militant suffrage movement, while praising his analysis of 'the wider implications ... the claim to full expression and experience'.[4]

Recent studies of the suffrage movement have demonstrated that the common image of its participants as being solely focused on winning the suffrage and blind to wider social issues concerning women and indeed other members of the community is extremely misleading. As Liz Stanley has pointed out in her study of Emily Wilding Davison, the women who were active in the suffrage struggle did not seek the vote for its own sake but (apart from its symbolic significance as representing full enfranchisement as a citizen) as a means by which women could eradicate or ameliorate a wide range of evils affecting women and children (and men) of all social classes.[5] June Hannam has demonstrated how closely entwined socialism and feminism were in the career of Isabella Ford, and how impossible it is to tease apart her commitment to equal rights from her awareness of the necessity for the recognition of women's special qualities, her devotion to the economic emancipation of women from her desire to reform domestic life and the conditions of motherhood.[6] The suffragette Teresa Billington-Greig saw the movement as embodying 'the spirit of emancipation, the great hunger for human progress and liberty which was seeking utterance through the channel of militancy',[7] and when she quit the militant suffrage campaign she considered that 'the choice of avenues of productive feminist work [outside the struggle for the vote] is only too great'.[8]

Stella, like a number of other activists, became somewhat disenchanted with the 'towering spiritual arrogance' she perceived in the WSPU leadership,[9] and the 'dogmatic and tyrannical' bureaucracy within the suffrage movement.[10] On the basis of personal experience she criticized the 'self-advertising *arrivisme* and snobbery' of 'arrant humbug[s]' within the movement, whose behaviour towards other women and men in a 'less advantageous social position' formed an 'illuminating commentary on [their] incessant protestations of feminism and democracy'.[11]

She was far from alone in quitting the WSPU in 1913. By that time many convinced supporters of the struggle were becoming alienated by the autocratic leadership style of the Pankhursts. In 1911 Billington-Greig (who had left the WSPU in 1907), publicly and in the full knowledge of the tendentiousness of her position, deplored the autocracy of the Pankhursts and what she perceived as their opportunistic political agenda leading to deleterious tactical shiftings of position. She delineated the militant movement as having taken on all the worst emotionalistic qualities of religious revivalism, becoming a 'system of mental and spiritual slavery' full of dangerously obsessed women mired in 'snobbery and narrowness and intolerance'.[12] These suggestions of a quality of self-glorificatory masochism among some sections of the movement were also hinted at by Edith How-Martyn when looking back to her days as a militant. She was moved to comment that 'causes can be very merciless things ... many fine workers are ruined in health quite uselessly'.[13] She further remarked on 'how we partly wasted much of our human material in laying too much stress on going to prison' and much more through 'overwork and overstrain'.[14] Many women became cynical about the way the militant campaign was run and refused to continue to give it their support, but did not abandon wider commitments to the emancipation of women.

Stella's comments about the suffrage leadership, which have sometimes been used to site her as hostile to the political aspects of emancipation and interested only in sexual liberation, need to be read in this context of a more widespread disillusionment with the direction in which the WSPU was moving. Like Billington-Greig, she did not find herself happy in a movement which had become 'socially exclusive, punctiliously correct, gracefully fashionable, ultra-respectable, and narrowly religious'.[15] While Stanley and Morley's study of Emily Wilding Davison and Sandra Holton's recent *Suffrage Days* caution against too monolithic an interpretation of the WSPU as a body and of its role in the suffrage movement as a whole,[16] it is clear that the leadership generated a certain degree of disfavour among some contemporaries.

Although women sought enfranchisement precisely so that they could abolish or ameliorate a vast range of evils which they believed women suffered uniquely, or to a far greater extent than men, British suffrage organizations were extremely chary of identifying themselves with any issue which might seem to associate the Cause with anything unrespectable. Some of these and their possible remedies from tactical necessity ought, it was believed, to remain inexplicit: as Billington-Greig put it – and not in any tone of approval – 'It pays for its one breach of decorum with additional circumspection in all other directions.'[17] Suffrage journals might consider questions of motherhood and the need to improve maternity services, and even touch on the evils of venereal disease. Debates on these issues, however, were predicated upon assumptions of the primacy of chaste monogamous marriage, threatened by male vice and hypocrisy, and upon perceptions of female sexuality as predominantly maternal. In 1931 Edith How-Martyn, herself a former activist in the Women's Freedom League, wrote to the American birth-control campaigner Margaret Sanger about the recent enfranchisement of Spanish women and expressed the opinion, doubtless based on her own experiences, that 'Women with a vote can defy the church and public opinion, without the vote they are afraid to speak out on b[irth] c[ontrol] as it may prevent them getting the vote.'[18]

Even so, a small section of the suffrage movement had been by tradition sympathetic to the cause of contraception. Dr Alice Vickery, the consort of Charles Robert Drysdale of the Malthusian League, the only British birth-control organization in existence before the First World War and in which she herself was a leading figure, was a feminist who had participated in many of the nineteenth-century struggles, including that for female medical education. She was a pillar of the Women's Freedom League and her writings for the Malthusian League put a feminist and not simply a standard economic case for birth control. There were a few other women like her who were veterans of both struggles and saw them as allied, and certainly Stella believed that 'The cause of Women's Enfranchisement is closely linked with Birth Control.'[19]

In fact there was a close relationship between feminism and a broad agenda of sexual reform going well beyond the concern for suffering motherhood which often actuated advocacy of birth control. The tradition of critique of male-dominated sexual mores has been delineated in Lucy Bland's recent *Banishing the Beast* and elsewhere, establishing that this critique cannot be divided neatly into a selfless philanthropic desire to eradicate prostitution and sexual abuse and the quest for a chaste bodily autonomy on the one hand, and a selfish agenda of personal sexual liberation on the other.[20] The institution of marriage was attacked, as well as sexual exploitation outside it; as Teresa Billington-Greig put it, 'the home ... is built upon the subjection of the woman and continued by the infringement of the rights of the child. ... Any woman who is really a rebel longs to destroy the conventions which bind her in the home.'[21] The need for open discussion of previously taboo topics was asserted: male suffragist and playwright Laurence Housman paid tribute to the fearlessness of the suffrage movement and its upsetting of outworn standards of modesty which made it possible to discuss 'an intimate and painful sex-problem' (presumably homosexuality) at a public meeting during 1913.[22]

From Stella's comments in the essay 'Some problems of sex' on the vociferous group among the suffragists advocating 'the reduction, almost the extirpation, of the sex impulse in men', the publication of Christabel Pankhurst's diatribe *The Great Scourge* in 1913 may have proved the last straw. While considering that the male sexual impulse needed to become 'more interwoven with the imagination and the affections, more altruistic and comradely, and above all, more instinctively discriminating', she did 'not believe that it would be a good thing if the majority of men *could* be subjected to the desexualising repression from which most women are only just emerging'.[23] She was not the only feminist appalled by the line taken by Pankhurst: Rebecca West was similarly horrified by her ferocity towards the male. While conceding that 'The fallen man may be something ... no woman wants as a lover ... too cheap and dirty to have much to do with', West pointed out that he was 'as much a victim of social conditions as the fallen woman'. She was depressed that 'a long and desperate struggle ... for women to write candidly on subjects such as these' had resulted in such 'old-fashioned and uncharitable views'.[24]

So it did not run counter to the spirit of the suffrage movement for women to move into more active engagement in the sphere of reproductive and sexual issues following the attainment of the vote, and many former suffrage activists did this (Edith How-Martyn's move into the birth control campaign has already been mentioned). Stella, however, had been explicitly advancing a feminist case not only for birth control but for the legalization of abortion since before the First World War. Many years later in 1937, presenting evidence to the Interdepartmental Committee on Abortion (the Birkett Committee), she described how she had become sensitized to this issue. During the period 1907–12 she had been employed as librarian at Morley College, which she described as 'an institution which looked after the mental and civic education of working people'. While there she had received confidences from other women (both working-class and professional) which gave her insight into the 'unnatural sufferings and complications in the lives of women'.[25] At a meeting of *The Freewoman* discussion circle in 1912 addressed by Dr Drysdale of the Malthusian League, Stella commented during the ensuing discussion that

> medical men received dozens of letters from frantic girls anxious to procure abortion, and if their humanity led them to comply, they were faced with ruin and penal servitude ... instruction in the means of prevention was the only method of avoiding this terrible dilemma.[26]

This seems to have been her first encounter with the Malthusian League and it is apparent that she was already a convinced feminist and suffragette, and evincing a concern with the problem of abortion, when she became involved with it.

However, she was by no means a single-issue fanatic and shared sympathies with a wide range of campaigns, for example speaking up on various occasions on the iniquities of regulated prostitution, a long-standing concern of the British feminist movement. She put her views, which did not differ substantially from those of Josephine Butler herself, in a 1912 letter to *The Freewoman*: 'State Regulation subtly but unmistakably debases the status of *all* women.' To achieve a real remedy for the evils of venereal disease required major changes in society and woman's role.[27] In 1918 she attempted to stimulate the British Society for the Study of Sex Psychology to protest against the inequitable regulation 40D under the Defence of the Realm Act, widely perceived by feminists as reinscribing the Contagious Diseases Acts under the guise of the necessities of the wartime situation.[28]

Stella clearly saw herself as part of an enduring tradition of resistance to male-created conventional moral standards inseparable from the struggle for political emancipation. In 1928 she commented that many supporters of birth control 'will have been active in the celebrations of the Josephine Butler centenary'. She praised Butler's 'proclamation of individuality and individual worth and choice' and her 'enormous courage against odds'. If an equal moral standard was not being worked out precisely along the lines anticipated by the Ladies' National Association for the Repeal of the Contagious Diseases Acts, there was still not, Stella suggested, 'so much steadfast courage or so much honest sex pride or solidarity among women, that we can afford to forget Mrs Butler's work'.[29] In the previous year she had paid tribute to Alison Neilans of the Association of Moral and Social Hygiene (as the Ladies' National Association had become), who had 'exactly expresse[d] the great objection to prostitution in general and licensed houses in particular, from the point of view of human individuality, quite apart from theological or conventional ideas'.[30]

Much of Stella's writing during the 1910s and 1920s was specifically directed to advancing the cause of birth control, and the largest amount appeared in *The Malthusian*, renamed *The New Generation* in 1922, a periodical specifically devoted to that cause. This may account for her apparent concentration on the issue; however, Stella would seem to have felt that many other aspects of women's emancipation were being adequately dealt with by others.

Stella was fully aware of and did not ignore the problems of single working women such as herself. In her article 'Women and the race', which appeared in *The Socialist Review* in 1917, responding to an anti-feminist article by male socialist S.H. Halford, Stella commented dryly, 'Mr Halford seems to me to over-estimate the magnificence and scope of women's economic prospects!'[31] This was a subject about which Stella, a graduate of Somerville and fluent in at least two foreign languages, knew a great deal: she never seems to have held a good job in her life, but had to do a lot of things, many quite uncongenial, in order to make a living. Although on pacifist principles she had eschewed war work, she was sensitive to the anomalous position of women who had assisted in the war effort. In 1918 a poem of hers entitled 'Scrapped: The Women Munition Workers of Britain, Before and After November 1918' was published in the socialist newspaper *The Call*:

> You have done well: To you we owe our lives
> Our soldiers' glory, and our prosperous days.
> Handmaids of Vulcan, sisters, heroes' wives!
> Our thanks shall match our praise.
>
> Well – as you see – inevitable quite,
> – ('Though very, very sad, of course, indeed!) –

> The world is ours! We've won our War for Right!
> Now, women, you can go! You've served our Need![32]

In an article in *The Communist* in 1922 she reiterated this point: 'the women who were gushed at as "splendid" and "saviours of the country" in war time are now realising that it is once more economically a crime to be a woman'. She additionally noted the way in which the 'economic position of women has been injured ... by the deliberate policy of the Government in playing off the temporary women clerks and the ex-servicemen against one another'.[33] In 1926 she reiterated cautions against tendencies to be 'far too sanguine about the present conditions and immediate prospects of financial independence for women' not only among many men but even among that minority of women already enjoying 'social and economic security'. Women, she suggested, had 'not advanced halfway towards economic justice'.[34]

Apart from her acute awareness of the specifically economic injustices which still bore hard on the unmarried working woman, she also, on several occasions, condemned the social pressures upon her to live, at least in appearance, a desexualized life. She deplored the fact that 'women of independent minds and ardent natures can find no publicly recognised and honoured form of sex union which meets both their needs'. Those who engaged in free unions, caught 'between the upper and nether millstones of legal marriage and prostitution', were often broken or degraded by this 'ceaseless, grinding, social pressure'.[35] Women who were 'unwilling to accept marriage – under present laws – or prostitution' had to struggle against 'the whole social order' for '[their] most precious personal right'. There was 'huge, persistent, indirect pressure on women of strong passions and fine brains' to find an emotional outlet with other women. Existing social arrangements, Stella suggested, repressed female sexual instincts and militated against women's forming either satisfactory and unstigmatized relationships with men or healthy relationships with one another.[36]

Although Stella clearly did not imagine that the single unmarried working woman was necessarily any better off than the overburdened married one, the main thrust of her activities throughout the 1920s was on behalf of married women, predominantly of the poorer classes. Denying any maternal instinct in herself, she yet worked for the good of overburdened mothers in a variety of ways. She was closely associated with the Workers' Birth Control Group, which from 1923 to 1930 campaigned vigorously to rescind the Ministry of Health's edict that birth control advice could not be given in local authority maternal welfare clinics, often the only source of medical advice available to working-class women. She articulated the case for birth control in a variety of publications. She was additionally active, as a leading member of the Chelsea Labour Party, in endeavouring to influence the party leadership to incorporate this measure onto its platform. And she addressed many meetings small and large, mixed and women-only, not only in the London area but all round the country, on the political issues of birth control and practical methods, and more generally on questions of women's health. As well as all this she managed to lead what she later described as a sexually and intellectually active life, make several significant translations of continental sexological texts, and keep up with modern writing in at least three languages. For a woman whose health was by no means robust, this was quite impressive!

For Stella, feminism was an intrinsic element within a wide-ranging agenda of political, social, economic and moral reform. She did not merely want herself or women like her to have a bigger slice of the existing cake: she wanted a different cake altogether. In perhaps her best-known work, the pamphlet *Sexual Variety and Variability among Women*, published by the British Society for the Study of Sex Psychology in 1917, based on a lecture she gave to the Society in 1915, she argued that no 'intelligent, humane, and self-respecting attitude towards sex' would be possible without major economic and social changes within society as a whole. She perceived the so-called double standard to be an 'integral part of a certain social order', and it was, she suggested, 'absurd' to repudiate it while continuing to accept that social order.[37]

Stella was an ardent socialist, a member of the British Socialist Party and later of the Communist Party, which she left in 1923 because of its refusal to incorporate birth control into its programme, though as a very left-wing member of the Labour Party she continued to be sympathetic to its aims. The women's organization of which she spoke most warmly was not any of the suffrage organizations or their successors of the 1920s, but the Women's Cooperative Guild. Certainly the causes with which Stella was identified, such as divorce law reform and maternity endowment, were those on which the Guild was also eloquent.

Perhaps the most extended and coherent statement of Stella's political position is to be found in her 1917 paper 'Women and birth control'. In this essay Stella deplored the recent upsurge of pronatalist propaganda in heated terms ('licensed imbecilities', 'senile tirades') and spoke up on behalf of 'the woman who claims to be, not a domestic utensil, but a citizen, a human being, and free in her motherhood and her love'. The nation-state as it existed was identified by Stella as monetarist, militarist and exclusively masculine in its structure. It gave women 'neither equality of opportunity, nor adequate special protection', yet demanded child-bearing with no reciprocal rights.

If women were to 'give their best energies' to bearing and rearing children, Stella argued, they ought at least to be able to do so under tolerable conditions and with the prospect of a tolerable existence for those children. Stella laid out a far-reaching manifesto of what would make this possible, taking in reforms in housing, food supply and agricultural policy, education and health provision, revision of the divorce and illegitimacy laws, and the granting of universal adult suffrage. A political system which disregarded women; an economic system which was 'iniquity and waste incarnate; and sexual institutions based on the needs and preferences of a primitive type of man' – these had 'no moral claim on women's bodies as instruments of propagation'. Stella stated in this article (and it was a reiterated theme in her birth control agitation of the 1920s) that 'it has never been safe for women to trust to the gratitude and justice of groups of men' – something she must have found exemplified by the pusillanimity of the Parliamentary Labour Party and Ramsay MacDonald's evasiveness over the giving of contraceptive advice in maternity clinics, in the face of overwhelming and repeated demands by Labour women.

Stella argued for voluntary motherhood, freely undertaken, based on free sexual selection by women. She put forward a case for the right to motherhood of those women of 'strongly maternal type' who were condemned to 'compulsory sterility' as others were to 'compulsory maternity', under the existing 'obsolescent patriarchal system' which insisted that only married women could become mothers and stigmatized and harassed the single mother and her illegitimate child. Women, Stella went on to state, had been the victims of 'masculine mythology suppressing and distorting all the facts of women's sexual and maternal emotions'. She was therefore speaking up not only on behalf of the 'many women exhausted by maternity' but also for those 'most intelligent, determined and morally elevated women' who rejected love and children under conditions which offended 'their own human dignity, conscience and reason'.[38]

Stella condemned, as a group and individually, privileged women who used their privileges selfishly or for the benefit of their own restricted circle. Lady Astor's 'nauseating humbug'[39] and Margot Asquith's 'dense ignorance'[40] were, perhaps predictably, subjected to caustic criticism. Astor was confronted with the accusation that 'Almost any prohibitive, punitive or repressive measure, dealing with sex, has found its champion in you',[41] while Asquith's objections to contraception were suggested to derive from the fact that 'Birth Control would have deprived the world of Mrs Asquith and her brother ... the youngest of a very large family. So that's that. Q.E.D.'[42] But apart from these particularly prominent figures, there were also 'women of the most expensively educated and publicly active type, whose initiative and independence on the private side of their lives as well as on Committees could be in no manner of doubt', who ignored the pressing needs of working women.[43] Such one-sided activism led Stella to attack the Six Point Group, for example, for apparently considering 'Lady Rhondda's right to sit and vote in the Upper House more urgent than working women's right to refuse to bear children they do not desire and cannot support'.[44] In 1926 she condemned *Time and Tide* for its exclusive concentration on political equality, calling its deploring of the preoccupation with birth control 'sexphobia', and 'hardly honest' for women 'themselves exceptionally energetic, articulate [and] fortunate'.[45]

However, in 1927 she conceded that the 'tardy and grudging concession' by the government of the franchise on the same terms to women as men could have been achieved only by the 'persistent agitation' of the National Union of Societies for Equal Citizenship (NUSEC) and the Six Point Group, and pointed out the lessons the birth control movement could learn from them.[46] She later referred to the franchise as an 'overrated but often helpful weapon', while paying homage to predecessors who, 'believing that we were really human beings, worked and suffered in that cause'.[47] When NUSEC finally swung over to support birth control she paid tribute to its members' 'immense political ability and experience'.[48] She praised NUSEC's contribution to the agitation in the following terms:

> When once they took the plunge, they worked with practised skill, with a conspicuous moderation in their actual demands, which reassured that timid creature, British Public Opinion, and with a most logical and effective synthesis of the demand for birth control knowledge with that advocacy of Family Endowment which Councillor Eleanor Rathbone has made her life work,

adding that this 'conclusively [gave] the lie to the imputation that women who are neither legal wives nor mothers are careless ... of the right of motherhood to free and decent treatment'.[49] For her the suffrage movement was a model of effective agitation, a struggle which had schooled women in the political skills necessary to fight a whole range of other causes.

If Stella chastised explicitly feminist groups for their lack of concern for reproductive issues, she also had no patience with women who had achieved power within the Labour Party but obsequiously followed the MacDonald line and ignored or rebuked the agitators for birth control. Ethel Bentham and Marion Phillips came off little better at Stella's hands than Lady Astor or Margot Asquith.[50] But no praise was too high for Dorothy Jewson: Stella paid many tributes to her comrade and friend as one who effectively combined genuine socialism with true feminism.[51]

Stella's vision of women's rights as an indivisible package comprising both civil and political recognition and respect for their biological role was confirmed in 1934, when she took part in a debate on whether 'the relationship of the sexes is better under communism than fascism' against William Joyce of the British Union of Fascists, later notorious as the Nazi broadcaster 'Lord Haw-Haw'. Stella, conceding that fascism honoured and provided for women as mothers, contended that it did so 'at the expense of their full humanity'. Under communism, however, women were admitted to 'a full share in industry, the professions and administration', while provision was also made for the child-bearer. Divorce was accessible, the status of illegitimacy had been abolished, and the right of refusal to bear unwanted children recognized. (Whatever Soviet communism actually achieved, this account depicts Stella's view of an ideal state of affairs.) She added that 'so long as women are regarded only in their relationship to men, as mothers or mates, nothing new [is] likely to evolve'.[52]

Stella's vision of the ideal society was one in which women were full participants and which built into its arrangements provision for women's particular needs: menstruation and menopause as well as maternity. She did not merely want the entry of a few women into an existing male-defined structure. She was thus engaged in a battle on several fronts, too militantly socialist and too concerned with unrespectable sexual issues for the mainstream feminist organizations, too feminist and similarly too concerned with unrespectable and politically perilous sexual questions for the Labour Party, and within the Malthusian League the Drysdales in particular flinched from her political sympathies. She seems to have felt it her duty, or her inclination, to fight for feminist agendas in mixed and not necessarily primarily feminist organizations. This may have been positively congenial given what she described in a letter to Havelock Ellis as her 'strong "red rag" temperament'.[53]

The Malthusian League had a strong strand of connection to mid-Victorian feminist struggles, both political and social, such as the campaign to repeal the Contagious Diseases Acts. However, it put forward the case for birth control predominantly in terms of a mid-nineteenth-century political economy argument which was increasingly coming to seem outdated and irrelevant in a period of growing state intervention in health and education. But until 1921, when Marie Stopes set up her Society for Constructive Birth Control, it was the only organization in Britain prepared to argue publicly for the spread of contraceptive knowledge (even if it was somewhat pusillanimous in actually providing practical information), and thus attracted Stella and others, such as Eden and Cedar Paul, the communist sex-reformers, and H.G. Wells, to whom the political and economic theories espoused by the Drysdales were anathema, because it was the only forum in which the issue was being discussed.

Even when other birth-control organizations had been established, Stella stuck with the Malthusian League. She did not, for example, formally join the Worker's Birth Control Group (WBCG), although she worked with it in close alliance. There were various reasons for this, including the desire of the WBCG to present itself as a body of working-class married mothers fighting for the cause of birth control, but – apart from the fact that she had a semi-official position with *The New Generation*, as it became, as a contributor – part of the attraction was surely that she was advancing the feminist (and socialist) case for birth control to an audience which might otherwise not have encountered it, and had contact with such networks as the League had built up, besides the ones she had with the Women's Cooperative Guild, Labour Party women's sections and so on.

Similarly Stella was extremely active for a number of years in the British Society for the Study of Sex Psychology (and continued to remain on good terms with it after her resignation from the committee). On several occasions she was reported in minutes as drawing the membership's attention to various topics of feminist import, such as the agitation already mentioned against section 40D of DORA (the Defence of the Realm Act), which penalized women, but not men, for communicating venereal disease. Besides giving papers in which she presented feminist arguments – her famous papers 'Sexual variety and variability' and 'Female inversion', a contribution entitled 'Women, birth control and the social order' to a symposium on birth control in 1922, and later, unpublished papers on both abortion and wider issues of female sexuality – it is clear that she was an active participant in the discussion of other speakers' papers. She also created and kept up contacts between the Society and various feminist organizations, for example persuading the International Suffrage Shop to stock the society's pamphlets.[54]

Throughout the 1930s Stella was a sought-after speaker, addressing such bodies as the Federation of Progressive Societies and Individuals and the Promethean Society as well as secular and ethical societies, the women's organizations already mentioned, and the British Sexology Society. On the basis of her 1935 essay 'The right to abortion'[55] and her contribution to the debate with the fascist Joyce, it can be assumed that her talks all manifested the many-faceted, no-compromise feminism already described. It can be argued that Stella took the vision of the suffrage generation to the younger generation of the 1930s, keeping alive a flame that is often believed to have been flickering feebly under the vicissitudes of this decade. Dora Russell, looking back to the early days of the Abortion Law Reform Association, described Stella as 'What we used to call a war-horse, a sort of militant suffrage type. ... Quite irrepressible at getting up and interrupting a meeting or asking questions.'[56]

In 1936 she helped to found the Abortion Law Reform Association (ALRA). Although the abortion problem was being discussed in the mid-1930s as an issue of maternal and child welfare (as indeed was birth control), Stella, in her 1935 essay, her evidence to the Birkett Committee and her work with ALRA, gave it a much more broadly feminist significance as an issue of female bodily autonomy, rejecting proposals to mete it out in 'deserving' cases and forcibly arguing for the woman's choice to be the paramount consideration.

She did not give up. Even when far from her comrades in struggle after her move to Liverpool in 1942, she continued for the rest of her life to remain in touch with ALRA, to write letters to a wide variety of periodicals, and generally support the cause. The suffrage struggle was one of her inspirations: she wrote to Alice Jenkins of ALRA in 1953, 'But surely you did not expect us to win *in the first round??* My goodness! when I remember the fights for Contraception, even in my time ...! also, the fights for suffrage, divorce reform, etc.'[57]

She was 75 and still a fighter when, sight going and mobility impaired by rheumatism, she died, twelve years before the passing of the Abortion Act – which, however, she would surely have thought did not go far enough. Indeed, barely a month before her death she wrote to Alice Jenkins that even though terminations on medical grounds seemed to be becoming more frequent, 'What a lot there is still to do!'[58]

Stella Browne, therefore, not only was inspired by the suffrage movement as a model of political agitation, but saw herself as carrying its essential meaning forward into a range of further struggles for women's existence as autonomous beings within society. She continued to count herself a feminist when this was an unfashionable and outmoded thing to be. Her career during a period in which it has been supposed that the energies of the suffrage struggle were dissipated leads us to reconsider what was actually happening once the vote had been achieved and feminists turned their attentions to an array of other injustices under which women continued to suffer. These were so many, and so entrenched, that it is perhaps no wonder that the struggles against them do not have the drama of the campaign for the vote; but we should not therefore imagine that feminism had died or was silent. Stella Browne's was one life and one voice which remind us that this was far from the case, and the analysis of the activities of other former suffrage campaigners following the concession of the vote in 1918 would surely reveal similar patterns.

Notes

1. See, for example, S. Jeffreys, *The Spinster and Her Enemies: Feminism and Sexuality, 1880-1930*, London, Pandora Press, 1985; M. Jackson, *The Real Facts of Life: Feminism and the Politics of Sexuality c. 1850-1940*, London, Taylor & Francis, 1994.

2. F. W. S. Browne, 'Some problems of sex', *International Journal of Ethics*, Vol. 27, 1916-17, pp. 464-71.

3. Annual reports of the Women's Social and Political Union, the Fawcett Library, London.

4. *English Review*, Vol. 13, 1912, p. 157.

5. L. Stanley with A. Morley, *The Life and Death of Emily Wilding Davison: A Biographical Detective Story*, London, Women's Press, 1988, pp. 83-5.

6. J. Hannam, *Isabella Ford*, Oxford, Basil Blackwell, 1989, pp. 98-107.

7. T. Billington-Greig, *The Militant Suffrage Movement: Emancipation in a Hurry* (first published 1911), in C. McPhee and A. Fitzgerald (eds), *The Non-Violent Militant: Selected Writings of Teresa Billington-Greig*, London, Routledge and Kegan Paul, 1987, p. 162.
8. *Ibid.*, p. 221.
9. F. W. S. Browne, 'Studies in feminine inversion', *Journal of Sexology and Psychoanalysis*, Vol. 1, 1923, pp. 51–8.
10. Browne, 'Some problems of sex'.
11. F. W. S. Browne, 'Women in industry' [letter], *New Age*, 22 July 1915, p. 293.
12. Billington-Greig, *The Militant Suffrage Movement*, p. 181.
13. E. How-Martyn to M. Sanger, 19 July 1915, Margaret Sanger papers in Library of Congress, Washington, DC, Vol. 21.
14. How-Martyn to Sanger, 27 July 1915.
15. Billington-Greig, *The Militant Suffrage Movement*, pp. 141–2.
16. Stanley with Morley, *The Life and Death of Emily Wilding Davison*; S. S. Holton, *Suffrage Days: Stories from the Women's Suffrage Movement*, London, Routledge, 1996.
17. Billington-Greig, *The Militant Suffrage Movement*, p. 142.
18. E. How-Martyn to M. Sanger, 6 October 1931: Margaret Sanger Papers in the Library of Congress, Washington, DC, Vol. 22, 'Great Britain'.
19. F. W. S. Browne, 'Marking time', *New Generation*, Vol. 6, 1927, p. 89.
20. L. Bland, *Banishing the Beast: English Feminism and Sexual Morality, 1885–1914*, London, Penguin, 1995; L. Hall, 'Sex, science, and suffrage', in M. Joannou and J. Purvis (eds), *The Women's Suffrage Movement: New Feminist Perspectives*, Manchester, Manchester University Press, 1998.
21. Billington-Greig, *The Militant Suffrage Movement*, pp. 197–8.
22. L. Housman to J. Ashbee, 23 August 1913, Ashbee Journals, Vol. 25, King's College Cambridge, Modern Records Centre.
23. Browne, 'Some problems of sex'.
24. R. West, 'On mentioning the unmentionable: an exhortation to Miss Pankhurst', first published in *The Clarion*, 26 September 1913, in J. Marcus, *The Young Rebecca: Writings of Rebecca West 1911–1917*, London, Macmillan, 1982, pp. 202–6.
25. Minutes of Evidence at the Eighth Meeting of the Interdepartmental Committee on Abortion, Ministry of Health, 17 November 1937: Evidence of Miss F. W. Stella Browne. Ministry of Health records (PRO: MH71/23), Public Record Office, Kew, London.
26. *The Malthusian*, September 1912.
27. F. W. S. Browne, 'The immorality of the marriage contract', *The Freewoman*, 4 July 1912, pp. 135–6.
28. L. Hall, '"Disinterested enthusiasm for sexual misconduct": the British Society for the Study of Sex Psychology, 1913–1947', *Journal of Contemporary History*, Vol. 30, 1995, pp. 665–86.

29. F. W. S. Browne, 'Current notes', *New Generation*, Vol. 7, 1928, p. 53.
30. F. W. S. Browne, 'Stocktaking', *New Generation*, Vol. 6, 1927, p. 102.
31. F. W. S. Browne, 'Women and the race', *Socialist Review: A Quarterly Review of Modern Thought*, Vol. 14, May-June 1917, pp. 151-7.
32. F. W. S. Browne, 'Scrapped: the women munition workers of Britain, before and after November 1918', *The Call*, 12 December 1918, p. 7.
33. F. W. S. Browne, 'The women's question', *The Communist*, 11 March 1922.
34. 'FWSB', 'Mr Joad's book', review of C. E. M. Joad, *Thrasymachus, or The Future of Morals*, *New Generation*, Vol. 5, 1926, p. 32.
35. F. W. S. Browne, 'Review: *The Sexual Crisis: A Critique of Our Sex Life*. By Grete Meisel-Hess', *The Malthusian*, 1917, p. 39.
36. Browne, 'Studies in feminine inversion'.
37. F. W. S. Browne, *The Sexual Variety and Variability among Women and Their Bearing upon Social Reconstruction*, London, British Society for the Study of Sex Psychology, 1917.
38. F. W. S. Browne, 'Women and birth control', in E. Paul and C. Paul (eds), *Population and Birth Control: A Symposium*, New York, The Critic and Guide Company, 1917, pp. 247-57.
39. F. W. S. Browne, 'An open letter to Lady Astor, MP', *New Generation*, Vol. 4, 1925, p. 65.
40. F. W. S. Browne, 'Friends and foes of birth control', *New Generation*, Vol. 3, 1924, p. 135.
41. Browne, 'An open letter to Lady Astor, MP'.
42. Browne, 'Friends and foes of birth control'.
43. Browne, 'Stocktaking'.
44. 'FWSB', 'Our movement', *New Generation*, Vol. 5, 1926, p. 53.
45. F. W. S. Browne, 'Birth control in Parliament', *New Generation*, Vol. 4, 1925, p. 76.
46. 'FWSB', 'Our movement'.
47. F. W. S. Browne, 'Current political notes', *New Generation*, Vol. 7, 1928, p. 44.
48. 'FWSB', 'Our movement'.
49. F. W. S. Browne, 'Victory – or compromise?', *New Generation*, Vol. 6, 1927, p. 39.
50. F. W. S. Browne, 'An open letter to Dr Ethel Bentham, by a socialist woman', *New Generation*, Vol. 2, 1924, p. 84; 'Climb-down or camouflage? Dr Marion Phillips answered', *New Generation*, Vol. 3, 1924, pp. 114-15; 'Dr Ethel Bentham answered', *New Generation*, Vol. 3, 1924, p. 128.
51. The most extensive is F. W. S. Browne, 'One of our liberators: Dorothy Jewson', *Medical Critic and Guide* (New York), August 1925, pp. 316-19.
52. 'FWSB', 'Lyceum Club debate', *New Generation*, Vol. 3, 1924, p. 47.
53. Stella Browne to Havelock Ellis, 6 March 1922, Additional Manu-

scripts 70539, Havelock Ellis Papers, Department of Manuscripts, British Library.

54. Hall, '"Disinterested enthusiasm for sexual misconduct"'; see also the archives of the British Sexology Society in the Harry Ransom Humanities Research Center, University of Texas at Austin.

55. F. W. S. Browne, A. M. Ludovici and H. Roberts, *Abortion (Three Essays)*, London, Allen and Unwin, 1935.

56. K. Hindell and M. Simms, *Abortion Law Reformed*, London, Peter Owen, 1971, p. 59.

57. S. Browne to A. Jenkins, 31 August 1953, Abortion Law Reform Association archives (SA/ALR/B.5.), Contemporary Medical Archives Centre, Wellcome Institute for the History of Medicine (hereafter CMAC).

58. S. Browne to A. Jenkins, 30 March 1955, SA/ALR/B.5, CMAC.

Index

Aboriginals 10, 164
abortion 190, 194, 201
Abortion Act (1967) 202
Abortion Law Reform Association (ALRA) 190, 201, 202
Actresses' Franchise League (AFL) 92, 94, 153
adult suffrage 25, 44, 127, 138, 139, 166, 170, 171
Adult Suffrage Society (ASS) 162, 170, 171
AFL, see Actresses' Franchise League
Allen, Mary 105, 108-13, 115, 116, 119
ALRA, see Abortion Law Reform Association
Amery, L. S. 152
Anderson, William 137
androcentrism 91
animal rights 29
Anthony, Susan B. 27
Anti-Corn Law campaign 70, 71
anti-slavery movement 70, 71
Artists' Suffrage League 91
Asquith, Herbert 6, 62, 63-4, 83, 155, 156
Asquith, Margot 198, 199
ASS, see Adult Suffrage Society
Association of Moral and Social Hygiene 195
Astor, Lady 111, 112, 198, 199
Augsburg, Anita 12
Austen, Jane 93, 96
Australia 1, 10, 12, 69, 164, 171
Australia First movement 113

Baldwin, H. A. 179
Baldwin, Stanley 113
Balfour, Clara Lucas 71
Balgarnie, Florence 79, 83
Ball, William 31
Barry, Florence 46, 47, 48
Bath 55, 56, 58, 60
Bath Ladies' Microscopical Society 55, 56

Baxter, Officer 117-18
BBC 115
BCL, see British Commonwealth League
BDWSU, see British Dominions Women's Suffrage Union
Becker, Lydia 26, 28
Beckett, John 182
Beethoven, Ludwig van 106
Belfast Women's Temperance Association 72
Bell, Doreen 118
Belt, George 172
Bentham, Ethel 199
Bernard, Mr 46
Besant, Sir Walter 99
Billington-Greig, Teresa 168, 191-2, 193
Birkett Committee 194, 201
Birrell, Augustine (Liberal Cabinet Minister) 61, 62
birth control 190, 192-201
   see also contraception
Black Friday (1910) 115, 156, 180, 183
Blackshirts 108, 114, 115, 119, 182, 183
Blathwayt, Emily 1, 53, 54, 55, 57, 58, 59, 61-5
Blathwayt, Colonel Linley 53, 54, 55, 61, 62
Blathwayt, Mary 53-6, 58, 60-4
Blathwayt, William 53
Blathwayt family 5, 8, 53-4, 57-65
Blease, W. Lyon 147
Blueshirt movement 109
Booth, Mrs Alfred 42
Bowring family 42
Box, F. M. 109
Boyle, Nina 14
Brailsford, H. N. 93
Bright, Jacob 71, 147
Bright, John 71
Bright, Mrs Allan 42
Bright, Ursula 71

Bright family 11, 69, 71
Bristol 7, 55, 56, 59, 61, 62
Britain
  Constitution 6
  democracy 5, 6
  imperialism 4-5, 15
  influences on the British experience 1
  regions 7-8, 16, 38, 48-9
  style of government 3
  temperance work 69-84
  transnational networks 11
  wartime patriotism 13
British Commonwealth League (BCL) 15
British, Continental and General Federation for the Abolition of Government Regulation of Prostitution 72
British Dominions Women's Suffrage Union (BDWSU) 162, 171
British Empire 7, 10, 15, 112
British Sexology Society 201
British Socialist Party 172, 197
British Society for the Study of Sex Psychology 158, 194, 197, 201
British Union of Fascists (BUF) 1, 105-20, 178, 182, 183, 184, 199
British Women's Temperance Association (BWTA) 9, 11, 69-83
Brontë, Charlotte 93
Brontë, Emily 93
Brontë family 96
Broughton, Ada 39, 47
Browne, Stella 4, 11, 14, 190-202
Browning, Elizabeth Barrett 93
Bryce, James, 1st Viscount 83
BUF, see British Union of Fascists
Burney, Fanny 93
Burton, Alice E. 38-40, 48
Burton, Antoinette 10-11
Butler, Josephine 26, 27, 42, 70, 71, 194, 195
BWTA, see British Women's Temperance Association

Cadbury family 69
Cady Stanton, Elizabeth 11
Caine, Barbara 5, 26
Canada 171
Cantonment Acts 77-8

capitalism 171, 182
Carlisle, Rosalind Howard, Countess of 70, 71, 79-83
Carlisle Women's Liberal Association 80
Carlyle, Thomas 30
Carrington-Wood, Mrs H. 117, 184
Carson, Sir Edward 21
Cassell, John 69
Castle Howard 79, 80-1
'Cat and Mouse' Committee 151
Catholic Women's Suffrage Society (CWSS) 37, 41, 45-8
Central National Society for Women's Suffrage 78, 147, 164
Chancellor, H. G. 155
Chant, Laura Ormiston 79, 83
Chapman, Adeline Mary 150-1
Chapman, Cecil 9, 145-59
Chapman, Reverend Hugh B. 149
Chartism 3, 10, 37, 146
Chesterton, A. K. 105-6
China 12, 13
chivalry 31, 150
Church, the 149
Church League for Women's Suffrage (CLWS) 41, 45-8
Church Leagues 9
Churchill, Sir Winston 7, 154, 156
citizenship 3, 15, 27, 44, 138, 139
Clark, Alice 30
Clayton, Joseph 93
CLWS, see Church League for Women's Suffrage
Cobb, Frances Power 26
Colquitt, Jane 42
communism 109, 112, 199-200
Communist Party of Great Britain 163, 172, 179, 197
Compton-Burnett, Ivy 92
Conciliation Bill 155, 183
Conservative Party 42, 107, 108
Conservative and Unionist Women's Franchise Association (CUWFA) 37, 41, 45, 48, 63, 64, 151, 153
Contagious Diseases Acts 27, 28, 70, 71, 72, 77-8, 79, 194, 195, 200
contraception 190, 193, 198, 202
  see also birth control
Cook, Thomas 69

Cooper, Selina 136
Cooperative movement 133
Council for the Representation of Women in the League of Nations 15
Covenanters 6
Craigen, Jessie 28
Criddle, Helah 47, 48
Cromwell, Oliver 180
Cruikshank, George 69
Currey, Muriel 119-20
CUWFA, see Conservative and Unionist Women's Franchise Association
CWSS, see Catholic Women's Suffrage Society

Daley, Caroline 1
Damer Dawson, Margaret 109, 112
Dangerfield, George 20-1
Davies, Emily 26, 182
Davison, Emily Wilding 29, 178, 191, 192
Dawson, Julia 165-6
De Rutzen, Sir Albert 151
Defence of the Realm Act (DORA) 194, 201
Defence Regulation 18B 106, 108, 110
Derby (1913) 29, 182
Despard, Charlotte 4, 14, 170, 180
Dickenson, Sarah 136
Dissenters 6
divorce 148, 149, 197, 200, 202
Divorce Reform Union 149
Docwra, Mary 76
DORA, see Defence of the Realm Act
Doughan, David 3
Drummond, Flora 112, 113, 114-15, 119
Drysdale, Charles Robert 193, 194, 200
DuBois, Ellen 11
Dugdale, Una 149
Duval, Victor 149

East London Federation of Suffragettes (ELFS) 20, 25, 171, 182
Edgeworth, Maria 93
Edinburgh 7
Edinburgh Society for Women's Suffrage 71
Edward VII, King 5
Edwards, John 44, 132

18B Advisory Committee 108
18B Detainees (British) Aid Fund 108
Elam, Bertha 39, 40
Elam, Dudley 107
Elam, Norah (Mrs Dacre Fox) 105, 107, 108, 110-13, 115-17, 118, 119
ELFS, see East London Federation of Suffragettes
Eliot, George 93, 96, 99
Eliot, T. S. 95
Ellis, Havelock 191, 200
Ellis, Mrs Havelock 93
Elmy, Elizabeth Wolstenholme 27, 28, 167, 169, 170
Enfranchisement Bill 137
England 6-7
equal suffrage 44, 83, 95, 138, 139
Europe 12, 13
Everett, Mary 57

Fabian Society 127
Faithful Begg bill 83
fascism 4, 14, 16, 105-25, 182, 184, 199
Fawcett, Millicent Garrett 6, 12, 13, 26, 30, 71, 83, 164, 171
FCSU, see Forward Cymric Suffrage Union
Federation of Progressive Societies 201
femininity 31, 98, 139, 150
feminism 14, 24, 93, 119, 150, 157, 162, 191, 197, 199, 201, 202
  and autobiographies 177
  Edwardian 38, 47
  first-wave 100
  nationalist 111
  networks 71
  'romantic' 30
  second-wave 91, 100
  and sexual reform 193
Fenwick Miller, Florence 78
Finland 1
First World War 2, 6, 13-14, 24, 30, 37, 41, 47, 64, 65, 94, 111, 112
Florence, Mary Sargent 98
forcible feeding 29, 31, 63, 115, 147, 156, 178, 180, 183
Ford, Isabella 191
Forward Cymric Suffrage Union (FCSU) 7

Fox, Dacre 107
France 1, 11
Frances, Hilary 5
Franchise Reform Bill 72
Franco, General Francisco 110
Franklin, Hugh 31, 156
French Revolution 29-30, 37
Freudian theory 21
full adult suffrage 4, 14

Galsworthy, John 94
Gee, Allen 133
gender identity 10, 30, 31, 136
gender relations 1, 5, 134, 136, 145, 149
George III, King 5
Germany 11, 106, 109, 112, 190
Gill, Elizabeth 183
Girton College 79
Gladstone, Herbert 152
Gladstone, Mrs 80
Glasgow Women's Labour Party 128
Glasier, John Bruce 138
Gleadle, Kathryn 3, 26
Goering, Hermann 109
Gore-Booth, Eva 136
Grand, Sarah 92, 93, 131
Grey, Sir Edward 78
Griggs, Anne Brock 119
Gueroul, Mrs 183
Guest, Arthur 151

Halford, S. H. 195
Hallett, Lilias Ashworth 59, 63
Hamilton, Cicely 13-14, 91, 96-9, 114, 177, 184
Hammersmith Society for Women's Suffrage 168
Hammersmith Suffrage Society 170
Hammill, Fred 130
Harcourt, Sir William 83
Hardie, Keir 126, 127, 129, 131, 132, 133, 138, 139
Harraden, Beatrice 92, 94
Hatton, Bessie 91, 92, 94
Haverfield, Honourable Mrs 153
Hawks, Olive 183
Healy, Tim 147
Heppler, Margaret 10
higher education 70
Hilton, Cecilia 39
Hilton family 69

Hinscliffe, Reverend C. 93
Historical Pageant 10
Hitler, Adolf 106-7, 109-10, 114
Holledge, Julie 28
Holloway Prison, London 39, 59, 108, 115, 117, 151, 169
Holtby, Winifred 114
Home Office 145, 151-7
Home Service Corps 47
Horne, Reverend Silvester 148
House of Lords 6, 178
Housman, Laurence 93, 158, 193
Hove Women's Suffrage Society 153
How-Martyn, Edith 192-3, 194
Howard, Lady Cecilia 83
Howard, Dorothy 80
Howard, Mary 80
Howard, Michael 80
Howey, Elsie 62-3
Hunt, Violet 92
Hunter, Archibald 130

ICW, *see* International Council of Women
ILP, *see* Independent Labour Party
Imagists 90
imperialism 3, 4-5, 11, 12, 15, 32, 108
Independent Labour Party (ILP) 16, 43, 44, 48, 108, 112, 114, 126-40, 166, 172, 179
Independent Order of Good Templars (IOGT) 70, 71, 72
India 11, 12, 78, 79
Interdepartmental Committee on Abortion (Birkett Committee) 194, 201
International Council of Women (ICW) 11, 12, 169
International Suffrage Club 157
International Women's Franchise Club 147
International Woman Suffrage Alliance (IWSA) 12, 169, 170
  British Overseas Committee 15
internationalist movement 24
IOGT, *see* Independent Order of Good Templars
Iota 131
Ireland 6-7, 21
Irish Home Rule 28, 79, 80, 112
Irving, Sir Henry 99

210 Index

Isle of Man 110
IWSA, *see* International Woman Suffrage Alliance

Jacobs, Herbert 146, 147, 148, 156, 157
Japan 12
Japp, Miss 42
Jenkins, Alice 202
Jewish League for Women's Suffrage 147
Jewson, Dorothy 199
Joint Standing Committee on the Criminal Law Amendment Bill 157
Joyce, William ('Lord Haw-Haw') 199

Kenney, Annie 5, 55, 56, 57, 59–64, 78, 83, 112, 168, 169
Kenney, Jessie 62
Ker, Dr Alice 47
Kipling, Rudyard 92
Kitchener, Lord 111
Knightley, Lady 151

Labouchere, Miss 43
Labouchere, Mr 169
Labour Church movement 131
labour movement 4, 22, 23, 25, 30, 129
Labour Party 21, 22, 24, 25, 108, 112, 132, 133, 179, 181, 182, 190, 196–7, 199, 200, 201
Labour Representation Committee (LRC) 132
Lacy, Reverend T. E. 149
Ladies' National Association for Repeal of the Contagious Diseases Acts 27, 195
Lancashire 8, 38, 43, 81, 109, 136
Lancashire and Cheshire Textile and Other Workers' Representation Committee (LCTOWRC) 23
Lawrence, D. H. 95
Leadley-Brown, Cicely 46–7
League of Nations 15
Leigh, Mrs 62
Leigh Smith, Barbara 27
Leneman, Leah 7
Lenin, Vladimir Ilyich 114
lesbians 157–8
Liberal Party 6, 42–5, 63, 64, 80–3, 115, 138, 154, 165

Liberal Women's Suffrage Union 37
Liberalism 42, 48, 162, 172
Licensing Act 82
Liddington, Jill 8, 23, 38, 43, 135
Linton, Jenny 183
Lintorn-Orman, Rotha 113
literary societies 90
Liverpool 8, 31, 39, 42, 46, 70, 75, 157, 201
Liverpool Labour Representation Committee 44
'Liverpool Prisoners' 39, 40
Liverpool Women's Suffrage Society (LWSS) 40–8
Lloyd, Councillor H. M. 147–8
Lloyd George, David 156
local government 4, 26
London 7, 38, 39, 40, 150, 151, 152, 169
London County Council 119
London and Provincial Anti-Vivisection Society 107
Longtown Women's Liberal Association 80
Lovell, Phyllis 46, 47
Lowndes, Marie Belloc 92, 93, 147
LRC, *see* Labour Representation Committee
Lucas, Margaret Bright 71–3, 76
LWSS, *see* Liverpool Women's Suffrage Society
Lytton, Lady Constance 178

MacDonald, Margaret 172
MacDonald, Ramsay 93, 138, 182, 198, 199
McLaren, Duncan 71
McLaren, Eva 79, 80
McLaren, Priscilla Bright 71
McLaren, Walter 155
MacNeill (pro-suffrage MP) 152
Magna Carta 5, 6, 146
Mahood, Hattie 46
Makgill, Lady Esther 108
male sexual violence 74
Malthusian League 193, 194, 200
Malthusianism 134
Manchester 7, 23, 75, 78, 128, 129, 167
Manchester Women's Suffrage Society 71
Manhood Suffrage Bill 155

Mansel, Mildred 151
Margetson, W. H. 94
Markievicz, Constance 111
marriage 11, 27, 28, 132, 133, 134, 148-51, 153, 190, 193, 196
Married Women's Property Acts 70
Marshall, Catherine 22-3
Martel, Nellie 38, 40
masculinity 31, 139, 150
Masefield, John 93
Maskelyne, Inez 58, 59
Mason, Bertha 78, 79, 80
Maxwell, Shaw 128
Men's Committee for Justice to Women 148
Men's League for Women's Suffrage (MLWS) 9, 38, 41, 145-50, 152-8
Men's Political Union for Women's Enfranchisement (MPU) 9, 155, 156
Merseyside 16, 38-49
Meynell, Alice 92, 93
Mill, John Stuart 71, 147
Ministry of Health 196
Mitchell, Albert 137
Mitchell, Hannah 21, 23
Mitford, Nancy 114
Mitford, Unity 114
Mitford sisters 113
MLWS, see Men's League for Women's Suffrage
Modernism 90
Montefiore, Dora 1, 4, 8, 12, 162-73
Montefiore, George Barrow 163
Morley College 194
Morris, Bessie 39
Morrissey, Alice 43, 44, 46
Mosley, Lady Diana 108, 117-18
Mosley, Lady Maud 109
Mosley, Sir Oswald 105-8, 112, 115, 116-17, 119, 182
MPU, see Men's Political Union for Women's Enfranchisement
Muller, Henrietta 167
Municipal Women's Association 44
Murray, Eunice 14
Mussolini, Benito 108, 114

National Administrative Council (of the Independent Labour Party) (NAC) 128, 136
National Club for Fascist Women 108
national identity 3, 6-7, 9-12, 15, 32
National Security Act 113
National Society for Women's Suffrage (NSWS) 27, 72, 78, 164
National Union of Societies for Equal Citizenship (NUSEC) 180, 199
National Union of Women Teachers 185
National Union of Women's Suffrage Societies (NUWSS) 12, 13, 21-4, 37, 38, 41-4, 46, 60, 63, 64, 93, 147, 162, 167
nationalism 1, 3, 15, 111
Nazism 106, 117
Needlework Guild 112
Neilans, Alison 195
Nevinson, Henry 57, 156, 157, 158-9
Nevinson, Margaret Wynne 153
New, Miss 62
New Constitutional Society for Women's Suffrage 151, 153, 157
New South Wales 164, 168
New Zealand 1, 10, 69, 171
Newcastle 70
Nolan, Melanie 1
Norris, Jill 8, 23, 38, 43, 135
North, Lord 180
North of England Society for Women's Suffrage 128
Northern Men's Federation for Women's Suffrage 9
NSWS, see National Society for Women's Suffrage
NUSEC, see National Union of Societies for Equal Citizenship
NUWSS, see National Union of Women's Suffrage Societies

O'Duffy, General 109
Ogden, G. K. 98
Oldfield, Sybil 28
Oldham Liberal Party 81
Olympia rally (1934) 183
Östberg, Kjell 1

Pageant of Empire 10
Pankhurst, Christabel 5, 6, 22, 24, 29, 47, 59, 60, 78, 92, 111, 112, 113, 136, 166, 169, 170, 178, 180, 182-3, 193

Pankhurst, Emmeline 22, 29–30, 39, 47, 59–60, 62, 63, 106, 111–15, 117, 128, 136, 147, 169–72, 178, 181, 183
Pankhurst, Richard 128, 147
Pankhurst, Sylvia 1, 20, 21, 22, 31, 32, 83, 113, 115, 169, 171, 182, 183, 184
Pankhurst family 40, 83, 111, 113, 114, 167, 169, 177, 191
Parker, James 136
patriotism 5, 12, 13, 14, 110
Paul, Cedar 200
Paul, Eden 200
peace movement 24, 70
Pearce, Isabella Bream 128
Penn, Mrs 178
People's Suffrage Federation 9, 37
Pethick-Lawrence, Emmeline 12, 59, 98–9, 114
Pethick-Lawrence, Frederick 93, 147
Pettit, June 11
Phillips, Margot 199
Phillips, Mary 7, 63
Picton family 42
Pioneer Players 94
police courts 150
politicization 4, 64, 163
Poor Law 153
Poor Law Guardians 26, 77, 84, 153
post-colonialism 32
Price, J. Arthur 146
Priestman sisters 30, 167
Priestman–Bright circle 27
Promethean Society 201
prostitution 194, 196

Quakers 69

radicalism 10, 32
Rathbone, Eleanor 40, 42, 44, 46, 199
Rayner Parkes, Bessie 27
Read, Saleeby 93
Red Cross 64
Reddish, Sarah 136
Redesdale, Lady 117
Reform Act (1832) 3
Reform Act (1867) 3
Reform Bill (1918) 64–5
Reformation 6
religious suffrage 45–6
Rendall, Jane 3, 26, 27

Representation of the People Act (1918) 14, 94, 107, 171
Rhondda, Viscountess 177, 198
Richardson, Mary 'Slasher' 1, 14, 105, 106, 108–11, 113, 115, 116, 177–85
Ridge, Pett 93
Risdon, Wilfred 182
Robins, Elizabeth 28, 91, 92, 93, 96–7, 99, 150
Roch, Walter 147
'Rokeby Venus' (Velázquez' *The Toilet of Venus*) 106, 116, 178, 179, 181
Rollitt, Sir Albert 74, 76
Roper, Esther 136
Rothermere, Viscount 182
Royal Albert Hall, London 39
Royal Commission on Divorce 148
Royal Commission on the Liquor Licensing Laws 78
Royal Commission on Prisons 146
Royal Society for the Prevention of Cruelty to Animals (RSPCA) 64
Rupp, Leila 12, 13

St George's Hall, Liverpool 38, 40
St Joan's Alliance 48
same-sex loving relationships 24, 27, 28–9
Sanger, Margaret 192
Schreiber, Lady Charlotte 151
Schreiner, Olive 92, 93
Scotland 6–7, 70, 75, 127, 132
Scott, Rose 164
SDF, see Social Democratic Federation
sectarianism 45, 46
Secular Society 56
'Seeing Through Suffrage' (Greenwich conference) 20
Selborne Society 64
sexology 28
sexual identity 96
sexual politics 27, 28, 30, 32
sexuality 11, 28, 132, 190, 201
Shackleton, David 136
Shakespeare, William 92, 106
Sharp, Evelyn 92, 150, 177
Sheepshanks, Mary 12, 13
Shetland 10
Sheur, F. J. 137
Sigerson, Professor George 146
Sinclair, May 13–14, 92, 93, 97

Six Point Group (SPG)   184, 198, 199
Slack, Agnes   83
Smart, Russell   140
Smillie, Robert   129
Smith, Harold   14
Snell, Harry   139
Snowden, Philip   126, 136
Social Democratic Federation
    (SDF)   126, 127, 166, 171, 172, 180
social equality   38
socialism   4, 29, 42-3, 44, 112, 127,
    130, 133-6, 139, 162, 171, 172, 179,
    182, 191, 199
Socialist League   127
socialist movement   22, 23, 25, 30, 131
Society for Constructive Birth
    Control   200
Society of Friends   167
Somerset, Lady Henry   71, 73-9, 81
South Africa   165, 171
SPG, see Six Point Group
Stanley of Alderley, Henrietta Maria,
    Lady   79
Steel, Flora Annie   93
Stewart, Eliza   70
Stewart, Louisa   76
Stewart, William   136-7
Stewart-Brown, Nessie   42, 43, 48
Stöcker, Dr Helen   11, 190
Stopes, Charlotte Carmichael   32
Stopes, Marie   200
Strachey, Ray   21, 32
Sturges family   69
Suffrage Atelier   91
Suffrage First Committee   152
suffrage newspapers   12-13
suffragette colours   55-6
Suffragette Fellowship   184
Sulkunen, Irma   1
Sutton, George   182
Swanwick, Helena   13, 24
Sweden   1

Tax Resistance League   63
taxation   5-6, 139, 151, 167-8
Taylor, Helen   28
Thompson, Louisa   10
Tod, Isabella   72
Tollemache, Aethel   56, 57, 58, 59, 63
Tollemache, Grace   57, 58, 63
Tollemache, Mrs   57

Tollemache family   59, 65
trade unions   8, 42-3, 132, 133, 136
Trevor, John   131
Troup, Sir Edward   154
Turner, Ben   133

UKA, see United Kingdom Alliance
Union of Practical Suffragists   162, 165
Unitarians   1, 26
United Kingdom Alliance (UKA)   82
United States   1, 11, 12, 24, 27, 69, 70,
    71, 73, 74, 76, 84, 183
United Suffragists (US)   25, 37, 41, 47
universal suffrage   25
University of Greenwich   31
University Settlement   42
US, see United Suffragists

vegetarianism   29
Velázquez: *The Toilet of Venus*   106
Vellacott, Jo   23, 24
VFWF, see Votes for Women
    Fellowship
Vickery, Dr Alice   193
Vorticists   90
Votes for Women Fellowship
    (VFWF)   37, 41

Wales   6-7, 112
Walpole, Sir Robert   5
Walsh, Adela Pankhurst   113
War Service Bureau   47
Ward, Arnold   153
Ward, Mrs Humphrey   92, 153
Warden, Gertrude   93
WBCG, see Workers' Birth Control
    Group
WCG, see Women's Co-operative Guild
WCTA, see Women's Christian
    Temperance Association
WCTU, see Women's Christian
    Temperance Union
WEA, see Workers' Educational
    Association
Wells, H. G.   200
Welsh Liberals   7
Wentworth, Vera   62-3
West, Rebecca   193-4
WFL, see Women's Freedom League
Whiteing, Richard   93
Wilding Davison, Emily   29

Willard, Frances   73-9, 81
WILPF, *see* Women's International League for Peace and Freedom
Wings (journal)   76, 77, 78
WLA, *see* Women's Liberal Association
WLF, *see* Women's Liberal Federation
Wollstonecraft, Mary   93
Wolmer, Lord   181
Womanhood Suffrage League of New South Wales   162, 163
Women Police   109, 112
women writers   8, 16, 28, 90
Women Writers' Suffrage League (WWSL)   8, 90-7, 99-100
Women's Auxiliary Service   109, 112
Women's Christian Temperance Association (WCTA)   78
Women's Christian Temperance Union (WCTU)   11, 70, 73, 74, 76, 78, 79
Women's Co-operative Guild (WCG)   8, 43, 44, 136, 197, 201
Women's Coronation Process   10
Women's Enfranchisement Bill   166
Women's Franchise League   32, 71
Women's Freedom League (WFL)   5, 8, 13, 14, 21, 24, 30, 37, 41, 48, 93, 128, 153, 171, 179, 180, 185, 192, 193
Women's Guild of Empire   113, 119
Women's International League for Peace and Freedom (WILPF)   13
Women's League Against War and Fascism   119
Women's Liberal Association (WLA)   71, 165
Women's Liberal Federation (WLF)   42, 43, 78, 79, 80, 82, 83, 165
Women's Local Government Society   165
women's movement   9, 21, 26, 56, 84, 115-16
'Women's Parliament', Caxton Hall, London   39, 59, 61
Women's Party   112
Women's Peace Conference (Hague, 1915)   12

Women's Police Force   109
Women's Police Reserve   109
Women's Propaganda Patrol   106
Women's Reserve   109
Women's Social and Political Union (WSPU)   7, 13, 20, 23, 24, 28, 29, 31, 37-41, 43-8, 54-65, 78, 83, 93, 98, 107, 108, 110, 112-18, 126, 139, 147, 153, 154, 157, 162, 167-70, 177, 178, 185, 190, 191, 192
Women's Socialist Circles   172
Women's Special Police   113
women's suffrage bill (Bright)   147
women's suffrage bill (Rollitt)   75
Women's Suffrage National Aid Corps   171
Women's Suffrage Society (WSS)   58, 59
Women's Tax Resistance League   5-6
Women's Total Abstinence Union (WTAU)   77, 78
Women's World Committee Against War and Fascism   184
Woodlock, Patricia   39, 46
Woods, Margaret   92
Woolf, Virginia   54, 97, 98
Workers' Birth Control Group (WBCG)   196, 200
Workers' Educational Association (WEA)   64
Workers' Suffrage Federation   171
Wright, Sir Almroth   92
WSPU, *see* Women's Social and Political Union
WSS, *see* Women's Suffrage Society
WTAU, *see* Women's Total Abstinence Union
WWSL, *see* Women Writers' Suffrage League

Yeats, W. B.   95

Zangwill, Edith   93
Zangwill, Israel   93